Red, Black, and Objective
Science, Sociology, and Anarchism

SAL RESTIVO
Rensselaer Polytechnic Institute, USA

Routledge
Taylor & Francis Group

LONDON AND NEW YORK

First published 2011 by Ashgate Publishing

2 Park Square, Milton Park, Abingdon, Oxon OX14 4RN
711 Third Avenue, New York, NY 10017, USA

Routledge is an imprint of the Taylor & Francis Group, an informa business

First issued in paperback 2016

British Library Cataloguing in Publication Data
Restivo, Sal P.
 Red, black, and objective : science, sociology, and
 anarchism.
 1. Science--Social aspects. 2. Objectivity. 3. Anarchism.
 I. Title
 306.4'5-dc22

Library of Congress Cataloging-in-Publication Data
Restivo, Sal P.
 Red, black, and objective : science, sociology, and anarchism / by Sal Restivo.
  p. cm.
 Includes bibliographical references and index.
 ISBN 978-1-4094-1039-3 (hardback)
 1. Social sciences--Philosophy. 2. Science--Social aspects. I. Title.

 H61.R4667 2011
 330.1--dc22

                                                                    2011011357

ISBN 978-1-4094-1039-3 (hbk)
ISBN 978-1-138-26094-8 (pbk)

RED, BLACK, AND OBJECTIVE

Contents

Acknowledgements

I acknowledge and appreciate that the "I" is – as Nietzsche was among the first to teach us – a grammatical illusion. The "social," by contrast, is not an illusion. I have drawn on my collaborative writings with Drs. Wenda Bauchspies, Jennifer Croissant, Deborah Sloan, Daryl Chubin, Randall Collins, and Julia Loughlin. They have been among my most enduring educators and collaborators but have no responsibility for the ways in which I have re-woven and integrated into this book our collaborative interrogative narratives on science, mathematics, and sociology. I have been fortunate to have counted among my friends and virtual teachers such saints of science as Joseph Needham, Mary Douglas, Dirk Struik, and David Bohm (all of whom have passed on), along with my colleagues in the sociology of science and other disciplines – notably, on a more personal level, Karin Knorr-Cetina, Randall Collins, Daryl Chubin, Peter Denton, Hilary and Steven Rose, the late Bernard Barber, Jerry Ravetz, Les Levidow, Leslie Brothers, Brian Martin, the late David Edge, the late Derek Price, the late Joseph Ben David, Steve Woolgar, Susan Cozzens, the late Leigh Star, Sharon Traweek, Aant Elzinga, Jean Paul Van Bendegem, Clifford Hooker, the late Donald T. Campbell, Ole Skovsmose, Ubi D'Ambrosio, and Jens Hoyrup. I have gained much intellectually and emotionally from knowing and working with the Michigan State University sociologists Herbert Karp and Christopher Vanderpool, long departed. I have also learned from and been provoked by knowing and reading Barry Barnes, David Bloor, Don Mackenzie, Sandra Harding, Elizabeth Fee, Evelyn Fox Keller, and Donna Haraway, the late Bob Merton, and Bruno Latour. Among my colleagues at RPI I have been closest to and most influenced by Michael Zenzen, Ellen Esrock, Audrey Bennett, Shirley Gorenstein, and Linnda Caporael. And I have been fortunate in working with graduate students whose values and intellect have helped them stand above the waves of commodification and commercialization that have been transforming what I once knew (without Platonic delusions) as "the university"; I mentioned Wenda and Jennifer (RPI STS Phds) above; the others are Gil Peach (Phd, NYU, sociology), Monica Mesquita (PhD, Lisbon, ethnomathematics), Colin Beech and Rachel Dowty (PhDs, RPI, STS), and Peter Bellomo (MS, RPI, STS). And just as I am completing this book, a brilliant young PhD student has come along to draw me into the roles of advisor, mentor, friend, and colleague: Sabrina Weiss. I had the pleasure of having an office at RPI next to one occupied at different times by the late David Weick and the late John Schumacher, friends, colleagues, and inspired anarchists. And the anarchist George Bennello, also long departed, was an occasional visitor to my home in southern Vermont and with me among the founding members of the humanist sociology movement.

I want to thank my undergraduate teaching fellows for assisting me in various ways in the classroom and with my research and writing over the last couple of years: Terry Cheng, Christine Eromenok, Ashley Lowe, Laura Henry, Leah Jakaitis, Eleanor Dunn, and Lorena Nicotra. I am especially grateful to Lorena for helping me with formatting problems during the final preparation of the manuscript.

As a young professor, I drifted away from organized Marxist, socialist, and anarchist organizations which I found generally uninviting for a variety of reasons. On the other hand, I was warmly but not uncritically embraced by and became one of the founding members of the science studies movement. I am grateful for the many ways in which the science studies community took me in when I was looking for a home as a young researcher. In the end, the truth is I have always felt homeless and marginalized, encouraged by many of life's contingencies to "do it my way". Paint me red, black, and objective.

I have drawn on several previously published articles and list them below. Readers interested in filling in the citation gaps in my narrative are referred to these sources. I have limited citations within the text and have not used footnotes or endnotes in the interest of narrative continuity. I have also included birth and death dates only in cases where I thought the person might not be widely known to readers or where it seemed important to locate the person in his or her historical context.

References

"Science, Social Problems, and Progressive Thought: Essays on the Tyranny of Science" (including "Technoscience or Tyrannoscience Rex", a review of Jurassic Park), pp. 39–87 in S.L. Star (ed.), *Ecologies of Science* (SUNY Press, Albany, 1995). With Jennifer Croissant.

"How to Criticize Science and Maintain Your Sanity", *Science as Culture*, 6, Part 3, 28 (Spring 1996), pp. 396–413. With Wenda K. Bauchspies.

"Science, Social Theory, and Science Criticism", *Communication and Cognition* (special issue on Popularization of Science: The Democratization of Knowledge in Perspective), 29, 2 (1996), pp. 249–272. With Wenda K. Bauchspies.

"The Invention of Science", *Cultural Dynamics*, 12, 2 (July, 2000), pp. 57–73. With Julia Loughlin.

"Building Labs and Building Lives", in *Degrees of Compromise: Industrial Interests and Academic Values* (SUNY Press, Albany, 2001). With Jennifer Croissant.

"The Will to Mathematics: Minds, Morals, and Numbers", *Foundations of Science*, 11, 1 and 2, special issue on *Mathematics: What Does It All Mean?* Edited by Jean Paul Van Bendegem, Bart Kerkhove, and Sal Restivo, March 2006, 197–215. With Wenda Bauchspies. Portuguese translation, Bauchspies, W. and Restivo, S. (2001) – "O arbítrio da matemática: mentes, moral e numerous", in *BOLEMA*, 16, pp. 102–124.

"Mechanical Mathematicians: The End of Proof as We Know It", review essay, *The Information Society*, 20, 1 (January, 2004), pp. 67–8.

"Theories of Mind, Social Science, And Mathematical Practice", pp. 61–79 in J.P. Van Bendegem and Bart Van Kerkhove (eds), *Perspectives on Mathematical Practices* (Kluwer, Dordrecht, 2005).

"Politics of Latour", review essay, *Organization and Environment*, 8, 1 (March, 2005), pp. 111–115.

"Social Constructionism in Science and Technology Studies", pp. 213–229 in Jim Holstein and Jaber Gubrium (eds), *Handbook of Constructionist Research,* edited by (Guilford, New York, 2007). With Jennifer Croissant.

"Sturm und Drang in Mathematics: Casualties, Consequences, and Contingencies in the Math Wars", *Philosophy of Mathematics Education Journal*, 20 (June 2007). With Deborah Sloan.

"Society, Social Construction, and the Sociological Imagination", invited commentary, *Constructivist Foundations* 3, 2 (2008), pp. 94–96.

"Minds, Morals, and Mathematics in the Wake of the Deaths of Plato and God: Reflections on What Social Constructionism Means, Really", pp. 37–43 in Anna Chronaki (ed.), *Mathematics, Technologies, Education: The Gender Perspective* (University of Thessaly Press, Volos, 2008/2010).

"Science Studies", *Cultural Theory*, M.K. Booker (editor), a volume in the *Encyclopedia of Literary and Cultural Theory*, M. Ryan (editor) (Blackwell, Oxford, 2010). With Jennifer Croissant.

"Bruno Latour: The Once and Future Philosopher", in George Ritzer and Jeffrey Stepinsky (eds), *The New Blackwell Companion to Major Social Theorists* (Blackwell, Boston, 2010).

A specter is haunting the sociology of science – the specter of anarchism. All the powers of the old and the new sociology of science have entered into a holy alliance to exorcise this specter: British relativists and American evolutionary epistemologists, Mertonians and Kuhnians, functionalists and Marxists.

Where is the paradigm in opposition that has not been descried as anarchistic by its opponents in power? Where is the opposition that has not hurled back the branding reproach of anarchism, against the more advanced opposition paradigms, as well as against its reactionary adversaries?

Two things result from this fact:

1. Anarchism is already acknowledged by all sociologists of science to be itself a power.
2. It is high time that anarchists should openly, in the face of the whole field, publish their views, their aims, their tendencies, and meet this nursery tale of the specter of anarchism with a manifesto of the paradigm itself.

Sal Restivo, Dubrovnik, 1990

Prologue

Here I stand. I come to the ideas, concepts, theories, and claims in this book by way of a life, a biography that has developed at the intersection of history and culture as they have unfolded between 1940 and 2010. I became disenchanted with religion early on in life and overly enchanted by science simultaneously. My voice today is not the voice of Everyman but of a relatively specialized and small thought collective, a collectivity of thinkers dead and alive. I don't know how to defend my claims in a way that meets all challenges and competitors. I do not know how to argue without rejecting out of hand the thoughts of those who think differently than me. I do not know what to do about the fact that I think I am right and they are wrong without appearing arrogant and intolerant. I struggle with a commitment to tolerance and pluralism that is constantly drawn up short by the recalcitrance of a reality that is more often than not intolerant and univocal. If the emperor has no clothes, the emperor has no clothes.

I am appalled by and analytical about rather than drawn to the emphasis some intellectuals place on mystery, what we do not and cannot know, on spiritual experiences, on the alleged "ineffables" of human experience. I think these experiences can be explained and that if we can't explain them we should be trying to while recognizing the powerful limits on our capacity to explain. But I also know one can pathologize knowledge, become overly arrogant with certainty, and that we need to protect ourselves from these dangers without giving up analysis, explanation, and theory. I do know that thinking the thoughts that make up this book is what I do, what I am; and I do know that I do not stand here alone, no matter how marginal and alone I may appear to myself as well as to others. I do think that something very significant, something novel, is afoot in terms of our individual and collective abilities to meet the challenges to our survival as a species. This book describes some of the ways I have come to think about this big problem. I have not been awed or stymied by experience-in-itself. I can in some sense feel the beauty of a sunset, a poem, a piece of music but also an equation. I have had what others would claim were spiritual, mystical, or religious experiences. They left me curious about what had just happened, not awed or overwhelmed. In the end, without apologies, I stand with Nietzsche when he writes that you must make your experiences "a matter of conscience for knowledge. 'What did I really experience? What happened in me and around me at that time? Was my reason bright enough? Was my will opposed to all deceptions of the senses and bold in resisting the fantastic?'" You must not, he writes, "thirst after things that *go against reason*" (Nietzsche, 1887/1974: 253):

> We others, who thirst after reason, are determined to scrutinize our experiences
> as severely as a scientific experiment – hour after hour, day after day. We
> ourselves wish to be our experiments and guinea pigs.

Here I stand, unawed and unwilling to be awed. By the time you reach the end
of this book, you should find that while I bend in the direction of reason and
science, I do so as someone who has heard the call of the poet, the artist, and the
musician. But I have not in those moments been rendered speechless. I know how
to engage and have engaged silence but I have never thought to make that a form
of life or a mode of inquiry. It takes a great deal of knowledge and philosophical
sophistication to argue for the virtues and values of the cloud of unknowing. The
very real dangers of the search for absolutes and certainties has driven great and
formidable minds to value the end of language, the limits of rational thought, the
apophatic state. I understand what drives people to this place but it seems to me
that when they get there they lose sight of the recalcitrance of the world that is
absolute and certain, the world where the cliff will not yield to the hurtling body,
where the rock wall will not give in to the fiercest unaided human strike, and
where death will take you no matter how much yoga you do, no matter how much
wonder you feel, no matter how sophisticated your defense of unreason and the
limits of knowing are. If there is room for wonder in my worldview it is never
in a way that bars unfettered inquiry, and fearless and courageous interrogation.
Perhaps those who defend the value of the cloud of unknowing remind us that
our inquiries and interrogations should pay attention to stop signs. Of course. But
stop signs are temporary and not places to live. Tolerance and pluralism should
not validate wrongheadedness, ignorance, and outright stupidity. It is one thing
for a Dostoevsky to defend 2+2=5; but we should teach students that 2+2=4
and educate them so that they come to understand Dostoevsky's position not to
mention Orwell's.

As an anarchist, I am at one with those postmodernists who have opposed
master narratives, Grand Theories, and the Grand Paradigm of universal science.
Such opposition, however, can only be a strength if it is part of a form of life
and inquiry guided by "ongoing critique" (Ferrell, 2009: 73; cf. Cohen, 1988).
We must learn to take our stands and defend our positions without committing
ourselves to master narratives, plans, and paradigms. Remember that this does not
eliminate the possibility of temporary and finite commitments where these may be
useful to ongoing critique.

Religion and god continue to be the principle fuel for the apophatics. My claim
is that the sociology and anthropology of religion and God change the rules of the
game. I will address this further in my final chapter. We "others" cannot afford to
encourage or be tolerant of, for example, Creationism and intelligent design in any
way whatsoever. Our reasoning here should not be based on the separation of the
realms of science and religion but rather on the separation of the realms of true and
false. The trick is to do this without subscribing to an oversimplified conception of
truth. This book offers some guidelines for navigating this territory.

Knowing things is empowering, not only for individuals but for the species. And knowledge is not equally distributed, or accessible. Tolerance, pluralism, polite conversation, and giving ourselves to wonder will necessarily be challenged and compromised in situations that threaten our survival. My claim is that we are in such a situation and that our ability to meet this challenge depends on how well we mobilize our best strategies and resources for adaptation, growth, development, and basic survival. I am not going to claim that I am in a position to dictate what those strategies and resources are. I am going to claim that I have access to some cultural capital that might bear on identifying, mobilizing, and utilizing such strategies and resources. I am also open to the argument that our "best strategies" in the most challenging circumstances will always have to include the very things I want to compromise from tolerance and pluralism to poetic and metaphysical imaginations. However, I want these always to be grounded in a sociological materialism, a realistic anarchist science. If this over privileges the material and the scientific, so be it. That's the way I think it has to be.

I am not going to associate myself with a particular school of thought or doctrine in the anarchist tradition. I am not going to enter into a dialogue with this tradition. I begin and end by adopting Peter Kropotkins's conception of anarchism as one of the social sciences. I then offer the following definition: if you champion the person as a social being dependent for self, thought, and consciousness on the social group or the community, if you champion and defend the rights of the person (as a social being) and the integrity and freedom of the person, if you are opposed to all forms of capitalized Authority, and if you oppose the state's claim that it owns (is the owner of last resort of) your body and labor, you are at one with the anarchist. As with many other anarchists, I do not draw strict boundaries to separate anarchism, communism, and socialism. Unless we blur these boundaries our doctrinaire and dogmatized debates will work against our shared interests in human survival, cultural growth, and ongoing critique.

My first exposure to progressive thinking came in college courses in which I read Karl Marx. By virtue of being drawn to Marx and given my working class roots, I have tended to start with class when considering the workings of society. Class continued to speak truth to me even after I digested Weber's analysis of class, party, status. This was especially the case the more I came to recognize that Weber and Marx were at one when it came to analyzing the "capitalist" economy.

I have been regularly reminded by one of my feminist sociologist friends that our positions in society and our sex and gender explain why she starts from gender and I start from class. Intersectional perspectives on race, class, sex, and gender complicate things but leave us both seeing the world through the primary lenses of class or gender respectively. It is difficult for me to privilege any social force or causal factor over class and power even while I grant the value of my friend's gender standpoint and the significance of intersectional analysis. I am sympathetic to May's (2009) distinction between exploitation and domination as respectively the central driving concepts behind Marxism and anarchism. I think it is more important to focus on how and where these standpoints converge than on how they stand apart. At the end of the day, I commit myself to the ways in which these standpoints stand apart and energize progressive analysis while I seek the convergence point and live with the contradictions imposed on me by my predispositions to begin all analysis and criticism with class and power.

If anarchism as a word, philosophy, program, practice, ideology, or idea frightens you, I invite you to open your eyes to the world around you. If you think the world works best in terms of markets, competition, and one or another political economy under the labels "capitalism" and "democracy", then I think the burden is on you to demonstrate that the world works at all and that in fact it works according to the rules and values of some form of capitalism and the free market (on why anarchists oppose markets, and profits as incentives to innovation see Duthel, 2010: 63-67, 201-217). Clearly this is not a good time to be defending these ideas. As I write, the largest environmental catastrophe in U.S. history is unfolding in the Gulf of Mexico in the wake of an oil rig accident. I write in the midst of the worst economic crisis since the Great Depression (and maybe if the economists were more attentive they might realize that this crisis is worse). Already, we have heard the voices of "the system" from French president Sarkozy to former treasury secretary Henry Paulson declare that ("raw") capitalism is dead. And yet the people charged with "saving" and "righting" the system are still showing an irrational commitment to the free market and capitalism. India, one of the most resilient economies during this period, is one of the nations not singing free market hymns.

The word "free" in free market is a slap in the face of reasoned economic discourse. It is a sign that someone is trying to pull the wool over your eyes and off your back. And "capitalism" is an ideological term not an economic concept. In its "pure form", capitalism is organized around "free markets" and "laissez-faire" competition among individualized – indeed, atomized – buyers and sellers operating according to the principle of self-interest, and guided by one goal and one goal only, maximizing profit. In this sense, capitalism has never existed, and indeed could never exist on this planet with these flora, fauna, resources, people and social relationships. Every effort to reform or otherwise modify "capitalism" eliminates one or more of its defining features. Capitalism cannot be saved by destroying what it means and what it stands for ideologically. An economy in which the goal has become to make money with money and not useful products and services actually represents the culmination of the profit motive that is at the heart of capitalism as an ideology.

The current situation as I write in 2010 is, I conjecture, an evolving economic black hole. The assumption that our situation is not as bad as the Great Depression underlies the remarks and analyses by the majority of today's pundits and professional economists. They may be wrong. The social theorist Kenneth Boulding (1970: 60-61) argued that the dialectical processes associated with scientific revolutions represent the heat of crystallization in a process of change; such processes are "costs". This idea can be extended to include the "cumulation of costs" and the progressive deterioration of the capacity of the scientific system to "recover" from the costs incurred during revolutionary changes, and hence to continue to "grow", "progress", "develop", or "evolve". I think this applies to the economy too. If we think of business cycles as processes of change that incur costs (environmental and broader ecological damage, human costs ranging from alienation and health risks to actual deaths, and institutional costs of the sort prominent in today's banking, insurance, and investment institutions), and we assume that those costs are cumulative in a world of limited and unrenewable resources, then I think we can make an argument for a contemporary black hole economy. The only way out that doesn't lead to a decrease in the carrying capacity of the planet relative to the human population is a radical development and deployment of new energy sources that do not require a massive overhaul of the existing infra-structure. That new energy source might be one that is way off the radar, magnetism for example.

Waste products, measured in human and environmental terms and physically and emotionally for humans, are growing exponentially and have been for decades. Consider what this means graphically. You walk past a pond every day in which algae are beginning to spread exponentially from the middle of the pond. You notice the growth but at first it really doesn't grab your attention. It's growing, it's growing. And then one day you notice that half the pond is covered. If that's the point at which you decide to do something, you are doomed because the pond will be completely covered the next day. I think we may be in for that kind of surprise. The concept of "behavioral sink" (introduced by John B. Calhoun, and discussed by the anthropologist Edward Hall in relation to urban environments) comes into play here too. Toxic products can build up in an animal population (say the citizens of New York City) and go unnoticed until one day most or all of the population drops dead.

In the sociology of science and mathematics sections of this book my goal is to cumulatively demonstrate that a case for science as an anarchistic enterprise can be made by focusing on scientific practice, science in action. If we understand science as the way of knowing of our species, it is not too much of a leap to the argument that social life is best organized according to the principles of anarchism, understood to be one of the sociological sciences.

The paths along which this narrative is going to unfold will introduce an open-systems perspective variously manifested in discussions of values and social organization. The open-systems perspective is the most general level of the analysis which I claim argues for an anarchistic approach to science and society. As we move along these paths, the reader should slowly realize that s/he is being led to understand the anarchist rationale. I travel some paths more than once, and sometimes move in circles. As always in my writings, this book is an invitation to walk and think with me, and this means to be an anarchist with me. Anarchism as a form of life is not something we aspire to but rather something we act out in every moment. To work toward an anarchist social order we must be anarchists step by step in our lives, in our thoughts, in our writing. On the other hand, we can think of the very idea of society as anarchistic "all the way down;" our very humanity, "being itself", may be anarchistic. If anarchism is one of the sociological sciences, then we must engage the idea that anarchism is ontologically grounded (de Acosta, 2009: 28; and see the Bibliographical Epilogue).

There will be moments in my remarks on science and knowledge when I will meet with criticisms, and where there will be openings for more or less conflictful or conciliatory dialogues. My remarks on religion and God, however, are likely to call forth labels like "arrogant", over-playing science, drawing on a "reductionist" sociology, or going well beyond what we know and can know about these subjects. From where I stand this reflects the consequences of wearing ideological blinders, simply not knowing enough about the historical sociology and anthropology of religion and God, and most important not understanding the sociological cogito. Furthermore, the interrogation of religion and God must be carried out fearlessly, courageously, without any thoughts of saving one's "soul" or whitewashing the eternal oblivion we all face. Not many people are ready to carry out this interrogation on such grounds. I expect and accept the labels which go with working on a frontier, pioneering, following the consiliency of evidences to their socio-logical conclusions. In the end, when all my arguments are rebuffed, I will be left with no other rationale for my standpoint but "Here I stand, shoulder to shoulder with my community of thinkers." Our motto is "The emperor has no clothes."

Chapter 1
Objectivity Revisited and Revised

I begin this book by exploring the terms of my title: objectivity, sociology, science, and anarchism. In the first two chapters, I consider the nature and meaning of objectivity. I will take the reader on a somewhat conventional tour of the subject but one that moves deliberately from the philosophical imagination toward the more revolutionary and empirical sociological understanding of objectivity. I begin by considering objectivity in the context of its conventional philosophical treatment, introducing the sociological imagination incrementally. The concept "objectivity" has been described as slippery and burdened by contradictory usages and inconclusive discussions. Contrary to its reputation in science as a basic goal, some critics have viewed it as a value and an ideology that manifests detachment and alienation from self, environment, and society. In some cases, the term "empirical" has come to be preferred over "objective". But objectivity as a value or ideology, and as a troublesome philosophical concept, should not be confused with objectivity as the affirmation of "objective reality". This affirmation is based on the fact that human beings do not and cannot know the nature of reality a priori and *per se*; they must exert mental, physical, and social effort to gain knowledge, to learn. In this sense, objectivity is generally viewed as the product of a social process, traditionally referred to as "intersubjective testing". The idea is readily paired with the norm that scientific evidence is public and communal.

My interest here is with the sociology of objectivity. But my sociological narrative necessarily unfolds against the background of the history of objectivity. Scientific virtues are contextual, and objectivity as the *sine qua non* virtue emerges only in the mid-nineteenth century. While objectivity has been "in the air" since the classical age in Greek philosophy, "truth-to-nature" and "trained judgment" prevailed in earlier eras as the key virtues of science. We owe a great debt to Lorraine Daston and Peter Galison (2007) for their notable efforts in contextualizing objectivity and unfolding its history in studied detail. Underlying this history is an ever-present struggle that pits objectivity in some form against some notion of subjectivity. This struggle, this tension, is of great significance in my project. It plays out against the history of sociology's opposition to psychological (and especially psychologistic) explanatory paradigms.

The classical social theory of objectivity rested on the assumption that communication and exchange in a public forum or community of scientists are necessary and effective means for insuring that we admit to science only statements that are valid approximations to objective reality and not products of abnormal perceptions, selective and unique subjective cognitions, or idiosyncratic and private introspections. The problem with this theory was that it treated the psychological level of scientific activity as problematic, but not the social level. The idea was that public tests, logic, and experiments or empirical observations gradually eliminate *personal* biases and mistakes. This leaves out the identification and elimination of *social* biases and mistakes which should be of at least equal concern. Before I turned my attention to the questions addressed in this book, one of my earliest efforts in the sociology of science was devoted to exploring what a sociologist could say about objectivity. This was the beginning of decades of work leading me in the direction of the positions I develop in this book. It is crucial that we have a robust sociological understanding of objectivity before we consider the relationship between anarchism and science.

Objectivity as a Social Fact

In his *Critique of Pure Reason*, Kant used the term "objective" to refer to knowledge that could be justified independently of any individual's whim. If a justification can, in principle, be tested and understood by anyone, it is objective. Karl Popper followed Kant in noting that the objectivity of a scientific statement is based on the fact that it can be intersubjectively tested. Objectivity, however, is not a product of universal human consensus. Practically, we tend to rely on corroboration by a limited number of persons, invested with the authority to establish "truth" by virtue of their "qualifications" and "credentials".

Classically, the extent to which a given definition of objectivity expressed its social nature varied from ideas such as "universal agreement", and "co-operative nature of scientific research" to various philosophical conceptions of "social institutions". Popper, for example, viewed laboratories, scientific periodicals, and congresses as the collective bases for generating scientific (objective) statements. He argued that an individual cannot simply decide to be "objective"; objectivity is a product of cooperation among scientists. Assume, Popper proposes, that an individual, trained in science but now alone and isolated from communication with others, succeeds in building laboratories and observatories. This Robinson Crusoe writes numerous papers based on his (or her) experiments and observations. He has unlimited time, and ultimately succeeds in developing scientific systems which coincide with those accepted by "our own scientists". Such a situation, Popper argues, would be nearly as accidental and miraculous as the case of science revealed to a clairvoyant. Before we turn to Popper's reasoning, it behooves us to note that Friday's co-presence on the island is and must be ignored here (along with various other locals Crusoe encounters) to make Popper's point cleanly. The reasons, then, are:

> **There is no one to check** this Crusoe's results.
> **There is no one to correct** the prejudices which unavoidably result from Crusoe's peculiar experiences.

No one can help Crusoe exploit the inherent possibilities of his results because such possibilities are often recognized in the course of adopting relatively irrelevant strategies in the face of the results.

Having no one to explain this work to, Crusoe is unable to develop the ability to communicate clear and reasoned results; this is a discipline that one learns only by having to explain one's work to others who have not done that work.

Crusoe can only discover his/her "personal equation" in a revealed way, by discovering changes in his/her reaction time and developing means for compensating; in "public" or "objective" science, reaction time is discovered when the contradictions among the results obtained by various observers are analyzed.

Popper concludes that objectivity is a social product, and not a product of an individual's impartiality. To the extent that such an impartiality exists, it is the result and not the source of the social nature of objectivity. Scientific criticism and scientific progress, according to Popper, depend on cooperation, intersubjectivity, and public method.

Norman Campbell, in a philosophical exercise similar to Popper's, concluded that a Crusoe *could* develop science even though the criterion of universal assent could not be applied. A scientific Crusoe could replace the intersubjective criterion with a subjective one by focusing on how satisfactory and coherent the laws were that one derived from the subject under study. This idea deserves serious attention. If it is meaningful to consider social factors which facilitate the production of objective statements, then a similar search could be undertaken to identify (social) psychological conditions which facilitate the production of objective statements. But Campbell's Crusoe would have to be socialized in some form of "scientific community" in order to later carry out his/her work in isolation. And it is with the nature of such a "community" that the sociology of objectivity is concerned. Campbell, of course, ignores the fact that his Crusoe is a social being and that living in isolation will take a toll on his/her humanity. The scientific self would lose its capacity to "do" science as the person declines emotionally and mentally, an inevitable consequence of isolation.

Having recognized that objectivity is a social fact, some students of science have gone on to ask what it is about the organization and values of science that accounts for its capacity to progressively generate objective statements. One response to this query has been to view science as an adventure in rugged individualism. Michael Polanyi was among the most articulate spokesmen for this *laissez-étudier* position. Polanyi argued that there is an "invisible hand" that coordinates the independent activities of individual scientists and leads to "unpremeditated" discoveries in science. Other examples of the *laissez-étudier* conception of science stress science as a democratic system with built in measures that prevent it from becoming political. Stated in its crudest and most sociologically vulnerable form this position requires scientists to do nothing but act in terms of what they consider their self-interests; the "invisible hand" is responsible for the beneficial societal outcomes of these independent acts of self-interest. But *laissez-étudier* sometimes gets linked to altruism and humanism, and scientists are portrayed as individuals whose self-interests happen to be broadly in line with the best interests of society at large.

In a more sophisticated approach to the problem of scientific progress, Thomas Kuhn argued that normal science is educationally narrow, rigid, and ill-designed to produce creative scientists. But he optimistically adds that individual rigidity is compatible with scientific progress. He does not consider whether rigidity is a social as well as an individual fact. Is the supply of scientific innovators – young scientists new to their fields – independent of social conditions within and outside of science? Can youth and newness become increasingly unlikely and ultimately impossible as individuals become more and more standardized and commodified, and as deviation becomes not merely less likely, but more intolerable and more at the mercy of agents and agencies of social control? Even if we assume the validity of Kuhn's model, certain "damping" effects on the cycles of scientific revolution and normal science can be hypothesized. The rigidifying effects of processes such as professionalization, bureaucratization, and routinization may lengthen the periods between revolutionary peaks, lessen the intensity of revolutions, progressively decrease periods of conceptual crisis in science, and progressively decrease the probabilities that *an individual scientist* will conceptualize a revolutionary idea, and that *such an idea will be recognized* and precipitate a crisis.

A second damping source is the "cost" associated with each revolution. Dialectical processes, as I noted earlier following Kenneth Boulding, incur costs. Such costs are cumulative and thus social systems, like biological systems, can progressively lose their capacity to recover and to continue to progress. This is part of the loss of adaptive potential that occurs as a species adapts to its ecological niche and eventually and inevitably fades off the evolutionary stage. This, incidentally, is one reason the business cycle model that locates the current economic crisis likely underestimates significantly the impact of the costs of this "cycle" on the nature of the recovery we can expect.

Science cannot be comprehended if social facts are ignored, treated naively, or approached with an optimism that obscures or denies their problematic nature. The full implications of the sociology of science must be recognized if science is to be genuinely comprehended as a social fact.

The Sociology of Knowledge

One of the basic objectives of sociologists of knowledge is establishing relationships between types of social structures and types of knowledge. A form of this idea had occurred to Francis Bacon. He identified values and interests associated with different types of institutions. Monarchies are associated with profit and pleasure, commonwealths with glory and vanity; universities are associated with sophistry and affectation, and cloisters incline to fables and unprofitable subtlety. He also speculated on whether the mind is more disabled by contemplation mixed with an active life or by a focus on contemplation. The systematic development of the sociology of knowledge in the late nineteenth and early twentieth centuries is associated with names such as Durkheim, Marx, Mannheim, Scheler, and Gurvitch. Scheler, for example, associated Plato's theory of ideas with the organization of the Platonic academy; he followed the Protestant theologian Ernst Troeltsch in arguing that Protestant beliefs determined and could only exist in the form of organization of the Protestant churches and sects; and he argued that *Gemeinschaft* societies generate a traditional, conclusive fund of knowledge rather than a form of knowledge which is continuously subject to discoveries and extensions.

The generalization of these types of hypotheses led to an intolerable relativism in the sociology of knowledge. If "scientific theories" are rooted in social milieux, then the prospect of obtaining warranted knowledge appears utterly futile. On this view, objectivity becomes an arbitrary mix of social conditions and relations, no more valid today than soothsaying in ancient Greece or Ptolemy's astronomy. Indeed, if we accept this perspective, what warrant is there for the sociology of knowledge, which must itself be "nothing but" a product of its particular social milieu?

One proposal for resolving this paradox is to assume that the sociology of knowledge can trace the emergence of different types of knowledge to different social milieux, but it cannot judge the truth-value of these systems. Furthermore, if types of knowledge are rooted in types of social milieux, we can set ourselves the task of discovering the social conditions under which "scientific" or "objective" knowledge is generated. The literature on science and society illustrates a number of approaches to this task. A stronger proposal, and the one I endorse, is to recognize that true and false knowledge is reached in the same way, by way of our interactions with others in our material environments with their earthly resources.

Science in some form has existed in all kinds of societies. The science referred to in the term "modern science", however, is assumed by many social thinkers to flourish in democratic contexts. This points to a crucial question: which societal type(s) facilitate(s) scientific development in the fullest measure? This question is often addressed by emphasizing external social forces and contexts that facilitate or obstruct scientific activity and scientific progress. Internal social forces and contexts that affect science as a social activity, process, organization, or institution were, in these traditional approaches, treated incidentally if at all. To fully comprehend science as a social fact, we must attend to internal factors. Professionalization and bureaucratization are examples of such forces and contexts. Both processes have been associated with the emergence of science as an autonomous, progressive social activity. Their continuing impact on science has stimulated some concern about dysfunctional consequences.

Scientists are normatively supposed to be rewarded for innovative and creative activities; bureaucratic norms value conformity over innovation and creativity. Bureaucratic organizations tend to exercise direct or indirect control over outsiders (or non-members). The more scientists become imbedded in bureaucracy the more their work norms become the work norms of the organization. The more "mature" the bureaucracy the more it tends to resist adapting to new conditions inside and outside the organization and the more it resists adopting innovative organizational and technological tools. One solution to this, practiced in some of the larger R&D firms, is to establish "off-campus" research sanctuaries where scientists identified as having the most creative potential work under conditions unfettered by conventional bureaucratic monitoring and oversight. Another solution is to keep organizationally off-line scientists on the payroll for ad hoc innovative projects.

Viewed in conventional social psychological terms, bureaucratization has a tendency to subordinate individual to collective decision-making, dividing responsibility for a given decision. This can easily lead to the negation of responsibility, and then to a failure to act effectively with regard to internal organizational problems, or broader "external" societal problems. Adopting a more strictly structural perspective would focus not on the conflict between "individual" and "collective" decision making but on the forms and substance of collective decision making. The conventional approach inherits the same problem we encountered in the unproblematized preference for intersubjectivity over subjectivity.

The dysfunctions of bureaucratization are reinforced by and reinforce the dysfunctions of professionalization. The two processes are linked at least to the extent that they are concomitant in the modern history of industrializing nations. Professionalization has been associated with the increasing specialization in the division of labor, the knowledge explosion, and the increasing demand for management expertise in highly technical and bureaucratized societies.

In the process of professionalization, an occupation becomes colleague-oriented, with practitioners seeking exclusive rights over naming and judging their mistakes. The goals of professionalization include standardizing, specializing, gaining status for occupational roles and services to society, and "objectivizing", limiting the impact of subjective elements on performance and service. One of the first, and among the foremost, students of professionalization, A.M. Carr-Saunders (1886-1966) concluded that professionalism was a hopeful feature of his time.

The dysfunctions of professionalization, however, arise precisely from the "hopeful" tendency toward occupational demarcation. This creates a volatile potential for subordinating reason to dogma. The structural basis for this is the closing off of the boundaries of the profession to outside influence. In medicine, for example, professional autonomy may have facilitated significant increments in knowledge about disease and treatment while simultaneously impeding the application of that knowledge. Professionalism tends to exempt the professional scientist from social responsibility, ethical codes notwithstanding. The negation of responsibility, as I noted earlier, has also been associated with bureaucratization.

The literature on professionals and complex organizations has traditionally stressed the conflicts inherent in linking the roles "professional" and "bureaucrat" based on differences between "professions" and "bureaucracies". This research focuses on the independent professional's resistance to bureaucratic standards, and his/her conditional loyalty to the bureaucracy. But there has been an increasing convergence of bureaucracies and professions, as bureaucrats become professionalized and professionals become bureaucratized. In this convergence, the dysfunctions of the two processes reinforce one another. Bureaucratization, for example, may reinforce tendencies in professionalization toward occupational closure and dogma with its demands for reliable responses and strict adherence to rules and regulations.

To the extent that the dysfunctions of bureaucratization and professionalization become increasingly salient and converge, we can expect a tendency toward occupational closure, an ethnocentrism of work, and a decrease in the capacity of individuals and organizations to respond to problems in critical and creative ways. This tends to undermine and eventually eliminate any pretentions to objectivity.

The important point to consider when thinking about the dysfunctions of professionalization and bureaucratization is not so much what it reflects about particular empirical realities, but the fact that it illustrates the mutability of social facts and the potential that exists in all social phenomena for dysfunctional or pathological transformation. Philosophers and other students of science have acknowledged the potential for evolutionary or progressive developmental change in science, but they have not given adequate attention to the potential for devolutionary change inherent in science as a social phenomenon. Students of "the crisis in science" in the 1960s and 1970s (including some philosophers) were, however, attentive to the dysfunctions of professionalization and bureaucratization.

The Crisis in Science

In the wake of the upheavals of the 1960s, some scientists and philosophers were asking questions by the early 1970s about the inhospitable climate for science. The title of a 1971 article in *Science* by the historian of science Arnold Thackray paraphrased Charles Babbage's 1830 *Reflections on the Decline of Science in England and on Some of its Causes.* Thackray confronted *Science* readers with his reflections on the decline of science in America, concluding that broadening social costs and implications demanded new forms of scientific organization.

J.D. Bernal (1939), writing early in the twentieth century, produced the first comprehensive report on the modern crisis in science. He wrote that the contemporary view of the "fruits of science" was dominated by images of war, economic chaos, the willful destruction of needed goods, and the fear of more and more terrible wars. Twenty-five years later, Bernal (1964) wrote that the potential of science for serving humanity was lower than it had ever been in a world burdened by class divisions and unprecedented levels of poverty, stupidity, and cruelty.

In the 1930s, Pitirim Sorokin (described by Robert K. Merton as a "sociological Jeremiah") regularly lectured on the decline of science. He warned prophetically that one day scientists would make it possible to destroy all life on earth, and then some of them would be curious to see what happens when the button is pressed. This is reminiscent of Fillipo Buounarroti's concern during the French Revolution that scientists would derive from their successes distinctions, a sense of superiority, and exemptions from the everyday burdens and responsibilities of the everyday citizen. The consequence might be indulging in enterprises that could be harmful to the interests of the masses.

Thinkers as varied as Francis Bacon, Thomas Huxley, H.D. Thoreau, and George Santayana have worried about the possible dangers to our imagination of the increasing abstractions that characterized modern science. I was a young man who like the young Thomas Huxley thought that science was somehow better, richer, and purer than other human activities. It *should be*, but the intrigues in science Huxley complained about in one of his letters led him to conclude that science was no better than other human activities.

The root of crises in science is the trivial fact that scientists are human beings. More to the point is the fact that science is a social activity and social process. It is an institution, and like all institutions is prone to become rigid and overly conforming over time. Under the impact of professionalization and bureaucratization, standards in science can lose their function as expressions and guarantors of excellence and become excuses for constraining originality and creativity. As the 1960s unfolded and the 1970s arrived, social, natural, and physical scientists began to pay increasing attention to the crisis. The late physicist John Ziman (1968: 65), a prominent figure in the science studies movement, warned of "closure" and "ecclesiasticism" in modern science arising as a consequence of the increasing control of certification in science by an "establishment". In science as in other social activities, professionalization and bureaucratization have tended to increase specialization to the point of overspecialization, and stimulated the development of excessive competition and a conflictful division of labor. This has led some scholars to speculate about possible decreases in the evolutionary (or if you prefer "developmental" or "progressive") potential of science. The resolution of the crisis in science – and the broader societal crisis to which it is related – is not guaranteed. A necessary condition, however, for resolving the crisis is rethinking the nature of science, and its relationship to values and social organization. In the next section, I consider the problem of value orientations and the generation of objective knowledge.

Science and Values

The goal of scientific activity is the comprehension (knowledge, understanding, explanation, and appreciation) of human experience and the application of that knowledge in solving problems of survival and cultural growth. It assumes a comprehensible reality. The form of this assumption varies. One can imagine, for example, a single physical reality "out there" which we can come to know progressively by creatively applying the tools of science (including observation, intuition, logic, and experiment). Or we can think of knowledge as the goal of an unending process that is never free of error. On this view, our scientific efforts produce fallible, corrigible, tentative truths and our knowledge continually increases by degrees. We are justified in assuming that our world and our universe in all their diversity is knowable in principle, but not in thinking that we can ever achieve unconditional and complete knowledge.

The truth of any given theory can only be approximate, conditional, and relative. But this does not mean that there is no "objective reality". Knowledge is not a simple matter of human goals, interests, and will. Nor is the lawfulness of nature a complete fantasy. Our experience shows that scientific knowledge and even laws have some objective content. My position here has been influenced by the views of the late David Bohm, one of the central figures in twentieth century physics. Our objective in science is to find more and more of the things of which matter in becoming is composed, to study the relationships among these things in better and better approximations, and to discover the conditions under which specific concepts and laws are applicable in greater and greater detail. Science approaches unreachable truths by studying multiplicities and diversities of an ever unfolding universe.

The question of the nature of objective reality can be examined in a broader historical and classical context by distinguishing between the hypotheses of Parmenides and Heraclitus. The Parmenidian hypothesis states that for the world to be knowable, reality must be eternally immutable. The Heraclitian hypothesis states that the Parmenidian hypothesis is formally true; but it offers no imperative for humans since reality is in constant flux and therefore unknowable. The contrast here is between absolutist and relativist perspectives on acquiring knowledge. These hypotheses or assumptions entail fixed minds, a fixed nature, and fixed principles. But it is clear that nature and principles have changed. This experience yields neither the Parmenidian nor the Heraclitian hypothesis, but the Bohmian hypothesis of variable minds comprehending variable nature using variable principles.

The concept of nature as an infinite diversity of things in becoming expresses more clearly than relatively static alternative conceptions of nature the need to conceptualize science and the "search for truth" as an endless process. The question then arises, what values must direct our activities if we are to engage in science, a dynamically cumulative and effectively endless process? In his pioneering work on the "norms of science" Merton attempted to derive the "ethos" of science from the goals and methods of science. Universalism, communism, disinterestedness, and organized skepticism were identified as the basic ingredients of the scientific ethos. Other notable contributions to the study of the norms of science were made by Parsons, Barber, and Storer. These contributions have been criticized on several counts.

> **They encourage a view of the norms** as those which do and should (logically) prevail in science; the relationship between ideal and actual behavior and orientation is ignored or obscured, and no provision is made for potential or actual changes in the norms due to changes in the organization and goals of science, changes in conceptions of the goals and methods of science, or changes in the social and cultural contexts of science;
> **The identification of the norms of science** should be based on systematic, continuous, and cumulative empirical and theoretical analyses.

The virtues of the norm studies are that they:

> **Contribute to the development** of a model of science and its logically associated values,

and

> **Do, in fact, identify** a number of orientations which must direct the pursuit of objective knowledge.

Due consideration, however, has not been given to the humanistic dimensions of the scientific ethos, and to whether this ethos is thriving or threatened by the external and internal social relations of science. Merton (1963), for one, does exhibit an awareness of these problems in his writings on the ambivalence of scientists and sociological ambivalence in general (cf. Mitroff, 1974). Mertonian sociology of science, however, does not linger on the human face of science and does not feed the radical science agenda.

The idea that scientific activity implies a certain set of values has been lucidly expressed by Jacob Bronowski (1965). If, he argues, the goal of scientific activity is to chase after truth, then scientists must be individually independent and collectively tolerant. These two "prime values" are the foundation for a set of values: "dissent, freedom of thought and speech, justice, honour, human dignity and self-respect". These values are inescapable as conditions of scientific activity. They are not derived from the virtues of scientists, nor from the self-aggrandizing codes of conduct professions use as moral and ethical reminders.

We need something more refined than professional codes of ethics, religious doctrines, or philosophical warrants to guarantee as much as we can the vital signs of science. Some observers from the radical science movement in the 1970s suggested one or another version of a general humanistic commitment. This was a new arena of inquiry in that period, and even today it is Abraham Maslow's (1971) humanistic psychology that provides some of the best insights into what such a commitment might mean.

Maslow's work in this area is especially interesting on two counts: first, because it is congruent with Bohm's "in-becoming" conception of nature; second, because it encompasses many, if not all, of the values associated by students of science from Merton to Bronowski with the scientific ethos. Maslow assumes the intrinsic value of truth, and views inquiry as a basic defining activity of human life. Among the so-called "being-values" Maslow associates with the "good person" and the "good society" are truth, goodness, beauty, wholeness, dichotomy-transcendence, aliveness, uniqueness, perfection, necessity, completion, justice, order, simplicity, richness, effortlessness, playfulness, and self-sufficiency.

The search for a humanistic ethos has often overlapped with some variety of "radicalism". The association of science with radicalism can be considered curious only by those who have not thought seriously about the nature and history of inquiry. The scientific ethos tends to conflict with the ethos of other social institutions. This conflict plays out in terms of ideals; realistically, science at any given time and place must be institutionally congruent with the prevailing values, norms, and beliefs of its social and cultural context.

Ideally, only science is associated with a full, uncompromising, unfettered commitment to pursuing knowledge. Scientific inquiry must be constantly pressed forward, driven by skepticism and the idea that even fundamental assumptions are ultimately subject to criticism and change. Nothing is protected from the basic query, Why? No other social activity – and in reality not even scientific activity itself – operates fully according to this imperative to inquiry. Scientific activity – "true science" – must inevitably be perceived as a radical activity relative to the other social activities in a society. When Tom Hayden, writing as a leader of the "new left" in the 1960s, defined the "radical style" he came intriguingly close to a definition of science. Radicalism as a style means penetrating a problem to its roots, to its real causes. It demands continually pressing forward under the guidance of the "why" question. Radicalism does not rest on conclusions, sees all answers as provisional, and is ready to discard conclusions and answers as evidence and conditions change. This was one of the moments in my intellectual biography that constitutes a birthing moment for ideas that led to this book. Notice that conservative resistance to "liberal" and "left-wing" tendencies in education and the academy reflect the fact that the interrogative disciplines and institutions are necessarily – in everyday political terms – left-wing and liberal activities, and indeed as I point out here, radical.

Bringing the radical perspective to its anarchistic conclusions should not be interpreted as an extension of the liberal agenda. Anarchists seek to develop social life from the ground up by way of direct cooperative organizations qualitatively different from and smaller in scale than the state (Suissa, 2006: 52-53).

In addition to humanistic and radical commitments, a related value orientation that must be considered in constructing a scientific ethos is "reflexivity". Reflexive sociology, like the sociological imagination, views the person as radically shaped at the intersection of biography, history, and culture in the context of evolving societies. It shares with Marx the view that while we are products of history and culture, we make history; but we do not make history any way we wish. Sociology has been haunted from its beginnings by a conflict between the concept of the "oversocialized self" and the idea that there is an inevitable "slippage" between self and society. I will work toward a resolution of this conflict in the course of this book. For the moment, let's consider reflexivity and why it is an important moment in radical sociology.

Reflexivity can be generalized as follows: a reflexive life is one in which the "things" of experience are all and always, at least in part, turned inward, and incorporated in our increasing awareness of who, what, and where we are. Physics can be learned reflexively by analyzing ourselves as physical systems. Astronomy and geology can be studied in terms of their meaning relative to our existence in and relationship to the universe – past, present, and future. The most so-called "abstract" human endeavors have reflexive potential. In the classical way of thinking about mathematics and logic, for example, such disciplines can be explored as themselves explorations in the structure and processes of thinking. Reflexivity is not a one way process. Its relevance for a scientific ethos lies in the fact that increased awareness is a condition of new perceptions and ultimately new conceptualizations and comprehensions.

Humanistic, radical, and reflexive commitments are bases for the construction of a scientific ethos. In a sense, they are the specification and elaboration of values apparent in ideal science, and in "good" scientific research. This complex of values emphasizes open-endedness, process, and change; it is in this sense consistent with Bohmian reality. It is also consistent with – and in part reflects – certain developments in the psychology of science and the theory of inquiry.

The Psychology of Science and the Theory of Inquiry

Abraham Maslow pioneered the development of a psychology of science that reflects the realities of human psychology and of scientific activity. He pointed out that scientific activity can be an anxiety-avoiding, anxiety-controlling mechanism and that it can be "neuroticized"; it then becomes more a defense mechanism and less a growth-motivated activity. The growth-motivated scientist can be at home with precision without being compulsive and rigid; s/he can pursue truth and beauty and at the same time value ambiguity, casualness, and even in the appropriate circumstances sloppiness. The education of scientists must expose them to techniques of caution *and* boldness.

Objectivity, according to Maslow, means seeing things "as they really are". He distinguishes between "not-caring", "*laissez-faire*" objectivity, and "caring" objectivity. Not-caring objectivity allows scientists to assert their freedom from a priori truths established by the church or state. "Caring" objectivity arises in situations where "not caring" is difficult or impossible. Such situations are not unknown in the scientist's relationship to physical and natural phenomena; but they emerge most clearly with the development of the human and social sciences.

In these sciences, the application of traditional canons of objectivity results in scientists trying to be objective about people, values, and themselves, things that they love and hate.

The basic thesis of "caring" objectivity is that loving someone or something enough means you will not want to interfere with him/her or it. By not interfering, you will perceive what you love as it is, without the contaminating effects of selfish goals. Such "contamination" can never be entirely avoided; but it is certainly possible to reduce the amount of physical manipulation used in exploring things. This aspect of science must be stressed because it has been subordinated to literal and theoretical "analyses into parts" for so long. Both approaches are necessary ingredients of science. Scientists must learn to live with control and lack of control, being tight and loose, sensible and crazy, and being sober or playful. The failure to teach and learn science in this way will damage the psychological health of the scientist as well as obstruct his/her creativity.

Considering these humanistic perspectives on science in the 1960s prompted some observers to begin making connections to the eastern religious and philosophical traditions. Maslow, for example, identified two polar activities in science: at one end, the scientist experiences and tries to comprehend concreteness; at the other end, s/he has to organize concrete experiences into comprehensible abstractions. In the atmosphere of the 1960s, it could appear with utter transparency that the activity of abstracting in science was like or no different than the Taoistic conception of non-intrusive, receptive contemplation. Thus, in addition to controlled experiments and quasi-experiments, comprehension of "objective reality" in its totality required a second mode of inquiry: receptive, contemplative, and non-interfering. In addition to the readily identified distinction between rationality and intuition, some students of the eastern ways now added a third category of knowing referred to as mystical, sage, or no-knowledge. In brief, then, a defense of new ways of knowing emerged and flourished in that period based on importing taoistic ideas into science. This idea is still a part of the intellectual landscape.

Scientists and philosophers have readily admitted intuition into the scientific process. But since intuition cannot, by definition, be incorporated into a paradigm (but see further on in this chapter) it has been accorded only cursory and anecdotal attention in the methodology of science. But the rational-intuitive process has limits. Beyond these limits, we are encouraged by mystically oriented inquirers to embrace the Tao. Describing what this means is not easy. The Tao transcends events and qualities; it has no shape or time. As a result it cannot be the object of ordinary knowledge. At the highest level of cognizance, the sage forgets distinctions between things. S/he lives in the silence of what remains in the undifferentiable whole. We face the same problem here that we do with respect to gaining intellectual access to an unknowable God. What does it mean to say that we can know in whatever sense you please unknowable things?

If science is the process of comprehending an "infinite variety of things" then the totality of human creative and critical intelligence must be tapped in order to deal with that infinite variety. The defenders of a Tao of science have contributed to the identification of the different modes human beings have used for comprehending reality and have provided a rationale for viewing these different modes as complementary, and as integrally related. These ideas can lead some advocates to make indefensible connections between mysticism and science. For the moment let's see if there is a way to think about this approach that might further our ways of thinking about science.

Let's assume then that rationality and intuition do not exhaust all our ways of knowing and that the taoistic approach captures the limits of rational and intuitive knowing. It is possible to conceive the scientific process represented by the concepts rationality, intuition, and no-knowledge (R-I-N) as one in which the R-I-N comprehension of reality at any given point in history and culture ultimately becomes assimilated into a rational structure, and gives rise to a new R-I-N comprehension. This idea is a least implicit in the theory of inquiry proposed by TenHouten and Kaplan (1973). They hypothesize the existence of a general class of nonscientific inquiries, called "synthetic" inquiries. Their thesis is that science involves perception but is primarily language based; synthetic inquiries involve language, but they are primarily perceptual. This distinction, they claim, has a neurological basis. We are faced here with another creation that emerged out of the revolutionary haze of the 1960s, the left-brain/right-brain paradigm. Let us follow up on the idea that there are two modes of inquiry without importing at the same time the notion that these modes are lateralized in the brain. The two modes of inquiry are propositional (scientific, analytical) and appositional (synthetic).

TenHouten and Kaplan admit that science is grounded primarily in propositional rationalities. Students of science and scientists themselves have tended to raise these propositional rationalities to the status of the rationalities of science. TenHouten and Kaplan claim that science in practice is not limited to propositional rationalities. Theory construction may involve integrating appositional and propositional modes. This does not seem too radical. They go further, however, and argue that creative science may transcend lateralized functions of the brain. Again, we can ignore this sort of "new age" cognitivism and still entertain the interesting idea that synthetic modes such as the Tarot and the I Ching complement propositional modes in science. The sociological viability of this idea is enhanced by eliminating the bi-lateral brain hypothesis and noticing that it has a parallel in Harold Garfinkel's (1967: 262-268) theory of rationalities. The four synthetic rationalities parallel the four rationalities of scientific method identified by Garfinkel. The synthetic (nonscientific) rationalities are present in the Tarot, I Ching, and in "primitive" inquiry (represented in the teachings of the magi, sorcerers, mystics, and traditional healers). The objective of this exercise is to expand the repertoire of scientific rationalties in a way that might ground an anarchistic anything goes philosophy or sociology of science. In the end we may have to jettison some or all of these strategies, some of which smell of 1960s "new age" indulgences. The benefit of carrying this exercise forward is that it will help us as anarchists by revealing embedded anarchisms in science-in-practice and identify areas where science needs to be modified in order to make it compatible with an anarchist agenda.

TenHouten and Kaplan (TK) propose the following "transformation" in which Garfinkel's (G) inventory of scientific rationalities is "mapped" or "mirrored" against an inventory of nonscientific rationalities.

Transformation A:
Compatibility of ends-means relationships with principles of formal logic (G).
Compatibility of means-ends relationships with layers of structural perception (TK).
Transformation B:
Semantic clarity and distinctness (G).
Semantic veiledness and complexity (TK).
Transformation C:
Clarity and distinctness "for their own sakes" (G).
Veiledness and complexity "for their own sakes" (TK).
Transformation D:
Compatibility of the definitions of a situation with scientific knowledge (G).
Compatibility of the perception of a situation with synthetic knowledge (TK).

TenHouten and Kaplan conclude that scientific theory construction, concept formation, and methodology involve essentially subjective synthetic rationalities. Objective rationalities are employed primarily in linguistic formulations. TenHouten and Kaplan affirm the analytic duality of objectivity-subjectivity (manifesting the hemispheric duality of the brain in their program), and the transcendence of this duality in total brain functions (physically rooted, perhaps, in the corpus callosum which links the hemispheres if we confine ourselves to their lateralization conjecture). Science represents a dialectical unification of objective and subjective rationalities. TenHouten and Kaplan's view of this process is similar to the view I outlined earlier of a rational, intuitive, no-knowledge dialectic. Indeed, it may be that TenHouten and Kaplan have given us a clue as to how intuition and no-knowledge can be rationalized. Instead of passively "waiting" for moments of insight or flashes of intuition, "paradigms" like the I Ching may be turned to when rational paradigms are exhausted. Such exercises might lead to the systematization, modification, and eventual rationalization in "objective" terms of the synthetic modes. This would in turn lead to the emergence of a new R-I-N, or, in TenHouten and Kaplan's terms, propositional-appositional framework. Rationalization or objectivization would provide "closer approximations" to reality, but would also create new frontiers for intuition and no-knowledge, or for appositional modes.

The crisis in science reflects in part the fact that the prevailing objectivity-subjectivity dichotomy is increasingly an obstruction to scientific inquiry. This reflects novel problems of the human and social sciences, and the emerging ecological-evolutionary challenges confronting the human species. These emerging problems demand a new set of problem-solving structures and values. Two things seem to be necessary for solving these problems in ways congruent with the enhancement of human life. One is a broader and at the same time more sophisticated conception of science, such as suggested in the works of Maslow, and TenHouten and Kaplan. This is strategy one; strategy two modifies strategy one based on the findings of the post-1970 sociology of science. The second is a generalization of this conception of science to other societal activities. The congruencies I discussed between the scientific ethos and humanistic, radical, and reflexive values should be examined carefully. Such an examination may support current speculations on the essential oneness of a scientific ethos emphasizing wisdom rather than simple technical prowess and efficiency, and a life-enhancing ethos. This in turn would bring science closer to the form of knowing compatible with an anarchist agenda. The next task is to examine bases for constructing organizations consistent with the values of science.

The Social Organization of Science

Proposals for resolving the crisis in science emphasize the necessity of achieving a closer realization of the ideal communal organization of science. These organizational proposals are usually linked, implicitly if not explicitly, to values which fit into the complex of humanistic, radical, and reflexive values discussed above. Examples of such proposals include Bernal's (1939) advocacy of "science as communism", Husserl's (1950/1970) association of "scientific culture" with thoughtfulness and enlightenment, and Jaspers' (1963) conception of science as a basis for world-unity, friendship, and trust where the fundamental drive of science turns common work into a foundation for friendship.

The "communistic" or "communal" theme is not radical in science; it has been identified as one of the norms of science. Merton used "communism" in "the nontechnical and extended sense of common ownership of goods", and referred to it as an "integral element of the scientific ethos". Writing in 1942, Merton noted that concerns about the "frustration of science" reflected the conflict between the communistic ethos and the definition of technology as "private property" in a capitalistic economy. He noted a variety of responses to the conflict: defensively patenting scientific work to ensure its public availability; urging the promotion of new businesses by scientists; and advocating socialism.

Wartofsky (1974) later outlined a rationale for socializing science. His argument rests on the assumption that science is reason. The rationality of science is the highest achievement of the evolutions of cognition. In spite of this, science seemed as the twentieth century unfolded increasingly dysfunctional or maladaptive. Wartofsky's vantage point is global ecological and evolutionary history. The question he raises is whether rationality, viewed as an adaptive mechanism, has begun to show the characteristic signs of a growth-mechanism that reaches the limits of its adaptive potential and becomes detrimental to survival. The dysfunctions of science, he says, are the result of reason being used as a tool in conflicts of interests and wills. The liberating features of science under such circumstances become repressive. His conclusion is consistent with advocacy of the communal ethos in science except in its emphasis on the sense of responsibility the ethos implies. If we consider his call for socializing reason and Merton's communal ethos, we can see the beginnings of a rationale for a more progressive form of science and necessarily a more progressive form of society. Against the background of associating science with democratic and socialist organizational forms and values and communistic or communalistic norms, the idea of an anarchist science should not seem so implausible.

When science is conceived as a social system unto itself, isolated from other human enterprises and from the social psychological and sociological realities of those enterprises, the communal ethos is also isolated; its relevance to broader socio-cultural concerns is obscured. An awareness of the reciprocal relations between science and society, and of the fact that science is a social activity and social process, leads inevitably to a generalization of the communal ethos. Just as this ethos was linked to the survival of science in isolation, it now becomes linked to the survival of the species. The fact that communality is advocated in the traditional-normative conception of science, and also in radical conceptions of socialized science is a strong rationale for considering communality a basic organizational imperative in science. Here it is important to recall that Darwin, who could be called the Durkheim of biology, emphasized cooperation as against competition as the key to adaptation and survival.

Progress is a second organizational imperative. Progress is not a function of optimism but a logical necessity in an infinitely diverse universe. In order to comprehend reality we must organize in such a way that we maximize actualization of our potential for achieving closer and closer approximations to reality. More generally, if science is conceived to encompass all activities which contribute to human progress and evolution, then the question we must answer is: How must human beings organize in order to adapt, progress, and evolve? Put this way, the idea of progress and the notion of closer and closer approximation to reality do not have much purchase in contemporary thought. However, let's see if we can find some way to re-imagine these ideas.

Following the sociologist Gerhard Lenski (1970: 59), I define progress as the process by which human beings raise the upper limit of their capacity for perceiving, conceptualizing, accumulating, processing, mobilizing, and utilizing information and energy in the adaptive-evolutionary process. The relationship between adaptation and evolution is a paradoxical one. On the one hand, survival depends on the capacity to adapt to surroundings; on the other hand, adaptation involves increasing specialization and decreasing evolutionary potential. Adaptation is a dead end. As a given entity adapts to a given set of conditions, it specializes to the point that it begins to lose any capacity for adapting to significant changes in those conditions. The anthropologists Sahlins and Service (1960: 95-97) summarize these ideas as follows:

> **Principle of Stabilization:** specific evolution (the increase in adaptive specialization by a given system) is ultimately self-limiting.
> **General evolution:** (progressive advance measured in absolute terms rather than in terms of degrees of adaptation in particular environments) occurs because of the emergence of new, relatively unspecialized forms.
> **Law of Evolutionary Potential:** increasing specialization narrows adaptive potential. The more specialized and adaptive a mechanism or form is at any given point in evolutionary history, the smaller is its potential for adapting to new situations and passing on to a new stage of development.

Sahlins and Service discuss the applicability of these principles to socio-cultural change. This was not and is not a new concern in sociology. What is noteworthy is that the revival of interest in evolutionary theory among sociologists is associated with an increasing interest in the sociological relevance of ecology (which by itself is also not a new concern among sociologists). Lenski's *Human Societies* (1970) outlined an evolutionary-ecological approach that represented a radical departure from mainstream introductions to sociology. John Leggett (1973) later outlined an evolutionary approach to political sociology. The attraction of evolutionary and ecological theories is that they are relatively more sophisticated than general sociological theories, and that they tend to converge. In both perspectives, for example, viability is associated with complexity, flexibility, and diversity. Contemporary evolutionary approaches to sociology (e.g., Sanderson, 2001; Lenski, 2005) should be distinguished from the developmental theories of Spencer, Durkheim, and Parsons.

   In some cases, sociological research seems to have uncovered the operation of principles of social organization that parallel evolutionary and ecological principles. All of this suggests the possibility of a general approach to systems and change that encompasses ecology, evolution, and social organization. In particular, given the theme of this chapter, an approach that manifested or otherwise allowed for the imperatives of community (as ecology might) and progress (as evolutionary theory might) in science would be ideal. One approach which recommends itself because of its generality and congruence with the open-endedness of reality, the Maslowian psychology of science, the TenHouten and Kaplan theory of inquiry, and the humanistic-radical-reflexive value complex, is dialectical sociology.

Dialectical Sociology

The pervasiveness of dialectical thinking (e.g., in Bohm, TenHouten and Kaplan, Maslow, and others) suggests the possibility that a dialectical perspective could ground the scientific worldview. My objective in the following discussion is the modest one of proposing a dialectical strategy for designing progressive scientific communities in the context of the concept of a progressive society.

If we begin by assuming a Bohmian reality, Maslow, and TenHouten and Kaplean recommend themselves because their ideas are consistent with the Bohmian view, part of, and conditions for comprehending that reality. Their ideas, and the value orientations I considered, have a dialectical quality congruent with Bohm's view of reality. It is reasonable to consider the hypothesis that Bohmian reality encompasses social reality. In that case, we can find sociological and philosophical perspectives that mirror or are otherwise compatible with Bohm's views. I should note that Bohm had a Marxist perspective and was influenced especially by Engels' ideas. Engels outlined a dialectical perspective on physical, natural, and social reality. According to Engels, the laws of dialects are abstracted from natural and social history. Following Hegel, Engels notes that these laws are simply the most general laws describing history and thought itself unfolding through time. These laws describe the transformation of quantity into quality and quality into quantity, the interpenetration of opposites, and the negation of the negation. I make no claims here about the clarity, precision, or logic of these ideas, nor their relationship to Hegel's philosophy. The point here is perspective, worldview, the big picture. Nonetheless, when we follow through on these ideas there is more substance than critics might imagine.

Gurvitch's (1957, 1963) view of social reality parallels Bohm's view of reality. He paints a picture of social reality in constant motion, filled with tension, always on the verge of revolution. Gurvitch adds some substance to the idea of the dialectic I am unfolding here by identifying five operational procedures.

Complementarily (contradictory alternatives turn out to be complementary; two polarities are connected by a continuum; polar points pull together, i.e., go in the same direction; and they pull apart, i.e., as a compensatory action).
Mutual implication (things that are heterogeneous or opposite exhibit mutuality and interdependency; they turn out to be imminent, at least partially, in one another).
Ambiguity (ambiguity can eventually lead to ambivalence, and then to polarization).
Polarization (tensions between social factors can resolve themselves into polarizations, or they can resolve into ambiguities, mutual implications, or complementarities).
Reciprocity of perspectives (total identification and separation are denied; mutual immanence, parallelism, and symmetry).

The affinity between the dialectical view of social reality and the dialectical views of Bohm, Maslow, and TenHouten and Kaplan makes it reasonable to allow dialectical assumptions to guide us, at least in part, in the construction of scientific organizations. I want to keep stressing lest the point becomes obscured that reconstructing science organizationally cannot be carried out in isolation from reconstructing society. Following Gurvitch's schema, the organizational imperative would be to coordinate his operational procedures with organizational structures and processes. One possible starting point for such coordination is the research on "creative organizations". This makes sense given the fact that science is paradigmatically creative and innovative. The characteristics of creative organizations show several points of coordination with Gurvitch's operational procedures, and the more general dialectical laws summarized by Engels. The use of ad hoc devices and approaches, contact with outside sources, a heterogeneous personnel policy, the inclusion of marginal and unusual individuals, assignments for non-specialists, allowances for eccentricity, experimentation, decentralization, a risk-taking ethos, cooperation between stable "philistines" and roaming "creators" are all characteristics which allow for the creation of and interplay between and among polarities, contradictory alternatives, ambiguities and ambivalences, and reciprocal perspectives. Creative organizations, in short, are structurally and dynamically dialectical and anarchistic.

Conclusion

Objectivity is a social fact. The achievement of closer, more detailed, and more exact approximations to objective reality in a universe of infinite diversity cannot be taken for granted. This has been recognized by students of the crisis in science. While this crisis *per se* is associated with an earlier period in our history, that crisis is still at large. The crisis in science is a species-level crisis, one that reflects the emergence of ecological and evolutionary challenges that are new in type and scale. Perhaps our species has reached the limits of its adaptability. What is the next step in evolution?

Annihilation is one possibility. What about the emergence of a post-homo sapien species? That species would already have to be in our midst if the global challenges we face are going to be met and there is no evidence that I know of that suggests this is realistic. Science fiction narratives and some postmodern technological narratives suggest that humans will be replaced by machines or a new human-machine hybrid – cyborgs or robosapiens. Evolution, however, is not only about biology and bio-technology; it is also about culture. We still have the option, in my view, of developing new value orientations and new forms of social organization and achieving new levels of cultural evolution. New levels of consciousness concerning the physical, natural, and social worlds must be achieved. This applies to our consciousness of science as a social reality. This sounds like I am separating consciousness and culture, but that is neither my intention nor is it the way consciousness and culture work. They co-evolve.

Our conception of science must be broadened to include all modes of inquiry and interrogation pursued indefatigably, identifying and encompassing more and more of objective reality. The facilitation of science – or inquiry – depends on developing an integrated perspective on (and, ultimately, theory of) the nature of reality, the social psychology, sociology, and anthropology of inquiry, and the relationship between inquiry, values, and social organization. The primary concern of the sociologist of science in this endeavor is with social organization and how it facilitates and/or obstructs inquiry. This concern has to be matched with a concern for the social and cultural contexts of science.

Among the tasks that lie immediately ahead are comparative studies of research organizations, theoretical studies of social organizations, and experiments in the design of scientific organizations. Following the strategy I have proposed, these studies would be guided by a dialectical paradigm. Other promising paradigms, such as general systems theory, should not be ignored. These studies must be guided by a sense of current and emerging ecological-evolutionary challenges, and an unwavering commitment to raising the probability of enhanced human living on this planet. I proposed a general theory of society that integrated dialectical sociology, general systems sociology, and ecological-evolutionary sociology in Restivo (1991: 79-98).

The present abounds in evolutionary and devolutionary tendencies. To encounter these tendencies without care and passion for one's self and one's community, to meet them technocratically and scientistically, or to sit back and rely on providential good will can only court disaster. A sociology of objectivity cannot insure that we will continue to do science, or participate indefinitely in the evolutionary process. It can, however, provide us with a better sense of what has to be done, and what (in terms of available resources) can be done. It can help us identify conditions of evolution and devolution, progression and regression. Only our participation in this process of uncertainties can determine whether "wisdom" (Jonas Salk), a "higher sanity", (Theodore Roszak), and "life and liberation" (Brian Easlea) can take root in this world.

In the early years of the science studies movement, David Bloor, Barry Barnes, and others resurrected the problem of the limits of the sociology of knowledge. As in the past, this problem arises in particular with regard to the sociology of scientific knowledge, and, especially, the sociology of mathematical knowledge. There are two aspects of this problem: (i) the problem of demarcating scientific and non-scientific knowledge, and (ii) the problem of accounting for objective knowledge given the assumption that knowledge is a social product, a social construction, and a social institution. The problem of "limits" is rooted in the prevailing assumptions of the sociology of knowledge, and a resolution of the problem requires rejecting or altering those assumptions. In particular, I propose a resolution based on rejecting or altering: (i) the "social theory of objectivity," that is, the idea that intersubjective testing and consensus guarantee objectivity, (ii) the conventional "one reality" assumption; (iii) the imperialistic tendency of the so-called "strong programme" championed by Bloor; and (iv) the privileged status of science and rationality in inquiry. The relativistic implication of this set of rejections, (v), is also rejected. My criticisms and the alternatives I recommend in each case constitute the basis for an alternative sociology of objective knowledge (objectivity). That this alternative is implicated in a theory of political economy, and more broadly, in a theory of lifestyles, values, and worldviews, should become evident as my argument unfolds. In this first chapter, I have taken the first steps toward an understanding of science in terms of an anarchist paradigm. Even the most conservative paradigms for and philosophies and sociologies of science tend to a view of science as an anarchistic anything goes enterprise. This first chapter has planted some of the seeds of an anarchist science that will come to fruition as we continue. In the next chapter, I will review some of the ground we've just gone over and move toward a more fully developed sociology of objectivity.

Chapter 2
The Social Theory of Objectivity
and Its Problems

Scientists and philosophers of science have generally assumed: (i) that there is some sort of "objective reality"; (ii) that this objective reality is not directly accessible to us, that is, we must operate on our world in a certain way in order to reveal objective reality; (iii) that, as individuals, we are subject to abnormal perceptions, selective and unique cognitions, biases, and mistakes; and (iv) that the fact of subjectivity is not a barrier to learning the secrets of nature because subjectivity can be transcended or neutralized in the public forum, or community, of science. I will refer to this resolution of the problem of objectivity as the social theory of objectivity. The two central ideas on which this theory rests are intersubjectivity and consensus.

Intersubjectivity

The social theory of objectivity is reflected in definitions of objectivity which refer to the cooperative nature of science and the collective bases of scientific statements. According to this theory, an individual cannot simply decide to be objective because objectivity is an intersubjective product. We saw in Chapter 1 how Karl Popper and Norman Campbell dramatized this problem using a Robinson Crusoe narrative and reached opposed conclusions. Recall Popper's three world concept: World 1 is the physical world, World 2 is the mental world, and World 3 is the world of intelligibles (objective ideas). Sociology is a difficult perspective to crack in modern cultures. This is especially the case for American culture, dominated as it is by individualistic predispositions. Such predispositions are readily transformed into philosophies that assume one head (one mind, one brain) is enough for grasping Popper's World 3. World 3 has a strong Platonic flavor and has a volatile potential for encouraging transcendental thinking. This means, for example, assuming that (i) knowledge is based on a strong objectivity that transcends intersubjectivity; and (ii) World 3 is populated by abstractions and therefore a very different world than the world of cultural objects. This raises the problem, however, of how a cultural process can generate an acultural, extra-cultural, or trans-cultural domain such as a Platonized World 3. The sociological imagination reveals the implausibility of such a position.

The social theory of objectivity appears to be a theory sociologists would welcome since it expresses an awareness of the social foundations of knowledge and standards of truth. The sociologically attractive argument is that public tests, logic, experiments, and empirical observations gradually eliminate personal biases and mistakes. The problem with the social theory of objectivity is that it covers up the problematic psychology of science with an unproblematic sociology. Intersubjectivity is a social process, and all social processes are problematic from a sociological viewpoint. Some science watchers view this process from the vantage point of biology. Science is an institution and, like all institutions, can be expected to age and to increasingly reveal rigidities and conformities. The pitfalls of this analogy can be avoided by noting that social processes such as professionalization and bureaucratization can transform standards in science from expressions and guarantors of excellence into constraints on original thought and means for restricting creativity within traditional boundaries. Why, then, don't all interested parties in the development of a social theory of objectivity consider the identification and elimination of social biases and mistakes to be a least as important as the identification and elimination of personal biases and mistakes? The tendency to treat the sociological realities of science as unproblematic is wide-spread. Kuhn, for example, argues that normal science is educationally narrow, rigid, and ill-designed to produce creative scientists. But, according to Kuhn, this is no barrier to scientific progress. He argues that the general tendency of normal science to promote individual rigidity cannot prevent some young scientists and scientists new to their field from introducing innovations, provoking crises, and precipitating "scientific revolutions". But Kuhn doesn't consider the potential impact of social structural changes on the possibilities for scientific change. For example, is the supply of Kuhn's "Bolsheviks of science" independent of social conditions within and outside of science? Can the creativity and novelty of youths and hybrids be suppressed by certain kinds of social control? Even if we assume the validity of Kuhn's general model of scientific change, certain "damping" effects on the cycles of scientific revolution and normal science can be hypothesized. Bureaucratization, for example, may lengthen the periods of normal science, lower the intensity of revolutions, attenuate conceptual crises, stifle individual creativity, and lower the probability of a revolutionary idea being recognized and thereby provoking a crisis. I discussed a second damping source earlier, Boulding's concept of the dialectically generated costs of revolutions. This idea can be extended to include the "cumulation of costs" and the progressive deterioration of the capacity of the scientific system to "recover" from the costs incurred during revolutionary changes, and hence to continue to "grow", "progress", "develop", or "evolve". Kuhn recognizes the rigidity of normal science; but his failure to consider the rigidity of social facts as a factor in scientific change is sociologically untenable. It is surprising that so many sociologists and other scholars and intellectuals have failed to recognize the lack of a problematic sociology in Kuhn. Kuhn himself is his best critic. He regularly resisted the imputed sociological implications of his work and indeed argued publically that *The Structure of Scientific Revolutions* was an homage to his teacher, the great internalist historian of science, Alexander Koyré. His post-*Structure* work in the history of science (notably his work on black body radiation) is indeed true to this view in terms of the internalist and, to some extent, positivistic perspectives he brings to this research. Where his defenders found an anti-Mertonian champion of the new science studies movement, Merton and Kuhn found themselves "at one" with each other as both explicitly recognized.

Consensus

Objectivity is associated with truth, or true belief. In other words, objectivity is a relationship between human beings and "objects of inquiry" that leads to truth. It is relatively easy to treat truth as trans-social, a product of the capacity for self- and social transcendence, that is, of the capacity to come to know what is true for "the world", the "universe", and not merely for one's community and not merely for one's self. But persons who have the basic mental faculties necessary for ascertaining truth, and who live in societies which stimulate and legitimate the development and facilitate the use of those faculties, may develop radically distinct and conflicting beliefs. In such cases, scholars who adopt this position argue, there must be a movement toward consensus. But this is part of the social theory of objectivity and raises again the problem of appealing to an unproblematic social activity and process.

What constitutes consensus? Is it the "universal agreement" referred to sometimes in the rhetoric of science? In fact, objectivity is never a matter of universal consensus but of a certain type of delimited consensus. Intersubjective consensus, for example, could be used to refer to the type of consensus that occurs among properly certified human beings whose sensory apparatuses are in "proper working order" and who in modern times have become known as scientists. They rely on this type of consensus in deciding whether given statements about reality are "objective". Even within the restricted universality of the scientific community, consensus can be limited. In any case, there are other types of consensus, all of them restricted in one way or another. Special consensus is associated with the so-called "man-of-knowledge", his apprentice, and his associates. Shamans are exemplary "men of knowledge". Individual consensus might be used to describe the result of achieving cognitive consistency: this type of consensus is the basis of idiosyncratic, personal, or subjective knowledge.

Types of consensus develop on personal, group, and sociocultural levels. They are the result of specific kinds of relationships between people and environments (physical, biological, and social), and they lead to the construction of distinguishable realities. It is important to note that all types of consensus involve some sort of intersubjective testing (even individual consensus, which can be conceived as a product of an internal dialogue). This should not be obscured by the fact that the term, "intersubjectivity", has to some extent been preempted by science and is not readily appropriated for more general usage. Social theorists have, of course, discussed the intersubjectivity of everyday life. The focus on everyday life more readily reveals the problematic nature of intersubjectivity and might serve as a model for the transformation of intersubjectivity in science from the taken-for-granted into the problematic. Incidentally it is conceivable that an advocate of the distinctive nature of intersubjective testing in science might argue that science is the only mode of knowing in which egalitarian and communal norms are operative. This argument would have to be rejected given the social stratification of the scientific community.

Intersubjectivity and consensus do not solve the problem of the demarcation of scientific and non-scientific knowledge and do not guarantee objectivity. The failure arises not because intersubjectivity and consensus have nothing to do with objectivity, but because they are treated as unproblematic. The awareness that intersubjectivity and consensus are problematic leads to the following problem: assuming that it is, in the first place, possible to define objectivity as a social fact, what type of intersubjectivity and what mode of consensus are most likely to stimulate the creation of objective statements about reality? This problem defines the focus of the sociology of objectivity. In order to attend to this problem it is necessary first to examine the relationship between reality and objectivity.

Reality or Realities?

In the 1960s, we became accustomed to such terms as alternate-, alternative-, separate-, and "multiple-realities" in many areas of intellectual life. These terms are kin to such terms as paradigms, glosses, and language games. They pose a challenge to the idea that there is "one reality" – an idea central in many philosophical and scientific quarters as the necessary condition for scientific inquiry. The premise of a single physical reality "out there" is widely viewed as a necessary condition for science. It generally follows then that truth (or true belief) is about that single reality. In such cases, the pluralist view of reality may appear to undermine the program for the scientific pursuit of truth (or objectivity). Consider, for example, a view that distinguishes an ordinary reality of separate objects, simultaneous happenings, and simple cause and effect relations from a relativistic reality of flowing events, relationships, and causal nexuses. Some people can walk on white-hot coals without burning their feet. Those of us who can't walk on hot coals operate in a different reality. There are different views of what alternate realities refer to. Among the shamans of the Navajo and Huichol, peyote was used as a shamanic "teacher plant" that gave access to an alternate spirit world. On the other hand, realities might be various but not discontinuous or separate.

In his *Principles of Psychology*, William James (1890) suggested that there are several, perhaps an infinite number of, realities; he called them "sub-universes". He distinguished the worlds of (i) sense (physical things, the paramount reality), (ii) science, (iii) ideal relations, (iv) "idols of the tribe", (v) mythology and religion (the supernatural), and (vi) individual opinion, sheer madness, and vagary. Alfred Schutz (1967, I: 207, 229-233) seized on James's suggestion as an important insight but freed it from its psychological context by developing the idea of finite provinces of meaning each of which may be given "the accent of reality". The property of finiteness implies that provinces of meaning – each characterized by a specific cognitive style and consistent set of experiences – are not mutually referable via transformation formulae. One "gets" from one province to another through what Kierkegaard called a "leap". Such a leap is subjectively experienced as a "shock", and is accomplished by modifying the tension of consciousness, that is, by changing one's attention *a la vie*. Schutz argues that there are an infinite number of planes in conscious life, ranging from the plane of action to the plane of dreams. The tension of consciousness is highest on the plane of action: here is where we are most concerned with meeting reality and its requirements head on and without error. This is the realm of "wide-awakedness" – attention is active and directed. The tension of consciousness is lowest on the plane of dreams – there, attention is passive. Here Schultz's meaning is congruent with some contemporary theories of attention and consciousness such as C. Evans' (1970) theory of absorptive and deflective attention, and Erika Bourguignon's (1973) theory of states of consciousness and degrees of nervous system arousal.

Each finite province of meaning has a specific tension, "*epoche*" (suspension of doubt), spontaneity, self-experience, sociality, and time perspective. The world of everyday life is the archetypal reality; all other finite provinces of meaning are modifications of that reality. Schutz suggested that we try to systematically group finite provinces of meaning in terms of their constitutive principle, their degree of consciousness-tension. It is reasonable to conclude, if we accept Schutz's point of view, that each finite province of meaning could be associated with a type of intersubjective testing and a mode of consensus.

The idea of alternate realities informs the dialogue on the relationships between science and other modes of knowing. One way of dealing with the problem of science and religion as alternate realities, for example, is to distinguish between the hypotheses of science and the dogma of a church, a more or less political distinction if we consider the early history of modern science. The physicist and philosopher Pierre Duhem (1861-1916) separated the two realities along more intellectual lines (though the distinction between political and intellectual here may be spurious). The Roman Catholic physicist argued that physical theory can neither support nor oppose any metaphysical assertion or religious dogma. More recently, some scientists and theologians have argued for convergence or complementarity between science and religion. Furthermore, the psychologist Lawrence LeShan and the physicist Fritjof Capra have proposed that ancient mysticism parallels, converges with, and is analogous to modern physics. Arguments relating ancient wisdom and contemporary knowledge are not unusual in the history of ideas, and there are notable parallels between the views and rhetoric of LeShan and Capra and those of earlier thinkers, such as Ficino, Pico, Bruno, and others in the Renaissance period. The conflicts and contradictions between the "one reality" and "many realities" view can and must be resolved in order to avoid the almost constant emergence of reality paradoxes. This resolution may be achieved by, first, accepting the Bohmian worldview. Reality is or is best viewed as if it is a process of things (including entities, properties, qualities, systems, levels), infinite in diversity and multiplicity, reciprocally related, and all in a state of becoming. Second, the resolution of the conflicts between the "one reality" and "many realities" views requires following the implication of something like the "bootstrap hypothesis" in elementary particle physics, the hypothesis that the universe is a self-consistent whole, or in Helier Robinson's (1975) words, a "singular possibility" and a "single polyadic relation" (i.e., a single structure which can be conceptually divided into substructures, and is so divided in, for example, rational modes of thought). Robinson's and Bohm's cosmological perspectives are at least mutually reinforcing if not structurally similar.

This proposed resolution is consistent with both the existence of an "objective reality" and the existence of "multiple realities". It is consistent with the existence of an "objective reality" at least in the negative sense that it does not contradict or preclude "lawful relationships" or the possibility of their discovery. This in part follows from our experience that actions and their consequences are not arbitrary. With regard to multiple realities, our ability to take different perspectives on reality in given states of consciousness and to have different experiences of reality in altered states of consciousness may be a manifestation of inexhaustibility and polyadicism and the source of notions about other realities besides so-called everyday reality. That is, a given phenomenon [a chair, for example] can be examined from different points of view in terms of (i) spatial relations, and (ii) disciplinary, cultural, or perspectival orientations. The different viewpoints and interests of an artist, a carpenter, a person looking for a place to sit, and a physicist will lead each of them to "see" something beyond what each of them in an ordinary (normophrenic) state of consciousness will describe as a "chair". This is not the same as experiencing the chair differently than others do (as a glowing, flowing set of snakes, for example) because you have altered ordinary perception and consciousness by ingesting a drug, or by some other consciousness altering regimen. Our ideas about multiple realities are, at least in the specialized world of astrophysicists, astronomers, and cosmologists, generated by the mathematics of these sciences. To some extent, at least, such mathematics generates conclusions that are more mathematics generating mathematics than they are mathematics generating empirically grounded and testable propositions. I call such conclusions mathegrammatical illusions. The multiple worlds hypotheses in quantum mechanics are more mathematics generating mathematics than mathematics representing something in the world of matter.

The reality we experience is always (constituted in) a relationship between ourselves, others, and things. The experience of reality always contains some "objective content" that transcends (but is not alienated from) the various unique qualities of self, setting, and time. The relationships between self, others, and things are adaptations; thus "realities" are adaptations. More generally, each reality is a worldview. Later I will generalize this to "theories". If there is, in the Bohmian sense, an "objective reality", does this mean that the problem of demarcating different modes of knowing is indeed one which we must solve? In a sense the answer is yes; but this does not imply that we know or can discover a demarcation rule in any conventional sense. The reason is that the Bohmian conception of reality leads to an unconventional conception of objectivity.

Objectivity as a Social Fact in a Bohmian Universe

There is an objective reality in the following sense: (i) our experiences can be summarized in "lawful relationships" (not necessarily simple "causal" ones), or "necessities", and (ii) there are "things" that existed before you and I were born, and that will continue to exist when we are dead, but that can never be experienced as "things-in-themselves". Objective reality is a relationship between inquirers and objects-of-inquiry; it is ever-changing, infinite in breadth and depth, and, as a whole, incomprehensible. It is an open-ended system. Information in a Bohmian universe is assumed to be always increasing (syntropy overrides entropy). This is a pragmatic assumption and nothing more. My use of the term "infinite", I should note, should be understood to mean effectively beyond our normal ability to comprehend large numbers. The literal idea of infinity has no meaning in the everyday human context.

If we want to find out as much as we can about our open-ended, ever-changing reality, we must behave and think in an open-ended, ever-changing way. If objectivity is a social fact, it must be an open-ended, ever-changing social fact. Individuals who want to be objective (engage in the process of objectivity) must strive to become open-ended, self-actualizing epistemic agents. We are, from this point of view, inquiring, self-reflective organisms (epistemic agents). Survival, and beyond that, the growth, expansion, and evolution of the quality of life, culture, and consciousness depend on our abilities to tap the effectively infinite capacity we have (individually and collectively) for critical, creative inquiry. The degree to which the societies we live in and the processes of socialization we experience are open ended will determine the degree to which we will be able to achieve open-ended living and thinking.

Open-endedness entails the continual generation of new information in the universe; in conjunction with inexhaustibility and polyadicism this insures the continual generation of new ways of comprehending our experiences. Whether this in any sense could be interpreted in terms of "closer and closer approximations to the true nature of things" is indeterminate and probably irrelevant. Values, lifestyles, and the conditions for objectivity are intimately interrelated and interdependent. In fact, the process of objectivity from this perspective appears as the process of human beings adapting to, transforming, and evolving in the world: the search for the conditions of objectivity is the search for the conditions of survival, adaptation, and evolution. Objectivities go with forms of life. There is no a priori universal objectivity but rather communities of objectivity. If you are set on achieving a universal objectivity you must settle for an objectivity that mirrors overlapping forms of life.

It should be obvious that there is no way to decide a priori whether reality is singular or plural; nor can we anticipate constructing a basis for such a decision in the future. However, on the basis of our negative experiences to date with finite and finalistic systems of thought and explanations; in the light of the various tendencies to rigidity which we encounter in the physical, biological, and social realms; and given the wide range of cases in which contemporary thinkers in intellectual and practical settings have turned to or come upon open-ended solutions and theories in response to a wide variety of problems, it seems reasonable to act as if reality is Bohmian (Campbell, 1957: 21).

The Rejection of Relativism, the Privileged Status of Science, and the Strong Programme

The acceptance of the idea of many realities and simultaneously the idea of an objective reality leads to the rejection of relativism. In its extreme form, relativism implies that the privileged status of a mode of knowing can only be established by virtue of, for example, its association with a center of political-economic power, its power of persuasion (independent of "universally" applicable standards of logic, rationality, or experience), and/or its power of prediction. But there is an objective reality that is infinitely unfolding, polyadic, and relational. The problematic nature of intersubjectivity and consensus thus comes to mean in this context that some types of intesubjectivity and consensus may be more fruitful than others for any given time and place in the unfolding of human inquiry. The open-ended view I have sketched is an imperative for incorporating the full range of modes of inquiry in the pursuit of objectivity. This should be done without giving a priori preference to one mode or another and without assuming that the sociology of scientific knowledge, or truth, or objectivity, must be a theory of rationality. In either case, the restriction of an a priori preference would interfere with the possibility of developing a full-fledged critique of science as a whole. This strategy would apply in the case of any prevailing mode of knowing; for the moment, it is the basis for rejecting the strong programme proposed by Bloor (1976).

Bloor argues that the best strategy to follow if we want to give an account of scientific knowledge is "to adopt the scientific method itself". This might be a reasonable position if there were some reason to believe that the "scientific method" is, first of all, a method and, furthermore, that it is a finished, universally valid method of inquiry whose levels of complexity are well-known and whose application is entirely straight-forward. From the assumption of a Bohmian reality, it follows that the study of science using its own methods exclusively can never reveal the limitations of science with respect to new horizons of inquiry. Even if reality is for all practical purposes static, it is so extensive and complex that it is difficult to imagine how we would go about convincing ourselves that we have discovered a universally valid and unchanging mode of inquiry.

The problem of the limits of the sociology of knowledge may arise in part on account of an implicit imperialism, that is, on account of the assumption or implication that a given statement or idea (in science, but also in mysticism or in any other given knowledge system) is solely, or ultimately, a social product. This assumption should be rejected on the grounds that sociology attends to limited aspects of human experience, and that the full range of factors in human experience must be drawn on to account for human creations. This does not resolve the problem of how we would go about testing the proportion of explanatory power that should be assigned to different disciplinary orientations and combinations thereof; and the problem may, in fact, change radically or disappear altogether if the disciplinary strategy is transformed or transcended (by some form of holistic inquiry, for example). Contrary to advocates of a rather orderly pursuit of truth, I conceive truth or objectivity as a process firmly rooted in intellectual conflict, contradictions, and dialectical processes. The conflict need not be violent or combative in any conventional sense; it can be of the kind which is constructive and based on mutual respect. But struggle and conflict are in any case conditions of social and intellectual change, and permanent features of Bohmian reality.

The Sociology of Objectivity

The sociology of knowledge can contribute to identifying the conditions under which knowledge systems undergo closure and stagnate. It can also help to identify the conditions under which knowledge systems resist closure. But resistance to closure implies open-endedness. Thus, the sociology of knowledge can help to identify the conditions under which human inquiry is most likely to resist stagnation, or, in other words, to be developmental, progressive, or evolutionary. This, given the Bohmian view of reality, must be considered a perpetual problem which allows only limited and regional solutions. The introduction of the general term, "inquiry", is necessary in order to avoid the two-pronged problem that science is (i) a historically and culturally-bound term, activity, and process, and (ii) subject to the stagnating and stifling effects of social processes such as bureaucratization.

The perspective I have sketched changes the nature of the problem of bias, whether personal or social. Bias is unavoidable. Inquiry in the best sense, that is, open-ended, developmental, progressive, or evolving inquiry, is characterized by the presence of a certain type of bias, not the absence of bias. This can perhaps be better appreciated if we recognize that knowledge systems can be construed as worldviews. Clifford Hooker (1975) has shown that philosophies of science such as empiricism and realism can be construed as worldviews; and similarly, as Michael Zenzen and I (Restivo and Zenzen, 1978) have shown, sociologies of knowledge and science under labels such as "Mertonian" and "Marxist" can be construed as worldviews. Revealing worldviews in science, or in philosophies and sociologies of science, involves a meta-inquiry into, for example, theories of reality, consciousness, and social action. If a knowledge system can be construed as a worldview, it cannot be free of bias since by definition it contains ideological and political dimensions, and is hence a value-laden system. Value-free and value-neutral inquiry as classically understood is, from this point of view, impossible.

Modes of knowing, including those of science, are worldviews and, therefore, as worldview, are value-laden. They are biased, but they vary in their capacity to (i) generate, over time, statements consistent with our changing experience of reality, and (ii) stimulate our involvement in reality as a dynamic process. These capacities are related to organizational and value aspects of modes of knowing.

The sociology of objectivity is the study of the social and cultural conditions of inquiry and how these conditions affect our individual and collective abilities to construct objective statements and develop objective knowledge. There is a need to conceptualize objectivity in a way that (i) avoids absolutism and relativism, and (ii) links commitment to truths (substantive, methodological, and theoretical) with perpetual openness to signals that may alter that commitment (which includes the possibility of becoming aware of new sensory apparatuses, biological, social, or mechanical). The notion of ideal or transcendental truths may be somewhat less stable but not as unstable as theoretical truths. However, since all three types of truths are interrelated and interdependent, it should be clear, even if somewhat paradoxical, why even the most obvious so-called truths or objective statements must be considered problematic. More generally, it might be useful to distinguish between informational and comprehensional objectivity. An objective statement might then be defined as one which is consistent with the full range of information possessed by the human species at a given time and "known" to a single ideal intelligence. Information exists to the degree that it is possible for human beings to achieve certain effects by carrying out certain actions in accordance with certain principles and to be able to do so repeatedly. Information tends to accumulate into relatively stable and increasingly universal "bundles" which can be pressed into operation in appropriate circumstances (for example, the objectivity of selecting and eating edible mushrooms). At this level, objectivity approaches limits defined by the boundaries of information niches. But the ability to be objective about mushrooms is not simply a matter of the "facts" about mushrooms; the ability is dependent on intersubjectivity and consensus probabilities.

Objectivity has a second dimension which I refer to as comprehension. It is in this sense that the concept of objectivity as a process is most clearly established. For we can learn to do things, and once we learn to do them, repeat them over and over, generation after generation, with comparable degrees of success: in this sense, we can say that we "know" something. But our comprehension of what we know and do can and does change; our theories change. They change because of new information in the form of new signals, new configurations of old information, or new sensory apparatuses which tune us in to new realms of information. Our theories become new worldviews, so that so-called "eternal" truths change in terms of how we "see" or comprehend them. Keep in mind that these ideas are consistent with movements in philosophy to eliminate the idea of fundamental grounds. Even the values of fundamental constants change over time. Fundamental grounds conjectures are not far removed from ideas about First Causes and God.

The degree of objectivity (objective content) in any given statement is determined by ascertaining the scope and depth of the information available to, or "in", a given individual, group, or community. Thus, the most objective statements that can be made at present about any human experience, can be made by the people, groups, and communities who, or which, have had the widest mental, emotional, and physical exposure to human experience as a whole, that is, in the present and in the past through exposure to historical accounts. The most objective statement possible about the nature of, for example, a star (the statement with the highest possible objective content) is constrained by the range of experiences it is possible to have as a human being or human community on this planet. The most objective mode of inquiry at any given time is the mode of inquiry practiced by those who have access to the widest possible range of human experiences, and who are oriented to exploring the limits of those experiences in order to expand their range. Note that while objective statements are referred to an ideal system (the omniscient knower or knowing community), they are not themselves conceived as "existing" in an ideal or transcendental form or realm. It is important to keep in mind that we are always talking about social institutions and social constructions.

Objectivity is more than just a matter of "statements". It is a complex, unfolding process of relationships, feeling, thoughts, intuitions, imponderables, and ineffables. A sociological theory of objectivity must take into account, for example, the prominence of "unreasonable" modes and motives in the history of science. Discoveries in science can be: (i) the result of "hard work and luck" even when the driving force appears to be mathematical or theoretical "reasonableness" (as in the case of, it now turns out, the discovery of Pluto); (ii) stimulated by unusual or bizarre experiences (as in the case of Poisson, whose interest in pendulums appears to derive from his childhood experience of swinging to and fro on a nail upon which he was sometimes hung for safety by a nurse who had to leave him alone for short periods); (iii) indirectly by personal traumas (the young Newton, for example, seems to have been stimulated to pursue his studies with greater dedication in order to overtake a boy who stood ahead of him in class – after that boy had kicked him in the stomach); and (iv) achieved by the suspension or alteration of conventional canons of logic and rigor (as in Wallis's treatment of infinitesimals). Once we get past positivistic and idealistic reconstructions of science, it becomes easy enough to read the history of science as a record of irrationalities, bizarre incidents, and improbable events. However, that history can also be read as an argument for reestablishing and sustaining conditions of open-endedness and pluralism. The stories about Newton, Poisson and others do not have to be historically true to serve as teaching moments.

The sociology of objectivity as I conceive it operates on the assumptions that (i) no objective statement or truth can ever be final or absolute; (ii) no system for arriving at truth can be universally valid and unchanging in its foundations; and (iii) a broader context for establishing truth always exists than that of any system of knowledge which is given or which is dominant. By definition, the first assumption is not an objective statement or truth; this, then, avoids a classical paradox! By virtue of these assumptions, the sociology of objectivity should contribute to generating new contexts and meanings for truth or objectivity. This perspective, incidentally, tends to dissolve the distinction between gnosio-sociology (DeGré, 1985: 27) and sociological theory of knowledge and eliminates the traditional role of the epistemologist.

Conclusion

The problem of the limits of the sociology of knowledge and the nature of the sociology of scientific knowledge (objective knowledge, truth, or true belief) can be resolved by rejecting or altering conventional conceptions of intersubjectivity, consensus, reality, science, rationality, relativism, and the strong programme. The alternative sociology of objectivity that I have sketched can be construed as a view of reality, a worldview, and a conjecture or a theory. It is an adaptive strategy relative (in a lesser sense) to a more or less circumscribed intellectual community, and relative (in a larger sense) to large-scale, long-term, evolutionary and devolutionary processes. Certain taken-for-granted aspects of inquiry are transformed into problematic aspects. From a sociological perspective, idealistic and transcendental conceptions of knowledge and truth have no material or mechanical ontological status; thus, the basis for viewing objectivity as a product of disinterestedness or detachment is undermined, and an argument for objectivity-as-engagement is substituted. Perhaps this notion can be clarified by distinguishing super-superstructure from superstructure and structure. The concept of a super-superstucture would help to clarify why it is possible, on the one hand, to conceive ideal, transcendental "realities", and why, on the other hand, such "realities" must be viewed as rooted in the world of social relationships. Their ontological status is symbolic and social.

In conclusion, let me sketch a few additional details of my conjecture. Reality is conceived to be a dynamic, relational, dialectical system (rather than something stable, static, and "out there"). The process of comprehension (encompassing explanation, knowledge, understanding, and appreciation) is a matter of (following Toulmin, 1972) variable minds inventing/discovering variable principles and applying them to variable nature (as opposed to a system of fixed minds, fixed principles, and fixed nature). The means for comprehending reality include, but are not restricted to, the realm of the rational, which, in any case, like other realms, changes as information and comprehension change. This implies changes in what we consider "everyday" reality and in what is considered to be in the "phenomenologically" accessible realm. Comprehension is a dialectically changing configuration of rational, intuitive, and other modes of knowing in various states of consciousness; the priority of any given mode or any given state is not a priori established. The value imperative is open-endedness. The organizational imperative is an open-ended communality which assigns priority to the person (self-actualization).

Finally, let me place my conjecture in its intellectual context. The sociology of objectivity which I have sketched builds on and contributes to (more or less) open-ended, relational-holistic theories, realities, worldviews, or conjectures that emerged in a wide variety of intellectual areas during the latter half of the twentieth century. Proponents of this perspective and their fields of inquiry include David Bohm (quantum mechanics), Clifford Hooker (philosophy of science), G. Radnitzky (metascience), Helier Robinson (metaphysics), J. Ogilvy (social philosophy), G. Bateson (cybernetic anthropology), A. Maslow (humanisitic psychology), G. Chew (bootstrap or hadron physics), J. Wheeler and J. Graves (geometrodynamics), E. Dunn Jr. (social and economic theory), and Claude Vallet (relational arithmetic). These developments represent the search for, and the development of, a new holistic thema (in G. Holton's sense (1973)) rather than simply another holism cycle in the history of ideas.

Objectivity-as-engagement as an intellectual strategy cannot be separated from my personal interests and struggles, nor from my involvement in the conflicts, contradictions, and struggles for power in social life. This is entailed in the worldview approach which I advocate, and which, by hypothesis, applies to all arguments. In order to have my conjecture exemplify Bohmian reality more adequately, I attach to it the statement that we have no justification for investing this hypothetical with positive or absolute belief. Following Hooker, this is designed to indicate that my conjectures, hypotheses, propositions, and claims, like everything else, are in flux and ripe with contradictions.

Classical and conventional ideas about the phenomenological world, the world of common sense, the world that appears to be accessible directly through our senses and especially through our eyes can no longer ground our epistemologies or theories of knowing. Modern physics alone has unseated naïve realism as a ground for inquiry. Nonetheless, let me be clear that whether we adopt a Bohmian realism or a model-dependent realism (Hawking), we are obliged to develop, test, and validate these complicated and common-sense defying ideas with our feet on the ground. That ground – the culturally layered earth, sociological and cultural materialism – is the only ground we have to stand on.

Chapter 3
Sociology: A Copernican Revolution Changes How We Think About Science and Mathematics

I first conceived of the crystallization of the sociological imagination as a Copernican revolution in 1994 while preparing a paper for a conference on the debate and discussions over new ways of conceiving the development of scientific and technological culture. The conception of scientific and technological culture at the center of that conference seemed to me to grow out of a traditional scientific worldview. One could even say more narrowly but more pointedly that it reflected a traditional ideology of science. This is an ideology grounded in the preeminence of the physical and natural sciences, and the experiences and achievements of physicists, chemists, and biologists. The idea that we needed new ways to think about the development of science, technology, and culture, however, opened the door for sociology (and anthropology), as well as for the sociology of science and technology. The issues around which the conference had been organized could not be addressed if sociology was left out of the conversation. Sociology has a history of being left out of the conversation. This book rests on the assumption that conversations about science that do not involve sociologists will be empty, repeat outworn ideas, and lead nowhere. This is true for many of the problems and issues we engage as intellectuals, scholars, and activists. This truth is exaggerated when science is the focus of our attention.

The fashionable term "technoscience" is one of the fruits of the interdisciplinary social studies of science and technology movement. That conception of the interdependence of science and technology will stand in the wings and perhaps hover about me while I concentrate on what is still recognizable as a distinct discourse, science. But what I say throughout must be understood to apply to technology and to technoscience.

In order to begin the inquiry I undertake in this book, I must first stress the significance of bringing sociology into our debates and discussions as a discovering science. But I do not want the term "discovering science" to be understood as making sociology a slave to or immature offspring of the physical and natural sciences. I use the words "discovery" and "science" nonetheless, but stress that in my usage they carry reconstructed meanings as a consequence of research in the new sociology of science, that is, the sociology of science that has emerged over the past 40 or so years. I want, then, to alert readers to an invisible revolution wrought by sociological discoveries and the new sociology of science they have spawned.

Sociology has a bad reputation. Much of what it has stood for has indeed been, as its critics claim, needlessly obtuse and empty. Even sociologists have wondered at times if they were saying anything. This is not unique in the histories of the sciences. And just as in other sciences that experience "identity crises", there is a core of significant worldview shifting discoveries at the center of sociology. These discoveries are associated with the high tradition. The low tradition is represented by the motley collection of titles in the sociology sections of shopping mall bookstores, images of sociology as a "soft science", a form of socialism or social work, and a pretentious inquiry that disguises common sense and the obvious in the jargon-infested trappings of a social science. Even the idea that sociology is a "hard science", to the extent that it imports a sexist and scientistic view of the field from the physical sciences, and stresses formal and methodological concerns over substantive social ones, is part of the low tradition. It is this low tradition that is behind the 11th commandment authored by the conservative political commentator George Will – "Thou shalt not commit a sociology".

Ironically, anyone who has listened to and/or read Dr. Will over the years will readily acknowledge that few pundits are as conversant with the social statistics produced by those who daily commit a sociology; and few pundits mobilize those statistics more expertly than Dr. Will (even where his conservatism leads his interpretations astray). The high tradition in sociology traces its roots to the revolutionary discoveries about self, society, and culture made between 1840 and 1920 by Karl Marx, Max Weber, Harriet Martineau, Emile Durkheim, George Herbert Mead, and others. The most important discoveries they made that bear on our understanding of the nature of science are that selves and minds are social structures, and that all forms of knowledge and belief are social and cultural constructions. This period of discovery reflects a general cultural climate which can be characterized in terms of the rejection of transcendence. It will be helpful, incidentally, in thinking about sociological discoveries, to learn from sociologists of science that discovery is not a simple matter of finding something new in the world. It is actually a rather complex and inventive social process that involves, among other factors, techniques of communication, negotiation and conflict, and crystallization of the discovery over time. "Discoverers" are often "political appointees" rather than original innovators.

The discoverers of society carried out a Copernican revolution that transformed our understanding of the social world. They identified the group, the collectivity, society, and culture as the centers of the human universe. Copernicus helped move the sun to the center of our solar system and the earth to a peripheral position. The sociologists helped move the group to the center of the human universe and the individual to the periphery. This achievement does not politically subordinate the individual to the group. Rather, it reveals how varieties of individual growth and development, and the formation of different types of persons, are dependent on forms of social organization and culture. Through its influence on the sociology of science, the Copernican sociological revolution has also had an impact on our understanding of science and of natural and physical realities. We are, in fact, in the midst of a second sociological revolution that is changing our conception of the nature of knowledge. The seeds of this revolution were planted during the earlier revolution, but it is only recently that sociologists have developed the appropriate experiences, tools, concepts, and orientations to pursue Marx's ideas on the social roots of knowledge, Durkheim's conjectures on the social nature of religion, logical concepts, and objectivity, Mead's reconstruction of our understanding of the self, and Spengler's insights on mathematics and culture. All of the ingredients of the invisible revolution I have been sketching here appear in the following excerpt from Marx's (1958: 104) *Economic and Philosophic Manuscripts of 1844*:

> Even when I carry out scientific work, etc., an activity which I can seldom conduct in direct association with others – I perform a social, because human, act. It is not only the material of my activity – like the language itself which the thinker uses – which is given to me as a social product. My own existence is a social activity.

Here, then, we have in the space of a few lines the ideas that the self, the mind, and science are social constructions. This perspective achieves its classical sociological form in the closing pages of Emile Durkheim's *The Elementary Forms of Religious Life*, where Durkheim introduces a non-obvious sociology of logical concepts. In the wake of contributing to the discovery of what the gods and religions are, Durkheim's sociology of logic grounds a movement that has ancient origins, the rejection of transcendence. The further articulation of this rejection was accomplished notably in Spengler's analysis of mathematics as a cultural phenomenon, and George Herbert Mead's theories of self and mind. Spengler's analysis would go virtually unnoticed until the emergence of the new sociology of science and in particular the programmatic sociology of mathematics introduced by David Bloor in 1976.

Randall Collins has been working within the framework of this invisible revolution to fashion a causal sociology of philosophies that is generalizable to intellectuals (including scientists), and it is worth summarizing some of the main points of his theory. Readers are urged to accept the challenge of Collins' monumental efforts in developing and presenting this paradigmatic sociological theory in order to appreciate the context of these generalizations:

1. major intellectual work tends to be concentrated in time, space, and social connections;
   1a. intellectual work is almost always concentrated in the same time period as other work of a similar degree of innovativeness and scope;
   1b. notable intellectual activity typically has been concentrated, at any given time, in a small number of places;
   1c. the most notable philosophers are not organizational isolates, but members of chains of teachers and students who are themselves known philosophers, and/or of circles of contemporary intellectuals;

2. the number of intellectually active schools of thought is almost always on the order of three to six (law of small numbers);
3. schools of thought rise and fall due to the fortunes of their organizational bases;
4. periods of greatest intellectual creativity are periods of major organizational transition;
5. factional loyalists produce a steadily lengthening corpus of scholastic materials;
6. conflict among rival positions produces a trend toward abstraction and self-conscious reflection on intellectual objects;
7. new positions are produced by negation of preexisting positions along the lines of greatest organizational rivalry.

I offer these generalizations as a gateway to the kinds of theoretical capital that sociology as a discovering science and an invisible Copernican revolution possesses. The intellectual resources I have identified so far in this chapter are not instances of nostalgia for the classical theorists, nor exaggerated estimates of the achievements of sociology but part of the contemporary fund of cultural capital that has helped us to fashion such counter-intuitive notions as the sociology of science, mathematics, god, truth, nature, reality, objectivity, and logic. There is a masculine Euro-American bias in the selection of certain men to represent this invisible revolution, but it is a revolution generated and sustained by working class men and women (as E.P. Thompson helped to document), and by sociological theorists from Harriet Martineau to Emma Goldman and from W.E.B. DuBois to Dorothy Smith.

What does science look like, then, from the perspective of the invisible sociological revolution? I want to sketch a portrait of science as a social construction. I will draw on my knowledge of mathematics to some extent as I unfold this sketch. Mathematical knowledge is not simply a "parade of syntactic variations", sets of "structural transformations", or "concatenations of pure form" to borrow some phrases from the anthropologist Clifford Geertz commenting on aesthetic objects, speech, and myths. The more we immerse ourselves ethnographically in math worlds, the more we are impressed by the way mathematical forms or objects increasingly come into view as sensibilities, collective formations, and worldviews. The foundations of mathematics are not located in logic or systems of axioms but rather in forms of life. Mathematical forms and objects embody math worlds. They contain – indeed they are – the social histories of their construction. They are produced in and by math worlds. It is, in the end, math worlds, not individual mathematicians, that manufacture mathematics.

This idea has not gone unnoticed by mathematicians and philosophers of mathematics. Their sociological understanding, however, is inevitably limited. Take, for example, philosopher Philip Kitcher's (1983) views on the nature of mathematical knowledge. Kitcher seems to understand that knowledge has to be explained in terms of communities of knowers, and that stories about knowledge can be told in ways that reveal how knowledge is acquired, transmitted, and extended. This is the only story Kitcher can tell; but he is intent on making his story confirm rationality and well-founded reasoning in mathematics.

Rationality and well-founded reasoning (and, more generally, cognition) cannot be separated from social action and culture. Where it appears that we have effected such a separation it will turn out that we have simply isolated mathematical work as a sociocultural system, and told a sociologically impoverished story about how that system works. The extent to which mathematics is an autonomous social system (institutionally speaking) will vary from time to time and place to place, and so then will the extent to which an empiricist epistemologist (e.g., Kitcher) can construct a rational explanation for mathematics. But "rational" refers to the rules governing a relatively well-organized social activity. "Rational" is synonymous with "social" and "cultural" as an explanatory account. Explaining the content of mathematics is not a matter of constructing a simple causal link between a mathematical object such as a theorem and a social structure. Jean Dieudonné's (cited in Nordon, 1981) challenge exposes a fundamental misunderstanding of sociological claims about science and mathematics:

> Celui qui m'expliquera pourquoi le milieu social des petites cours allemandes du XVIIIe siècle où vivait Gauss devait inévitablement le conduire à s'occuper de la construction du polygone régulier à 17 côtés, eh bien, je lui donnerai une médaille ou chocolat.

> [Whoever can tell me how the social circles of the 18th century minor German courts in which Gauss lived drove him to construct the regular 17-sided polygon, well, I'll give that person a chocolate medal].

The sociological way is first to look to both "external" and "internal" contexts, networks, and organizations. Dieudonné's error is to imagine that only "external" milieux hold social influences. Second, the sociological task is to unpack the social histories and social worlds embodied in objects such as theorems. Mathematical objects must be treated as things that are produced by, manufactured by, social beings through social means in social settings. There is no reason why an object such as a theorem should be treated any differently than a sculpture, a teapot, or a skyscraper. Only alienated and alienating social worlds could give rise to the idea that mathematical objects are independent, free-standing creations, and that the essence of mathematics is realized in unmediated and conceptually unreconstructed (that is, "pure") technical talk. Technical talk, rightly understood, is always social talk.

Notations and symbols are tools, materials, and in general resources that are socially constructed around social interests and oriented to social goals. They take their meaning from the history of their construction and usage, the ways they are used in the present, the consequences of their usage inside and outside of mathematics, and the network of ideas they are part of. Here I anticipate an idea

I will turn to later in this book, that we need to abandon the distinction between "abstract" and "concrete" or else we will be prone to make reference errors and category mistakes that can lead us dangerously astray.

Mathematics, science, and knowledge in general (and as more and less differentiated activities) are crucial resources in all societies. Systems of knowledge therefore tend to develop and change in ways that serve the interests of the most powerful groups in society. Once societies become stratified, the nature and transmission of knowledge begins to reflect social inequalities. And once knowledge professions emerge, professional boundaries tend to shield practitioners from the realities of their broader social roles even while they define a realm of systemically (institutionally) autonomous work. Science and math curricula in such contexts are certainly influenced by professional interests and goals, but they are also conditioned by the social functions of educational and professionalizing systems in stratified societies.

Science worlds are social worlds, and we must ask what kinds of social worlds they are. How do they fit into the larger cultural scheme of things? Whose interests do they serve? What kinds of human beings inhabit science worlds? What sorts of values do science worlds create and sustain? Scientific change in and out of the classroom must always be examined closely in order to understand its relationship to wider social changes. It follows from all I have said that reforms and changes in general cannot be effectively carried out in isolation from broader issues of power, social structure, and values. If, on the other hand, we adopt conventional scientific tools and ways of working to help solve social, personal, and environmental problems we will fall short of our goals. It is therefore unreasonable to suppose that social reformers and revolutionaries could *eliminate* science from society, and equally unreasonable to suppose that science reformers and revolutionaries could *force* science as we know it today into some "alternative" shape independently of broader social and cultural changes.

Platonism, apriorism, and foundationalism (along with God) are dead. But the protective, awe-inspired, worshipful orientation to science survives. This is understandable, readily as a vestigial homage to the culture and conversation of the West (as in the works of Richard Rorty, the John Wayne of epistemology, for example), less readily as a vestigial homage to the God of the West (as Spengler realized). One can see historically, from Mannheim and Scheler to Donald Campbell, that the dialogue between the sociology of knowledge and epistemology has flirted with a radical sociological reconstruction of our understanding of science and culture. It is futile to try to construct an epistemologically relevant sociology that falls short of a full-fledged worldview analysis, critique, and reconstruction of science and culture.

It appears that until we fully extricate ourselves from the hold that Plato has had on us, we will never be able to fully appreciate sociology and anthropology as the revolutionary sciences (or forms of life) they are. When we make this move, we will find ourselves confronted with the end of a certain way of doing inquiry, and finally with the end of a certain way of living. The death of God presages the death of epistemology and of philosophy. For the moment, sociology and anthropology stand ready to take their place as the most important cultural productions of industrial civilization. They may go the way of natural philosophy eventually, but attacks that promise their premature demise are attacks that undermine our future as a culture capable of meeting the challenges of the global, multicultural society.

Kafka's assertion in *The Trial*, "Logic is doubtless unshakeable, but it cannot withstand a man who wants to go on living" would find ready endorsements from Dostoevsky, Nietzsche, and others. These thinkers held such views not because they were "relativists" or under-appreciated the value of inquiry but rather because they appreciated the dialectical complexities of social structures and cultures. They were critics of the "Cult of Science" and that cult's intense "faith in science". In order to appreciate this, we must recognize that when we talk about science, truth, logic, and related ideas, we are always talking about social relations.

This way of seeing sensitizes us to the progressive and regressive aspects and potentials of words, concepts, and ideas that as social relations can embody inequalities, destroy environments, inhibit individual growth and development and undermine inquiry. The next time someone wants to ask an expert about the nature of science or God, s/he had better turn to a sociologist or anthropologist instead of a physicist, astronomer, chemist, or biologist if s/he wants to escape Plato's clutches and learn something. The tensions between the form of sociology I champion here and what sometimes passes for sociology in contemporary science studies is illustrated by the efforts of Bruno Latour to construct an alternative to the social constructionist paradigm in science studies. I will shortly turn my attention to Latour in some detail because of the enormous influence he has had across the intellectual spectrum. His audiences are often predisposed to embrace anti-sociological musings and clever sounding defenses of psychology, philosophy, and metaphysics disguised as sociology.

Social Construction Unbound: What it Really Means

The foundations of mathematics are not located in logic or systems of axioms but rather in forms of life. Mathematics embodies mathematical worlds, and mathematical worlds are configured by societal and cultural worlds. The more professionalized mathematics becomes, the more it embodies itself, its own world of professional objects. This is the source of that mysterious sense of beauty and transcendence that infects mathematicians and philosophers. It is caused by the difficulty of locating everyday referents for mathematics. The situation is analogous to why the gods tend to be located outside of ourselves instead of within our social formations and why they tend to be experienced as beautiful and awesome.

Recall Dieudonné's error in imagining that only "external" milieux hold social influences. This is of a piece with the idea that the term "social", as in "social construction", is a synonym for "political", "religious", "economic", or "ideological"; and that it means, essentially, "false" or "arbitrary". I want to remind the scientists, the Steven Weinbergs, Lewis Wolperts, and Richard Dawkins, that to say that science and mathematics are socially constructed is *not* to say they are false, arbitrary, fabricated out of thin air, or the direct product of external political, religious, economic, or ideological forces, causes, or influences. The sociological task is not to make such claims but rather to unpack the social histories and social worlds embodied in, for example, mathematical objects. The objective of this "unpacking" should be to allow us to move more freely in the world mathematicians have collectively created.

Every emancipation restores the social world and social relationships to ourselves, to paraphrase Marx. Social constructionism (sociology) is just such an emancipation. It de-alienates and de-fetishizes representation, reference, cognition, knowledge, and belief. This is not simply an intellectual emancipation, but a political one.

In the next section I review the contributions of Bruno Latour in some detail. The detailed focus on Latour will allow me to clarify the nature of sociology by demonstrating the limitations of Latour's "alternative" sociology. Even under the constraints of his weak brand of sociology, he can add something to our understanding of science as a social activity. And his work also affords us an opportunity to explore the contemporary social and cultural contexts that are provoking anarchist agendas in studies of society, culture, and science. There is even reason to see in Latour's playful creativity elements of an epistemological if not a political anarchism.

Sociological Tensions in Contemporary Science Studies

Bruno Latour: The Once and Future Philosopher

Latour and Woolgar's pioneering laboratory ethnography *Laboratory Life: The Social Construction of Scientific Facts* (1979) helped launch the field of science and technology studies, already by then a developing research arena still trying to find its way onto the academic stage after a decade of research, publications, and meetings. This book (reissued in 1986) contained an agenda that unfolded into a career that has taken Latour far beyond science studies. Woolgar has become an intensely creative bright but lesser light, an Oxford don who has continued to spin science studies and sociology as ethnomethodological (see below) creations and demonstrated a formidable capacity for connecting the academy to business ventures.

Latour's career has followed to some extent at least the path to becoming a dominant French philosopher schematized in sociologist Michelle Lamont's (1987) analysis of the career of Jacques Derrida. Briefly, some of the factors Lamont mentions that apply to Latour are: strong theoretical trademark; diffusion potential based on being ambiguous and adaptable; addressing fundamental questions and transcending classical works; and diffusion by prestigious scholars and journals.

Reviewers consistently describe his works as provocative and important, radically original, witty, stylistically dazzling, and bold in their approach to problems everyone has become embroiled in. These problems have been generated in the contexts of structuralism, postmodernism, grammatology, narrative, and social and cultural critiques of history and theory.

In an intellectual world characterized by widespread skepticism about the status of sociology as a science (a skepticism that has a foothold even within the sociological community), Latour's criticism of the scientific claims of traditional sociology has been readily embraced and his status enhanced. His antipathy to sociology and to causal science has driven him away from sociology and anthropology (in spite of his self-definitions) and toward philosophy.

Latour presented some initial findings from the Salk study at the first meeting of the Society for Social Studies of Science (November 1976) in a paper titled "Including Citation Counting in the System of Actions of Scientific Papers". There are already hints in this paper of an actor-network theory (ANT), Latour's major contribution to social theory (e.g., as explicated most recently in Latour, 2005). But by the time *Laboratory Life* was published, Karin Knorr-Cetina, Steve Woolgar, Doug McKegney, Sal Restivo (with Michael Zenzen), and a few others were already engaged in field studies of science. Sharon Traweek, who would become one of the most prominent anthropologists of science, was already working outside of this network at the SLAC national accelerator laboratory in Stanford, California. By the early 1980s, the work of the ethnographers had revolutionized our understanding of scientific practice. In combination with the studies undertaken by Harry Collins, Trevor Pinch, David Edge, Michael Mulkay, Nigel Gilbert, David Bloor, Donald MacKenzie, Andy Pickering, Steve Shapin and others (primarily representing the Edinburgh and Bath schools) on replication, reflexivity, discourse, mathematics, and social histories of science, the ethnographies of science produced a new narrative in answer to the question "What is science?"

Latour is one of the most prominent guides to our liminal times. The liminality of our era reaches to most of the fundamental categories and classifications that have guided human cultures for millennia in some cases and for the last few hundred years in the case of industrial societies. This liminality is driving some of the most significant and influential intellectual movements of our era. Nature-society, human-machine, male-female, person-fetus, mind-body, and life-death are among the powerful dualisms that have become dramatically problematic. The very idea of science (along with those "good" terms rationality, truth, and objectivity) has been embraced by this liminality that threatens to engulf all of our values, goals, and gods.

Traditional dichotomies have given way to complexities, non-linearities, and chaotic, fractal, and multi-logical ways of thinking, speaking, and seeing. We have encountered new phenomena across time and space on and off the planet; engaged new ideas, experiences, and values from east to west and north to south (politically, economically, and culturally); and we have endured enormous leaps in our knowledge about how the world around us works. The result is that we have been forced into new epistemological and ontological territories. It is important not to ignore the cultural inertia that sustains classical dichotomies. That inertia is fuel for caution when reading Latour's criticisms and challenges. Nonetheless it is difficult to ignore the signs of worldview and paradigm shifts and essential tensions that are widely visible features of our everyday and professional lives.

Our liminal era is producing hybrid ideas and concepts and monstrous entities on a new scale. One day we are accosted by cyborgs, the next day by robosapiens; cloned sheep march with "natural" cows and horses; mice are patented; some women sell their eggs, some men donate their sperm. No one has exploited this situation on the public and professional stages better than Latour. His prominence has tended to obscure the innovative contributions in this arena by feminist social theorists, beginning with Mary Daly in the 1970s and including scholars such as Donna Haraway, Gloria Andalzua, and Susan Leigh Star. Latour, nonetheless, has been a leader in exploring new ways of reworking our systems of categories and classifications. He has been among the leaders documenting the changes in worldview our emerging human ecologies are calling forth. Such efforts, now as in all liminal eras, necessarily strike us as awkward, counterintuitive, and obscure to different degrees. Latour's particular mix of counter-intuitives, even where his critics consider him wrongheaded and misguided, has the virtue of drawing our attention to the limits of our reigning categories and classifications. In a world of hybrids, monsters, and uncertainties it should not surprise us that Latour has produced theories and concepts that are themselves hybrids, monsters, and embodiments of uncertainty.

Latour can appear on the one hand as a charlatan and on the other as a creative strategist in the midst of uncertainties and complexities. Like science in one of his best known graphics, he is Janus-faced. One face knows, the other face does not know yet. This image gives us "science and technology" on the one hand and technoscience on the other hand. Perhaps to understand Latour we must look both ways – forward and backward in time. His advice is to recognize that we need to shift our activities and viewpoints just as science, nature, and actors/actants in general shift theirs. Here we have the foundation for a strategy that avoids dichotomies old and new as we move through time and space. Latour is not dogmatically opposed to dichotomies *per se*, only to those that are uninteresting and obstruct our research.

Prior to the emergence of science and technology studies (variously science studies, technology studies, social studies of science and technology, and the new sociology of science) in the late 1960s, the question "What is science?" was primarily addressed by scientists themselves, philosophers and historians of science, and science writers. Sociologists of science also studied science but they were not seen by scientists as encroaching on their jurisdiction because (1) they championed science and viewed themselves as scientists, (2) they studied the sciences scientists themselves viewed as embodying the best of what science could offer the world, especially physics, and (3) they did not claim any analytical purchase on the content of science.

The new sociologists of science associated with science studies included social critics of science (such as Restivo, Ravetz, H. and S. Rose, Arditti, Young, and Levidow) but for the most part still adopted an uncritical to worshipful orientation to science (in the works, for example, of Bloor and H. Collins). But it was their claim that they were now prepared to study the actual content of science that would eventually upset some scientists and many philosophers and historians of science. Latour became the whipping boy for these defenders of the faith because he was so outspoken, and so widely and wildly visible through his writings, lectures, and interviews. Underneath the attacks on Latour and science studies was a fervent resistance to sociology as a science, discipline, and profession and a widespread ignorance about the nature and findings of sociology. The so-called "science warriors" who initiated the science wars (see, for example and notably, Gross and Levitt, 1994) read postmodernism in general and the idea that science was socially constructed as meaning that science was arbitrary, not objective, and more fiction than truth. The science wars of the 1990s brought some scientists and philosophers into open conflict with social scientists and humanities scholars over the nature of science. Briefly, the conflict pitted "realists" (who believed in an objective "reality out there") against "social constructionists" whom they assumed (incorrectly) to be making relativist claims and challenging the validity of science (for the details of this controversy, see Restivo and Croissant, 2007: 225ff.). Latour, while trying in different ways to mollify the scientists and philosophers, has at the same time joined them in opposing a certain kind of sociology or perhaps sociology *per se*. Latour does not want to alienate the scientists who are his "subjects" and an important segment of the audience he wants to cultivate. One of the things he shares with many physical and natural scientists is a skepticism about the value and even the possibility of a scientific sociology.

Laboratory Life, Latour's best known work (co-authored with Woolgar), was part of a movement that reworked our conventional ideas about how science works. In *Science in Action* (1988), Latour offered readers a systematic rendering of this reworking, and showed us how to think anew about science and technology. He tied together the major achievements of science studies, namely the emphasis on practice, construction, the central role of inscription, and the institutional context of modern science. Latour turned these achievements into a general theory of science as a network building activity. With this book, we are a few steps closer to articulating the actor-network theory adumbrated in *Laboratory Life*. Latour's next book, *The Pasteurization of France* (1988), contributed to the development of actor-network theory by demonstrating that it takes more than a great man to produce and ground a discovery. Louis Pasteur (1822-1895) is best known to the general public for inventing pasteurization. He contributed to reducing deaths due to puerperal fever, and developed the first rabies vaccine. Latour demonstrates that Pasteur's success in developing pasteurization was dependent on a network of forces that included public hygiene actors, physicians, and government interests.

Pasteur's triumph – substantively and methodologically – was the outcome of competing forces and interests within a specific historical context. Pasteur's success (as an actant in a network of actants) in relation to other microbiologists was dependent on mobilizing various elements of the French public from farmers and industrialists to scientists and politicians.

Latour argues that society and scientific facts co-create each other simultaneously. Two Latourian axioms begin to come into sharper focus in this book. One is that it doesn't make sense to think in terms of "science and society", the other is that there is no way to "reduce" the case of Pasteur to disciplinary sociology. But where Latour and his acolytes see the triumph of "irreductionism" over sociological reductionism, some critics see just another example of sociological analysis (e.g., see especially Restivo, 2005, but also Star and Griesemer, 1989; Amsterdamska, 1990). The problem here turns once again on the assumptions ethnomethodologists make about the world compared to the assumptions of scientific sociologists. Latour does not admit social facts amenable in the manner of Durkheim to scientific *qua* theoretical analysis. Therefore, Latour views sociology as reducing social life to scientific explanations; thus his alternative notion of "irreductionism". If we think of this sort of strategy in relation to physics instead of sociology, what could be made of an ethnomethodological physics? The very idea is self-destructive. If one assumes the reality of a physical world, the analysis of that world in terms of disciplinary physics is not reductionist. If one assumes the reality of a social world, the analysis of that world in terms of disciplinary sociology is not reductionist. Latour does not admit such a social reality, so in his terms scientific sociology is by definition reductionist (see the discussion on the debate between Latour and Bloor below).

In *We Have Never Been Modern* (1993), Latour continues to confound the taken for granted boundaries that separates humans and things, the physical and the social sciences, and the sciences and the humanities. Where hybrids abound, the myth of modernity totters. This book is a way station on Latour's path to an increasingly systematic and well-articulated actor-network theory. If modernity is a myth so must be one of its defining features, the idea of progress

Latour's *Aramis* (1996) is a cautionary tale about technology and progress. Reviewers have described the book as "quirky" and filled with "stylistic excrescences" on the one hand, and as "eminently readable" and "strange and deep" on the other. Latour tells the story of a robotic transit system the French government designed for Paris during the 1970s and early 1980s. He tells this story by inventing a new genre, "scientifiction". The book interweaves fictional and real characters into a Rashomonesque tapestry designed to demonstrate once again the limits of sociology and the promise of actor-network theory. This book more than anything else Latour has written demonstrates his impressive capacity to mobilize wit, style, concepts, perspectives, bibliographies, empirical facts, and theoretical resources to create challenging hybrid theories. Even those who do not agree with his understanding of the sociological enterprise must conjure with an approach to reality which adopts sociology as one and only one of the resources to be brought to bear on a question or problem. It is difficult to argue with this approach, one that Nietzsche (1887/1956: 255) long ago anticipated when he argued that the more eyes one brings to a situation the more objective the viewing will be. The heterogeneity of sociology itself affords us many different sociological eyes with which to view social reality. Symbolic interactionism in particular offers an important approach to the social that is in some ways competitive with ANT and in others a resource for ANT.

Pandora's Hope (1999) is purportedly Latour's reply to a scientist friend's question: "Do you believe in reality?" Latour mobilizes ANT in defense of the reality of science studies and the flawed nature of his friend's question. He begins by rehearsing the contributions of science studies to our understanding of science and reality. This is followed by case studies in which Latour's dictum "follow the scientists" is the research imperative. Latour's account of science studies is designed to answer skeptics and critics of the field. From the very beginning, science studies has been about documenting in ethnographic detail and with Geertzian "thick descriptions" (Geertz, 1973: 3-30) the details of scientific practice. Latour, more than most of his colleagues, is concerned to bring into sharp relief the ways in which technology and science, the material and the human merge as our pictures of reality emerge, evolve, transform, and stabilize. Where and why given all this complexity did the idea that there is a reality we can fathom that is independent of our humanity come from? Latour wants to be the champion of ordinary people who are submissive to and intimidated by the warring claimants to "the facts" and ultimate truths.

Politics of Nature: How to Bring the Sciences into Democracy (2004) evidences the culmination of Latour's evolution from philosopher to sociologist and anthropologist to über-philosopher and naked metaphysician. Even if and where his metaphysics is in some self-contradictory sense "empirical", it is a philosophy more idealistic than realistic. The title and subtitle sizzle with the promise of saving us from ourselves, or more correctly from our categories and classifications, and from political tendencies driven by outmoded worldviews. Despite his penchant for the empirical, his profound understanding of science and technology as interwoven practices, and his decades of critically dismantling our conventional ideas about science and society, in the end he has divorced himself from real problems, practical solutions, and the guidelines of the ecological-sociological imagination. We nonetheless are forced to engage with the limits of our taken for granted categories and classifications, and this is why Latour always demands our attention.

Latour, who has traditionally shown little concern for a normative politics, now turns to a politics rooted in Plato's allegory of the Cave. He argues that that myth has given the West its ideas about science and society and the concept of the philosopher-scientist. Unlike the rest of humanity who only have access to the Cave's shadows, the philosopher-scientist can travel between the world of truth and the world of shadows, the social world. The myth of the Cave becomes a new starting point for an old idea in science studies: we have to distinguish the myth of Science from the actual practices of the sciences. Latour argues further that we have to on similar grounds distinguish the power politics of the Cave from politics in action. These distinctions flow from and reinforce the Latourian project of blurring the distinction between nature and society and between things and humans.

The point of his argument is that we should reach our views on reality, the external world, and nature not by way of the travels and tales of scientists moving between the worlds of truth and the social world but rather through a representative "due process". In place of an assembly of things and an assembly of humans, Latour proposes a new constitutional politics in which there are no special envoys and no barrier to go over and come back from. The sciences and one could say "the politics" are no longer concerned respectively with nature and with interests. Scientists and politicians now work together to construct our view of reality. Curiously (but in a way that is consistent with the ethnomethodological program), the due process that gives us reality with representation leads us to all of the old forms – a reality out there, subjects and objects, humans, a cosmos – we constructed under the old constitution.

What in fact has happened to Latour is that he has gone back to his philosophical roots and now works on a plane of inquiry that is far removed from the social and political realities of everyday social life. There is something grossly Platonic and transcendental in his plan for bringing the sciences into "democracy". Democracy? Surely you're joking, Mr. Latour! The term appears immediately in the book's subtitle, but does not rate a definition in the glossary. This is a book that is written in the philosophical tradition that worries more about bats, armadillos, and Martians than about real human beings and then applies the "insights" of these worries to humans and their societies.

The democracy that Latour writes about perhaps "exists" in some imaginary Platonic realm of ideas but nowhere on earth that I am aware of. The results inevitably reflect elegant literacy, are logically clever (or cleverly logical), and challenge the reader to distinguish brilliant insights from frivolous word play. The sociologist of knowledge would not be hard pressed to see Latour's elite upbringing guiding him here. Latour sees himself as a champion of novel insights on science, society, and nature that bear on the most pressing human problems, locally and globally. His admirers seem to be hypnotized by his neologisms, doodles, and wit, while his critics find him obscure and self-indulgent. His insights on the distinction between Science and science (see below) are enough, however, to make this an important book for students of the social relations of science and technology. His style is reminiscent of a Rousseau or Hobbes; he writes with a naïve self-confidence about society, innocent (after the fact in this case) of or dismissive of the perspectives and findings of the social sciences.

Latour (2004: 246) begins by claiming bluntly that political ecology has nothing to do with nature. "Political ecology" designates "the understanding of ecological crises that no longer uses nature to account for the tasks to be accomplished". Perhaps the reader now expects the book as a whole to demonstrate the basis and implications of this claim, and surely to some extent that expectation is realized. But Latour immediately raises a cautionary flag – against this reasoned expectation of some sort of dialogue with the reader, he reveals that perhaps this is nothing more than Latour raising questions for himself and himself alone about nature, science, and politics, and what they have to do with each other. Even if and where this is an exercise in solipsism, it can be worth your while to follow Latour around while he muses and amuses. Inevitably, one must navigate around variations on clichés ("human beings are born free; everywhere they are in chains"), pithy confucianisms ("today's enemy is tomorrow's ally"), and the occasional Latin seasoning (*"Non nova sed nove"*) in order to stay the course.

The more dangerous navigation is through the counterintuitives that abound in Latour's writings. The danger is that the reader will dismiss counterintuitives that are grounded in the empirical research of the science studies movement and sociology along with counterintuitives that are idiosyncratic products of Latour's philosophical imagination. When he tries to draw you into a game of plurals – sciences, natures, politics – you might be tempted to resist because you think of Science and Nature and not sciences and natures. But this is exactly where Latour is on the most solid grounds. His criticisms of Science and Nature reflect nearly half a century of research in the sociology and anthropology of science carried out by a variety of interdisciplinary scholars.

Latour is characteristically either sloppy or consciously inconsistent depending on how charitable the reader wants to be. Within the space of two pages he says first that he has no definitive answer to the opening query ("What is to be done with political ecology?"), and then that even though political ecology is already practically speaking doing what he claims it should be doing it requires his intervention. This is part of the Latourian game – keep the reader on his/her toes, caution him/her (correctly, let us acknowledge) that there are difficulties and complexities everywhere. When he then tells us that he has provided a six page "crib sheet" for "readers in a hurry" (perhaps you don't remember that he has already warned you that we need to proceed like the tortoise to beat the hare, or that he has promised you a meticulously organized argument), we are left to wonder why we shouldn't just read the crib sheet.

Latour's politics begins with Plato's allegory of the Cave. That allegory defines the relations between Science and Society in the West. The myth, Latour writes, constructs an absolute difference between the world of truth and the social world. At the same time, the myth creates a philosopher-scientist who can travel back and forth at will between the world of truth and the social world. The rest of humanity are prisoners, witness only to the Cave's shadows. This allegory has given us Science. Science Studies, by empirically investigating the nature and grounds of this Science, has given us the practical reality of the sciences. The classical idea of Science embodied in the Unity of Science movement has been displaced on empirical grounds by a new awareness of the Disunity of Science. This is in my view indisputable. The old ideologies and myths of science, the classical philosophies of science, the old sociologies and histories of science, the journalistic, anecdotal, and heroic stories of science have not survived the empirical sociologists and anthropologists of science. Latour, however, is going to draw an additional lesson from these results that requires eliminating sociology from our toolkit of methods of inquiry. This is where he and I (in company with David Bloor, Karin Knorr-Cetina, and other science studies scholars) part company. Latour, of course, will want to view our disagreement as nothing more sinister than a difference to be played out in the new agora as the field of "politics". He argues for something akin to philosopher Richard Rorty's idea that if we keep the conversation going all will be well. But it is the conversation of the West, and a polite one besides, that Rorty wants us to continue. This is the conversation that Latour too wants us to continue, a conversation that cannot sever the umbilical cord that ties our intellectual lives to the very Cave he wants us to escape.

Now just as we have to distinguish Science from the sciences, we have to distinguish the power politics of the Cave from politics, the "progressive composition of the common world". Philosophers like Rorty and Latour are liberal interpreters of the old myths of the West, weaving benign philosophies of academic discourse that do not sweat, urinate, or defecate, and that do not have recourse to conflict, let alone violence. This sort of liberal discourse promises to deliver us from the evils, issues, and troubles of our all-too-human world by marching lightly under the conservative Willian banner of "Thou shalt not commit a sociology".

Part of the process of distinguishing politics from power politics involves distinguishing next between "militant ecology" and "the philosophy of ecology" (or *Naturpolitik*, which mimics the concept of *Realpolitik*). Latour's (2004: 19) criticism of the ecology movements is that "under the pretext of protecting nature, [they] have also retained the conception of nature that makes their political struggle hopeless". The argument from this point on becomes rather dense, especially for those who have not followed closely either Latour's writings or developments in science studies. The main point is that here, as in his earlier writings, Latour wants to blur the distinction between nature and society and between things and humans. On the question of nature, he wants to exorcise (a) the nature based on the idea of primary qualities (as opposed to secondary qualities); (b) the "warm and green" nature of *Naturpolitik;* and (c) the "red and bloody" nature of political economics. Regarding things and humans, Latour wants to legislate equal opportunity. He does not argue that things should or can speak for themselves or exhibit a humanoid agency (although he can be maddingly confusing about this point). Rather, he is opposed to scientists being the sole interpreters of the world of things, of experts taking upon themselves the job of "speaking for" the mute objects of the natural world. The point of all this is to reach our views on reality, the external world, and the unity of nature not by way of the travels and tales of the scientists moving between the worlds of truth and the social world but rather through "due process". This brings Latour into the world of constitutional politics.

Latour's cleverly understated defense of the constitutional metaphor fails to hide the philosophical assurance he projects that he has hit on a solution to nothing less than the crises of our time. He becomes the savior of our "public life". Until now, public life – under the influence of the Cave allegory – was ruled by a bicameral political model. The two houses of "nature" and "society" were constituted respectively of an assembly of things and an assembly of humans. Latour wants now to eliminate the distinction between nature and the representations we make of nature. This is the culmination of a process that emerged in the second edition of the pioneering ethnography of the Salk Institute, *Laboratory Life*, written by Latour and Steve Woolgar.

The subtitle of the first edition, published in 1979, was "the social construction of scientific facts". For the second edition, published in 1986, the subtitle was changed to "the construction of scientific facts". Now Latour claims that science studies "in combination with militant ecology", shows us how to break away from the "deceptive self-evidence of the social sciences". This means "abandoning" social constructionism. According to Latour, we need to change our notion of the social. In place of "the social world as prison" we put "the social world as association". Recall that the allegory of the Cave gave us a world – a universe – in which special envoys called "scientists" could move between nature and society to provide the rest of us with objective renderings or representations of the mute objects of nature. In Latour's new constitution, there are no such special envoys and there is no barrier to go over and come back from. The sciences and (one could say) the politics are no longer concerned respectively with nature and with interests. Scientists and politicians now work as equals on the six functions of the collective. These functions are: perplexity, consultation, hierarchy, institution, maintenance of the separation of powers, and scenarization of the whole. Defining these terms here and summarizing their grounds is beyond the scope of this chapter, but the "reader in a hurry" will find all of these terms defined in Latour's glossary.

What do we have, then? All of the institutions that manifest Latour's proposed constitution, he notes, already exist in tentative form; and all of the old forms – subjects and objects, the external world, humans, and a cosmos – will be back, products of due process and not given, once and for all, at the beginning before due process. "No reality", Latour proclaims, "without representation!" This is one of the two major allusions that perversely tie Latour's liberal metaphysics to revolutionary theory and practice. He also echoes the famous title of Lenin's essay, "What is to be done?" (which in turn recycled the title of Nicholas Chernyshevsky's 1863 novel) and which has been a staple slogan in radical politics for nearly a century. The problem Latour addresses is: what is to be done with political ecology? He concludes his book with the stronger Leninism: What is to be done? Political ecology! Latour is revolutionary the way Thomas Kuhn (in *The Structure of Scientific Revolutions*) was revolutionary – not through his own efforts but rather through the tortured efforts of his acolytes.

These are liminal times. Perhaps all times are liminal in some way. But when we say "our time" is liminal here at the beginning of the second millennium we do so with a level of awareness of the flux of categories and classifications unavailable in earlier periods. And the categories and classifications at stake at this juncture of history and culture are the foundation of the world's culture's values, interests, and goals. Social movements and social changes in general have made such primordial classifications as male-female, person-fetus, and life-death problematic. I don't mean to ignore earlier examples of this sort of problematic but rather to suggest that we are engaged in more fundamental problems in part on account of the scope of the historical and cross-cultural information we have access to. Nature-society and human-machine are among those challenged classifications. The very idea of science has become problematic as Western modes of thought become increasingly engaged with non-Western modes of thought. Dichotomous thinking across the spectrum of intellectual life has given way to thinking in terms of complexities, non-linearities, chaos, and fractals. Networks and the circulation of information have come to rule theory.

One of the characteristics of liminal times is the proliferation of hybrids and monsters, that is, hybrid ideas and concepts and monstrous entities. We are everywhere in and out of the academy accosted by inter-, multi-, and transdisciplinarities. Cyborgs, robosapiens, and clones abound. We have more and more real life examples of human-machine hybrids from the iconic Stephen Hawking to the self-styled chip implant pioneer and "cyborg", Kevin Warwick. Latour has exploited this situation better than many (perhaps all) of his colleagues and competitors. At least, he has recognized the potential for exploitation. Competing exploiters are charged with exploring new ways of organizing our categories and classifications and serving as the source eventually of a new worldview, a new way of ordering the world that works for our changed circumstances. These efforts will in general strike us as awkward, counterintuitive, and obscure. Latour's mix of counterintuitives, even where some of us consider him wrongheaded and misguided, deserves our attention if for no other reason than that he draws out attention to the need to reconsider reigning categories and classifications. If sociology too has to be reconfigured, so be it. I am not opposed to such a strategy. Latour, however, has tried to do this without understanding first what it is that sociologists do. He has abandoned social constructivism (or constructionism) without persuading me and some of my science studies colleagues that he has discovered an alternative to the constituting activities of social relations. And that, after all is what social construction means: we have no recourse outside of our interactions – our social humanity – for constituting the world.

In *Reassembling the Social* (2007), Latour mobilizes all of his resources to mount a focused challenge to reigning ideas about society and "the social". He reiterates his claim that following Durkheim's imperative to explain social facts with social facts means "explaining" stable things in terms of other stable things. However useful this methodology may have been historically it is now obstructing and obscuring our ability to understand social life. The old theories and methods left out too many "things" or "facts" that enter into the social domain. These other things and facts cannot be taken into account if we think of the social as a kind of thing, a level of reified material reality. To understand scientists, we must follow them and document all the connections they make and engage; to understand society, we must follow it everywhere it goes and document all the connections it makes and engages. Notice the difference in kind Latour ignores when he treats following scientists and following society as presenting the same methodological challenge. According to Latour, the new social science must focus on the process of assembling the social without prejudging what is and what is not social. Here, then, is the introduction to actor-network theory that many of Latour's admirers and critics have been waiting for. Here is Latour assembling actor-network theory.

Working out actor-network theory has leveraged Latour's development of an alternative sociology, a sociology of associations opposed to a sociology of the social. Latour views this distinction as parallel to pre-relativistic physics (conventional sociology with its Durkheimian roots) versus relativistic physics (the sociology of associations, grounded in ethnomethodology, material-semiotics, and most recently in the work of Durkheim's contemporary Gabriel Tarde).

I leave aside the failure of this Einsteinian analogy, which ignores the fact that relativity is a theory of invariance and was originally, in German, *Invarianttheorie*. The main methodological principle emerging out of Latour's studies and made explicit in *Science in Action* (1987) was "follow the scientists and engineers". This was the portal that led to ANT.

Already in the first chapter of *Laboratory Life*, Latour (with Woolgar) begins to dismantle the very idea of the social. Their concern with "the social" is different, they stress, from that of traditional (notably Mertonian) sociologists of science. It has become increasingly clear that Latour's understanding of "the social" is not just different from that of sociologists of science but that of sociologists in general. The focus on "the social" in *Laboratory Life* emphasizes the construction of "sense" in science, rather than the sorts of variables the Mertonians addressed (such as norms, rewards, and competition).

What, then, are the socially available procedures for constructing ordered accounts out of practices, discourses, and environments that appear initially to be chaotic? Some of Latour's colleagues discuss this in terms of contructing facts out of contingencies. Latour has mounted a formidable attack on cultural patterns of practice and discourse, categories and classifications that have concretized over centuries and resist our efforts to learn anew, to adapt to new situations, and to strategize politically in the wake of new political and ecological imperatives. It is important to recognize that while the laboratory scientists are constructing order out of disorder, Latour and Woolgar are constructing an orderly account out of the initial appearance of disorder in the laboratory. Later, Latour (1988: 161) would say that one order is being created out of other orders. On the surface, the effort to make this approach seem like something innovative is belied by how closely it imitates classical ethnographies. At least some sociologists of the social appear to operate essentially as Latourian sociologists of associations but without losing the Durkheimian sense of the social.

It is instructive here to review accounts of anthropologists engaging a culture for the first time. Raymond Firth's (1936) introduction to *We, the Tikopia*, for example, clearly describes a process of creating order out of disorder or out of other orders. Such accounts demonstrate that Latour's effort to create a new sociology has continuities with classical ethnography. The Firth example is one of many more one could point to that demonstrate that Latour's sociology has been a part of classical and modern sociology all along. What *is* innovative is the idea that the account given by Latour and Woolgar is not privileged over the accounts given by the scientists themselves in terms of giving us access to a sociology of science. Even here, however, we hear echoes of ethnomethodology and anticipations of the new ethnography and the commitment to making anthropology the science of giving a voice to the Other. In *Laboratory Life,* this strategy plants the seeds of an assault on Durkheimian sociology and of the future science wars.

The marks of ethnomethodology pervade this account, and postmodern French philosophy (notably the works of de Certeau and Serres) underwrites the emphasis Latour and Woolgar place on science as the production of "fictions", connoting here literature and writing accounts and not falsehoods. After all the exegesis and critical evaluation is completed, it will turn out that Latour and Woolgar have made an invaluable contribution to the sociology of science, independent of the distinction between the social and associations. That is, they have neither denied the "out-thereness" of reality, nor the existence of facts; but they have stressed and empirically demonstrated that facts and realities are social accomplishments, the result of the practical, discursive work of scientists. On this point, they are at one with their post-Mertonian colleagues (including Bloor, Knorr-Cetina, R. Collins, Leigh Star, and Restivo), all of whom however distance themselves from Latour's claims about the demise of the social.

In the 1986 edition of *Laboratory Life* Latour and Woolgar added a postscript and eliminated the word "social" from the subtitle. In a section on "The Demise of the Social," Latour and Woolgar carry out the promise of their original study to understand how scientists themselves distinguish between "social" and "technical" factors. The idea of the social was useful to the Mertonians in their development of the concept of science as a social institution. It was equally useful to the Edinburgh School in its development of a sociology of scientific knowledge (SSK), constructed on the foundation of Bloor's "strong programme". Latour and Woolgar now claim that "the social" is no longer useful.

Perhaps the single most important focus for critics of ANT is that it seems to assign agency to nonhumans. ANT has been described by its founders as a material-semiotic method that maps relations between things and between concepts simultaneously. This means that the interactions we can observe in a bank, for example, are not just the interactions between people, but rather the network of interactions involving people, their ideas and concepts, and technologies. It is not clear why, when ANT is described in this way, it is any different from the way anthropologists view culture holistically in terms of the network of relations between socifacts, mentifacts, and artifacts (to use David Bidney's [1967] categories). This is a good place to recall the work of Ludwik Fleck (1935/1979) who anticipated so much of Latour, not to mention Fleck's contributions to Kuhn's (1962) thinking. The anthropologist Mary Douglas (1986) has succinctly explicated the significance of Fleck and Durkheim for any sociology of knowledge.

Latour identifies more closely with anthropology than with sociology. The foil he makes of sociology from this position is somewhat forced. Opposing sociology from the anthropological perspective is based on a distinction without a difference, a matter of professional, disciplinary, and historical contingencies. His identification with anthropology as an interpretive discipline (as opposed to sociology-as-science) probably allows him to mobilize more humanities scholars, and anti-quantitative STS scholars and social scientists.

Let's look again at the example of the bank. In ANT terms, the bank is a network that can under certain conditions be treated as a unity, as an actor/actant. ANT stresses that networks are transient, constantly engaged in making and re-making themselves. Our relationships and our networks constantly have to be reconstituted, re-produced. Again, it is not clear what this idea achieves that hasn't already been achieved by sociologists like Harold Garfinkel and Erving Goffman. These two exemplars might readily be dismissed because they are idiosyncratic in the context of mainstream sociology. But we could as easily demonstrate the point with Weber and the sociologists who have followed in his wake, Merton no less than R. Collins.

Basic Concepts in Actor-Network Theory

ANT's focus is on actants. The term "actant" appears in the work of Lucien Tesnière as early as 1959. It is also associated with the works of Greimas (1966) and Kristeva (1967). Latour introduced the term "actant" into science studies to avoid speaking of "actors" acting or systems behaving. It is characteristically difficult to pin Latour down on definitions which seem to flow from him like zen koans (cf. Zammito, 2004: 189). Giving him the benefit of the doubt, we can argue that this is just what is necessary in order to capture something about a world of great complexity and uncertainty that seems constantly to be outrunning our efforts to stabilize it conceptually. Latour's critics see shallow maneuvering, comic effects, and attention-getting strategies in his work. It doesn't help the matter when Latour himself refers to his work as a joke, and tweaks his readers with ambiguities and contradictions. We, however, have to consider whether he has hit on a strategy that has at least temporary relevance for a period in which worldviews are undergoing stress and change (cf. Restivo, 1985: 129-156). It is important to keep in mind that the heritage of the laboratory studies has been to keep the focus on matters that are not yet settled, not yet closed, and still mired in different degrees of controversy. This is part of a postmodern disease that wants to view everything as open-ended and unsettled. The result is that many contemporary thinkers seem to think we are living in a conceptual world that is constantly experiencing earthquakes. In such a world, we could hardly live let alone stabilize language and concepts. The open-ended strategy I recommend in this book only works if we live in a world characterized by fundamental stabilities. As we walk from one room to the next in a house the properties of squares and rectangles don't keep changing. To suggest as some postmodern thinkers do that everything is always in flux is simply not true. Things stabilize and can be captured in recognized patterns, lawful relations, predictable outcomes of actions. To ignore these stabilities in the interest of an interesting postmodern game that only wants to play with chaos comes perilously close to a form of nihilism. Causality may be complicated, but it is possible to address those complexities and dangerous to deny them.

The critiques leveled against Latour often mischaracterize his position. Indeed, these are critiques that have been leveled against science studies researchers in general (notably in the science wars). Latour (1999: 299-300) claims explicitly that his critics are attacking someone with his name who defends all the absurdities he disputes: that science is socially constructed, that science is nothing more than discourse, that there is no "reality out there", that "everything goes" in science, that science is conceptually empty, that the more ignorant you are the better; that everything is political; that subjectivity and objectivity are inter-mingled; and "that the mightiest, manliest, and hairiest scientist always wins provided he has enough 'allies' in high places".

How is it that critics could make such a mistake? One answer is that Latour demands with the authority of the ethnographer that we rethink ideas about science that have gone unexamined; another is that science studies has invaded territories long held by more traditional disciplines; and finally, we can't dismiss the possibility that the very idea of a sociology of science breaches powerful ideologies of science.

Already in his presentation at the first meeting of the Society for Social Studies of Science (1976), Latour is at work redefining things in the world of science so as to extend what it includes; he begins to draw the outlines of what he will later capture in the term "actant". In his 4S paper, he defines "literature" as a continuum which includes drafts, corrected manuscripts, private and public preprints, oral presentations of papers, posters, abstracts, and the finally published papers, reprints and copies. The very process of ethnography forces Latour to focus on the frontiers of science, watching unsettled science where we find chains of conflict, controversy, and modalities. What Latour sees in his Salk laboratory study is not facts plain and simple, but a continuous chain of activities.

In *The Pasteurization of France*, Latour mobilizes ANT in the interest of providing what amounts to a "thick description" of actants, of an actor-network. Society is not formed with the social alone; in this particular case, for example, we have to add the action of microbes. We cannot speak of something – science – done in laboratories and then speak of groups, classes, interests, and laws in a separate narrative. Instead we have to speak of actor-networks, and instead of thinking in terms of "forces" that cause this or that, we must think and speak of "weaknesses", "entelechies", "monads", or more generally "actants". Latour uses "actor", "agent", or "actant" without assuming actions or properties. They are "autonomous figures", and they can be individuals or crowds, figurative or nonfigurative.

These ideas can be very confusing, but the main thing is to avoid using the term "actor" which is often limited to humans; the virtue of the term "actant" is that it can refer to humans and nonhumans. People and things have "spokespersons" in the assemblage of an ANT and Latour borrows the term "actant" from semiotics to describe what the spokesperson represents. He now can describe the power of the scientific laboratory in terms of the number of actants it can mobilize around its findings and interests. In general, then, power is a function of the number of allies "the laboratory" or anyone, or any network can shape and enroll – mobilize – to support its findings and interests in an agonistic arena. If Pasteur speaks for microbes, the Curies can be said to speak for plutonium, Cantor for transfinite numbers, Einstein for photons, and so on. Perhaps the simplest definition of actant is the one Latour offers in the glossary for *Politics of Nature*; but he once again confuses his readers by pairing actor and actant as one entry. Actant applies to humans and nonhumans, he writes. This is followed by "an actor is any activity that modifies another activity in a trial". Presumably, this is what he means by "actant", the non-anthropomorphic sibling of "actor". It helps to reflect on the use of the concept of actant in semiotics to reveal more clearly what Latour is trying to accomplish.

Originally, the concept of actant was invented to help readers of stories identify characters as one sort of actant or another: helper or opponent (the conflict axis); subject or object (the project axis); and sender or receiver (the communication axis). Characters could also be combinations of two or more actants. This framework offers a primitive narrative organization for a fairy tale. Something or someone is missing as the result of a villainous act. The subject lacks this object. The sender and the receiver contract to retrieve the missing object. The sender is high on the hierarchies of status, power, and privilege, which means the receiver incurs an obligation in this contract. The subject, with or without a helper, retrieves the object in combat with an anti-subject (opponent). This is known as "the test" (Hawkes, 1977; Tesnière, 1959). Latour (1987: 89-90) has translated this framework and imported it into science studies. The "things" that stand behind the texts of science are like the heroes of our epics. In some stories, heroes defeat dragons and save maidens. In some stories, hero scientists "resist precipitation" or "triumph over bismuth". The essence of the hero does not appear to us all at once but over time and retrospectively. What at one point is a list of actions eventually becomes clear as an essence.

Actants are characters, and they require spokespersons to turn them into actors (Akrich and Latour, 1992). By pairing humans and nonhumans, Latour makes it possible to assemble the greatest number of actants in a single world, an assembling carried out by the collective. The result is that there is no longer any need "to defend the subject against reification, or to defend the object against social construction. Things no longer threaten subjects. Social construction no longer weakens objects" (Latour, 2004: 80-81). The creation of an actor-network is known as "translation". Notice that Latour considers it useful to focus on a single actor (read "actant") and to see translation from that actor's perspective.

The process of translation occurs in four stages. First a focal actor identifies and aligns itself with other actors who share its identities and interests. The focal actor sets itself as an "obligatory passage point" (OPP), and in this way renders itself "indispensable" (Callon, 1986). This is known as the problematizing stage. At the interessement stage, the focal actor is engaged in convincing others to accept its definition(s) of identities and interests. The stage in which the others accept the focal actor's definition(s) is known as enrollment. The fourth stage, mobilization, solidifies the shape, form, and scope of the network.

Six additional concepts help to flesh out the basic conceptual skeleton of ANT: inscription, irreversibility, punctualization, depunctualization, token, and technoscience. Inscription creates technologies designed to protect the interests of actors and networks (cryptography technologies are a transparent exemplar). Keeping in mind that interessement involves interrupting and ultimately triumphing over competing definitions, the idea of irreversibility refers to how likely it is to return to a situation in which alternative possibilities exist. As Hardy, Phillips and Clegg (2001: 538) note: "These strategies help to create convergence by locking actors into the network. The more fixed or stable it appears, the more 'real' and durable it becomes, and the less controversy and ambiguity are evident...The aim, then, is to put relations between actors into 'black boxes' where they become a matter of indifference – scientific 'facts', technical artifacts, modes of thought, habits, forces, objects." The laboratory studies, viewed from this perspective, describe the process of translation from macrocosm (larger "outside" world) to microcosm (the laboratory), from laboratory activity to laboratory inscriptions, and from the laboratory back to the outside world.

Punctualization refers to the fact that the components of complex systems, such as those of an automobile, are hidden from the view of the user. If a car breaks down, this can provoke the driver to recognize that the car is a collection of parts rather than just a vehicle that s/he can drive from place to place. This kind of awareness can also be kindled when parts of a network begin working in conflict with the network as a whole. This is referred to as "depunctualization". Social order in general and the working automobile in the example above are achievements of the actants interacting within actor-networks. Such creations are known as "tokens" or "quasi-objects" and they get passed from actants/actors to actants/actors across actor-networks. The more tokens circulate through a network the more they get punctualized and reified; a decrease in the circulation of a token results in depunctualization and a decrease in reification.

Early on in *Science in Action*, Latour (1987: 29, 174-175) "forges" the word "technoscience" in order to avoid endlessly writing "science and technology". Technoscience refers to "all the elements tied to the scientific contents no matter how dirty, unexpected or foreign they seem". This leaves "science and technology" (in quotes) "to designate *what is kept of technoscience* once all the trials of responsibility have been settled". We can see Latour's ANT strategy at work here. The term "technoscience" appears to have been introduced into philosophy by the Belgian philosopher Gilbert Hottois (1984) in the late 1970s. Hottois' concept of technoscience was not tied to a social theory of science but rather to Percy Bridgeman's notion of operationalization. In both cases, the term technoscience is designed to broaden our notions of science and technology. Notice that for Latour, technoscience implies a stage as well as a new stability. It is a stage within which science and technology are composed of many different kinds of elements (or actants). Once the trials of responsibility are settled, we can once more distinguish science and technology (or in Latour's more exact terms, "science and technology"). Latour's translations within science studies revolve around mobilizing the concept of the actant and ANT and result in a clear separation between ANT and the strong programme (hereafter SP) in the sociology of scientific knowledge. Latour's principle antagonist is the author of SP, David Bloor. Latour's theory and critique of "the social" achieves a dramatic focus in his "vehement" (Bloor, 1999: 81) criticism of the sociology of knowledge and of SP. Bloor (1999: 82) claims that Latour's criticism of SP systematically misrepresents the programme and his alternative, "in so far as it is different, is unworkable". Latour and Bloor differ on what to do about the "subject-object schema". Latourian sociology simply rejects the schema. Bloor points out that there are many levels and interpretations of the schema, and that at least one is sociologically viable.

Latour versus Bloor

Latour criticizes sociology and SP for relying on "Society" to explain things. He is opposed to a Durkheimian sociology that explains social facts with social facts, and a SP that uses Society to explain Nature (Latour, 1992: 278). The issue for Latour is that sociology and SP do not take into account the ways in which non-social things and processes contribute to "Society", that is, to the social organization of our lives. Latour adopts the term "anthropology" for a project that is non-sociological, non-reductionist, non-naturalistic, and non-causal and not anything like the anthropological tradition that runs from Durkheim to Mary Douglas. That tradition is central to SP. Latour mistakenly assumes that the goal of SP is to use society to explain nature. The goal of SP is in fact to explain not nature but "shared beliefs about nature" (Bloor, 1999: 87). The debate between Bloor and Latour is not easily resolved. The reason in part is that differences in metaphysics (as Latour recognizes) and more broadly differences in worldview are at issue. We must in the end compare and contrast entire worldviews rather than little bits and pieces of epistemology, methodology, and ontology, a general strategy elegantly outlined by the philosopher of science Clifford Hooker (1975).

Latour wants to interrogate everything philosophically: science, nature, society, causality, the subject and the object, politics. Bloor wants to carry out interrogations on the grounds of the successful sciences. Parenthetically, notice that this could easily degenerate into a conflict between a Latourian antagonism to causal science and a Bloorian scientism. In his reply to Bloor, Latour raises the banner of anti-absolutism, the very banner Bloor waves in the face of those SP critics who understand relativism as the opposite of realism. Bloor has consistently stressed that relativism in SP is opposed to absolutism and even defined relativism as "distinterested research" (a classic philosophical and sociological definition of science; see Barnes and Bloor, 1982: 47n).

Could it be that the result of this debate is to demonstrate that Bloor and Latour are at one on the nature of science and society? This would not be an unusual outcome. After all of his efforts to distance himself from Lakatos in *Against Method* (1975), Feyerabend joins him. And all radical appearances to the contrary, the more Kuhn explains Kuhn the clearer he makes it that he is more a traditional internalist historian of science than a classical sociologist of knowledge or new sociologist of science. The outcome of all of Latour's interrogations is that he lands on Bloor's territory. When we have interrogated all of the old forms – the subject/object schema, external reality, society, and nature using Latour's (2004) proposed new constitution and parliament, in the wake of the due process he demands, all of the old forms will be back. Latour's slogan is "No reality without representation". If all the forms are the same before and after representation, before and after due process, what has Latour added to our discourse except the strong programme and SSK? According to Latour (1999: 113) Bloor, indeed, claims just this, that Latour has given us SSK "couched in a fancy vocabulary".

Critique and Opposition

Four main questions have occupied Latour's acolytes and critics – is he a constructionist (social or otherwise); is he a relativist; does he grant machines and material objects agency; and what discipline can he be assigned to? Latour himself claims that he is not a *social* constructionist; he is a relativist only in the same way, he says, that Einstein is a relativist (recall that Einstein's theory is a theory of invariance); he is frustratingly ambivalent about the agency of objects; and if not a dominant French philosopher he is at least an über-denker. Forced to discipline him, I would choose philosophy over sociology or anthropology. Let's look more closely at Latour and social constructionism.

Latour's early education and training in philosophy and theology and his continuing exercise of philosophical analytical and discursive strategies in his research and writing underpin his defense of metaphysical narratives. His view of how the world works and what it "is" bears some resemblance to the views of the late physicist David Bohm. Bohm was at least as sensitive as Latour to the volatility and dynamics of the material world and the world of humans, their languages, and their cultures. Bohm's science is strikingly consistent with Latour's metaphysics (Restivo, 1985: 121-125).

As we approached the second millennium, the flux of categories and classifications and the proliferation of hybrids and monsters, increasingly came to dominate our everyday lives and the horizons of humanity. These are times that require great courage and imagination to engage, so it is it not surprising that only a few thinkers like Latour come to the fore. But his work and his ideas are strengthened by the fact that a thinker like Bohm, stressing science as opposed to metaphysics, has seen contemporary liminal dynamics through the very lenses that Latour is seeking to change. Bohm (1976) even championed a verb based language as one way of coordinating language and reality.

Does Latour consider himself a relativist? Yes and no. Is his sociology more metaphysics than science? Yes and no. Do machines have agency? Yes and no. It's easy to view Latour as a sort of zen master, prying open black boxes, challenging the taken-for-granted, shaking us out of our complacency about everyday language – by drowning us in language games designed to enlighten us. There is method behind what sometimes can appear to be zen sociology or less charitably, just a little joking. When the philosopher Graham Harman described Latour as an empirical metaphysician, Latour countered by stressing that while philosophy and metaphysics are significant aspects of his research program the main thrust of his approach is to engage in empirical research. He accepted with good humor someone's description of him as a "serial re-describer". Latour's approach has roots in ethnomethodology, arguably a methodology of translation (translating phenomena into the language of ethnomethodology) but certainly not a scientific methodology. Ethnomethodology has this characteristic because it focuses on describing how people use language in constructing their lives and not on the standpoint of the "outsider" theorist or analyst. Latour's book *Politics of Nature* is nothing if not an exercise in unadulterated metaphysics rooted in ethnomethodology. He addresses issues ranging from science and philosophy to world politics, ecology, and the body. He is always "trespassing" onto the territories of other scholars and specialties. This is, on the one hand, characteristic of the general theorist, and especially of the philosopher. On the other, this opens Latour up to attacks on many different fronts.

The difference between the sociologists of the social and the sociologists of associations is a red herring. Latour claims that the former can be called on to study stable social orders, but that the latter are needed to study and understand social orders in process. But there is no reason to make such a distinction unless one is ready to defend the claim that in any field of study you need two different sciences to study statics and dynamics. For the Durkheimian "sociologists of the social", the other issue is that if we make "everything" social, we lose sight of the unique qualities that obtain in the social interactions of humans – the ties that bind: belongingness, community, solidarity, imitation, emotional coupling, engaging the other. Indeed, when he chooses Tarde over Durkheim as his starting point, he reveals why his social theory does not rise to the level of a scientific sociology. At the same time, he ignores the influence of Tarde on pragmatism and Chicago school sociology. Tarde is a more subtle sociologist than I can demonstrate here, but see Tarde (1899/2009).

The problem for the Durkheimian sociologist is that Tarde locates the origin of social changes in the "individual" and the "single mind" (Latour, 2005: 15). For Durkheim, society precedes the individual; the individual is a social unit, a social fact. Humans come onto the evolutionary scene not as individuals who then at some Hobbesian point choose to come together socially by way, for example, of a social contract. Rather, humans emerge everywhere, always, and already social. Latour's preference for Gabriel Tarde over Emile Durkheim amounts to an attack on the sociological imagination (C. Wright Mills), the sociological cogito (Randall Collins), social constructionism (Sal Restivo, Karin Knorr-Cetina), and the form of symbolic interactionism inspired by Anselm Strauss. In Latour's defense, it is important to note that the sociology of associations stresses the in-betweenness of things classically held to be inside individuals. Emotions, for example, are in-between, relational; so is consciousness. When humans and objects interact, relational phenomena emerge. There are forms of emotion that characterize our relations with the shells we pick up as we stroll along a beach, and with the computers and robots we interact with. The more interactive and the more humanoid the object the more salient the emotional relationship will be, the more it will imitate human-human emotions. In this sense, then, the concept of actants and networks of actants can be enlightening. The problem is not to lose sight of the unique nature of the relationships between human beings, and the roots of a certain privileged form of being human in those relationships. We are different kinds of humans interacting with each other than we are interacting with objects.

Latour is a formidable social theorist, but this does not automatically make his work sociological. His criticism of the sociologists of the social ignores the fact that sociologists as different as George Lundberg, Nicolai Bukharin, Howard Becker, and Randall Collins have addressed the very issues and problems Latour claims require ANT. Like many philosophers, he is prepared to claim jurisdiction over a discipline (sociology in this case) and to idiosyncratically define the nature and subject matter of the field. If sociology has to be reconfigured, so be it. Latour, however, has tried to do this without understanding first what it is that sociologists do. He has abandoned social constructivism/ionism without persuading many of his science studies colleagues that he has discovered an alternative to the constituting activities of social relations. And that, after all, is what social construction means: we have no recourse outside of our interactions – our social humanity – for constituting the world (Restivo, 2005).

Latour has underestimated the diversity of contemporary "sociology". This has trapped him in a caricature of a universe he doesn't inhabit and sees only from afar. It is important to continuously keep in mind that the issues here turn on whether we accept ethnomethodology as a mode or school of sociology or rather as an opponent of or alternative to sociology.

David Berreby (1994) conjured the image of a boxing match when he titled an essay, "And now [one can almost hear the implied "in this corner"], overcoming all binary oppositions…that damned elusive Bruno Latour." Latour's elusiveness is due in great part to the increasingly philosophical voice he has adopted combined with the wider and wider scope of the issues he has taken on. His philosophy, once unambiguously empirically grounded, has moved onto a metaphysical plane divorced from the social and political realities of everyday life. If he started his career with the promise of helping to fashion a Copernican revolution in the sociology of science, he has evolved into a thinker who reminds us more of Rousseau or Hobbes. This helps explain his ready dismissal of the perspectives and findings of the social sciences. His plan for bringing the sciences into "democracy" is more Platonic and transcendental than empirical. Science studies has given us the sciences as social practices and discourses. This empirically grounded view of the sciences that Latour explicates and defends is indisputable. The further lesson that Latour draws from science studies, that sociology's conventional toolkit must be eliminated, is far less convincing. The disagreements on this point and on the social construction conjecture with Bloor, Restivo, Knorr-Cetina, and others do not trouble Latour. The pluralism in Latour's theory, to the extent that it is salient, does not rise to the level of the pluralist theories developed by the feminists, black and queer social theorists, and women and minority voices in Brazil, Africa, India, and elsewhere outside the Euro-American sphere.

Latour continues the conversation of the Western philosophers, and does so politely under the rules of a gentlemen's club. It is, however, hard to ignore the vocabulary of warfare that marks Latour's rhetoric. If this rhetoric was derived from sociological theory, from conflict theory for example, it might be more persuasive. In Latour's hands, this rhetoric is just another strategy for mobilizing adherents and a philosophical undertaking rather than an empirically grounded political economy.

His most recent philosophy cum metaphysics – empirical or not, science-like or not – is more like the story-telling he advised as an alternative to explanation early in his career. At the end of the day, it will fall to Latour's readers to balance the applause of his most adoring acolytes against the damnations of his most volatile critics. This won't be easy because Latour transforms ANT as he goes. In Latour (1999: 1), four things do not work with ANT: actor, network, theory, and the hyphen; in Latour (2005: 9), ANT fits Latour's project "very well". Are networks, indexed in Latour (2005), the key idea, or is circulation, not indexed in that same volume, more to the point (Latour, 1999: 19)? If, however, the balance is true, and readers weigh the pros and cons fairly, they might readily and reasonably conclude that Latour is a social theorist to conjure with, a social theorist to think with, and one of the most learned and eloquent guides to our time and place as the twenty-first century unfolds. But in the wake of the Copernican social science revolution, Latour is a false prophet. For confirmation of my reading of Latour as a philosopher by Latour himself, see Latour (2010), "Coming out as a philosopher".

Latour's place in my narrative is dictated as much by his contributions to science studies and his challenge to sociology as it is by a kind of playful anarchism it is hard not to admire. Against the background of this critical review of Latour, I turn to the general impact sociological thinking and social criticism have had on the nature and shape of the science studies movement.

Chapter 4
Science Studies: Sociological Theory and Social Criticism

Until the 1970s the philosophy, sociology, and history of science tended in general to reinforce the idea that modern science is a progressive enterprise. With the emergence of science studies as a hybrid discipline, modern science came under more critical scrutiny, and scientific knowledge itself became an object of social inquiry. But there is a considerable degree of continuity across the 1970s watershed. One key to this continuity is the myth of the Kuhnian revolution in science studies. The Kuhnians, to the extent that they have stayed true to Kuhn, have sustained the traditional uncritical belief in modern science as a well-functioning and progressive social system. Thus, in spite of important advances in science studies, it is still widely believed that "normal science" (in Kuhn's sense) is an efficient and productive autonomous research community governed by negotiation; that there are privileged value-free sciences – notably physics and mathematics; and that whatever the social problems of science, they could be solved if only science could be purified or socialized, or if the external contexts within which science operates could be so purified or socialized. One idea is that science can be democratized. This idea ignores the social fact that science is an institution embedded and nourished in a wider social context. But "normal science" is an instance of and a factor in the reproduction of a society burdened by oppressive and alienating work; modern science is intimately coupled to structures of class, race, gender, and power; there are robber barons, entrepreneurs, statespersons, and lobbyists in science who link the interests of science and the state; and conflict is a crucial fuel in the dynamic of science.

It is easy to see some of the basic reasons for the continuity in worldview that links "old" and "new" social studies of science. The very existence of science studies as a profession is dependent on the goodwill of scientists as respondents and objects of observation and analysis, and the belief among scientists, intellectuals, scholars in general, and the general public that science "works" and produces benefits for society. It is also clear that many of us assume that because "scientific methods" seem to be the only "reasonable" methods to adopt in inquiry, we must also adopt the competitiveness, elitism, alienation, machismo, and other social trappings of modern science (and society). This viewpoint is so deeply imbedded that even when we set out to criticize modern science, we adopt the "scientific approach" with all of its social baggage. And how many of us can afford, psychologically and professionally, to recognize (let alone act on the recognition) that the rationality of modern science is a piece with the Alice-in-Wonderland form of authority that has infiltrated every sphere of modern social life?

The new discipline of science studies has helped to uncover important social realities of science based on the seemingly trivial notion that scientists are human and that science is a human activity. We have learned a great deal about such things as the ways in which choosing particular technical assumptions can, to use Brian Martin's phrase, "push an argument". We have deepened our understanding of the nature and significance of selecting, interpreting, and using evidence. We know that in a specialized form of intellectual labor such as science, presuppositions seem to be missing (one reason why science appears to be value-free or unquestionably objective) only because they have become built into scientific practice itself and into the very technologies of science. And the more we inquire about why scientific research is carried out, who does it, who can use it, and what it justifies, the more connections to "society" (empirically, the structures of power and inequalities) we uncover in terms of the social ties between science and the power centers of society. Science is selectively and institutionally biased toward supporting the technological commodity base on which the lives of the rich and powerful unfold and dictate the life chances and life styles of the working classes.

If we look at discussions of modern science that treat it as a well-functioning and progressive enterprise, we will see that they entail a certain worldview and in particular a theory of social relations. This theory of social relations – which justifies elitism, competition, the alienated activity of "normal science", and the separation of science from ethics and values – is a barrier to social progress. Max Weber described the rationalization of worldviews as a universal, but above all a European historical process. Rationalization goes hand in hand with the modernization of the state. In these processes, an other-wordly authority, God, is transformed into a this-wordly authority, reason into an immanent principle. This carries with it the potential for the separation of rationality and science from ethics.

Researchers in science studies have had to stop thinking, publicly or privately, of "science" as "physics". The tendency to equate science and physics has traditionally obscured the significant discoveries of the social sciences, and made sciences such as ecology, biology, and chemistry second-class modes of inquiry. This equation, along with a psychologistic, ahistorical, and asocial conception of consciousness and behavior, has fueled misguided efforts to link scientific and mystical traditions. This has undermined the potential value of examining alternative cognitive strategies.

We need to pay more attention to the role of ideology in modern science. To say that there is an ideology of modern science means in part that there is a dogmatic support for modern science as a way of life, and a collective cultivation of false consciousness that conceals from scientists the psychological, social, and cultural grounds and consequences of their activities. False consciousness can also manifest itself as a mistaken interpretation of self and social role. The ideology of modern science sustains struggles for power and status, institutional survival, and the use of science (to the extent that it overemphasizes quantification, rigor, control, and prediction) as a resource for reducing personal anxieties and fears.

The pursuit of "science for its own sake" generally requires a commitment to work and profession guided and reinforced by the less enlightened aspects of professionalism (for example, the "publish or perish" imperative, and "grantsmanship"). This makes it difficult to find time for outside activities and intensifies the ideological hold of modern (professionalized, bureaucratized) science on scientists and on society. The convergence of the dysfunctions of professionalization and bureaucratization tends to increase specialization and overspecialization in a conflictful division of labor. Occupational and organizational closure (autonomy) increases under these conditions, and creative, critical intelligence, along with the more enlightened motives, are eroded. Ultimately, the ability of people socialized under such conditions to distinguish illusion and reality, hallucinations and material events (or even to know about these distinctions) is threatened. The final price of runaway professionalization, in conjunction with bureaucratization, and the mechanization and commodification of the self must be first the routinization of rationality, and then the loss of the critical faculties. A more critical view of science and society in science studies would help bridge the gap between science and values, and help us identify the social conditions that simultaneously facilitate progressive inquiry and social progress.

Progress – And Social Progress

The Scientific Revolution made "science", "progress", and "rationality" synonymous. In what is generally recognized as the first modern secular treatise on the theory of progress, *Digression on the Ancients and the Moderns* (1688), Fontenelle argued that scientific growth represented the clearest, most reliable mark of progress. This relationship between science and progress was expressed in the works of Comte and Spencer. Rousseau, by contrast, argued that "our minds have been corrupted in proportion as the arts and sciences have improved". Progress in our time has come to mean putting men on the moon, splitting atoms, and promising the prolific flow of commodities through the lives of the privileged to the struggling masses of the earth. It is difficult to sustain the idea of progress in the face of the wide range of problems we are burdened with. The essence of the crisis is that the very forces of production we depend on to mark progress are interlocked with the very problems that make us doubt whether there has been any progress. Treating drug abuse and mental illness are the ways we try to tune up, service, and put back into efficient operation humans whose lives are constantly taking them and ourselves to the brink of a complete breakdown of the social order.

It is interesting to view the way in which the optimism rooted in the idea of progress and the idea of science is affected by the unavoidable realities of human experience. For example, in 1957 a panel of distinguished scientists gathered to celebrate – of all things – the centennial of Joseph E. Seagram & Sons, Inc. They were asked to speculate on "The Next Hundred Years". The idea – or better, the ideology – of science and progress required that the scientists speculate optimistically. What is interesting is the way many of them introduced their speculations. The geneticist and Nobel laureate Herman J. Muller said that the future would be rosy if we could avoid war, dictatorship, overpopulation, or fanaticism. Harrison Brown prefaced his remarks with the words, "if we survive the next century"; John Weir began, "If man survives". The most bizarre opening sentence was Wernher von Braun's, "I believe the intercontinental ballistic missile is actually merely a humble beginning of much greater things to come."

The idea of scientific and intellectual progress was fueled by the seventeenth-century advances in science and literature by such cultural giants as Galileo, Newton, Descartes, Moliere, and Racine. The idea of social progress was added later. Early in the eighteenth century, the Abbé de Saint Pierre advocated establishing political and ethical academies to promote social progress. Saint Pierre and Turgot influenced the Encyclopedists. It was at this point that social progress became mated to the values of industrialization and incorporated in the ideology of the bourgeoisie. Scientific, intellectual, and social progress were all aspects of the ideology of industrial civilization. But there have been attempts to identify a type of progress that is independent of material or technological criteria. Veblen, for example, argued that the various sciences could be distinguished in terms of their proximity to the domain of technology. Thus, the physical sciences were closest to that domain, even integral with it, whereas such areas as political theory and economics were farther afield. We have entered an era of machine discipline unlike any in human history. And now we stand on the threshold of machines that will discipline us with conscious awareness and values, the robosapiens.

Progress, then, can be viewed in terms of "amelioration" or "improvement" in a social or ethical sense. Are we more advanced than cultures that are less dominated by machines and machine culture? How do we measure the primacy of the person and how do we sustain it in any given culture? Can we bring it to fruition and nourish it in any culture, or are some more friendly to the primacy of the person than others? These issues are really matters of degree associated with the degree to which individuation has progressed in any given society.

Editorials in *Technology Review* (Marcus, 1993) and *Science* (Nicholson, 1993) express the professional concerns of engineers and science directly. The first review asks that scientists and engineers "climb off the pedestals", while the second is concerned with the anti-science threat that "The Postmodern Movement" presents. This last is especially curious, especially given the use of capital letters.

The term modern science refers to the institutionalization of inquiry in the West since the scientific and industrial revolutions. Science is a heterogeneous, changing institution, caught up in contemporary transformations of the social order. However, despite numerous intellectual assaults on the hegemony of science, its rhetorical and ideological power and legitimacy – and its power to legitimate – have been extraordinarily resilient.

There are a number of progressive agendas that engage science. Three in particular are perennially and preeminently engaged with science as social relations and an ambivalence about science; Marxism, anarchism, and feminism. Others, such as the U.S. civil rights movement or worldwide anti-colonialism agendas reflect similar ambivalence about science and technology. This is often made evident in intra-movement conflicts among affirmative action, reformist, or assimilative strategies and more revolutionary agendas, or in contradictory uses and critiques of science and scientific information.

I doubt that many anarchists, Marxists, and feminists who have embraced science and technology in their programs for social progress, human emancipation, and individual liberty would agree with the notion that progress based on the primacy of the person could be independent of material or technological progress. The very development of the idea of the primacy of the person seems to be dependent on a certain level of social development grounded in scientific and technological advances.

Theodore Roszak (1972), one of the foremost critics of modern science and of the very idea of scientific objectivity, distinguished two types of progress. One type is associated with "reductionist science and power-ridden technology". This type of progress refers to the "necessary evils" that attend the unfolding promises of industrial society, from technocratic elitism and alienation to environmental destruction and the global threats posed by nuclear armaments. The second type of progress, defined in a way that many anarchists might find too mystical, too richly clothed in mystery, is called "the way back", variously described as "the Way", "the eight-fold path", and the journey to the Godhead.

This is another example, then, of the effort to conceive of progress in terms of ideas about dignity, liberty, integrity, creativity, community-mindedness, and ecological consciousness. My notion of social progress originates in such examples but seeks to eliminate any roots that attach this idea to mysticism, mystery, spiritualism, and more generally the transcendental.

Social progress involves an increase in the capacity of human beings individually and collectively to identify, process, store, retrieve, mobilize, and utilize information and knowledge; it is simultaneously measured by the degree to which a community or society has established the sanctity of human life, the dignity of human beings, and the right to liberty, well-being, and self-actualization. Some of the anarchists defend the individual against suffocation by the corporate mass. This is a laudable goal but it invites in the specter of the individual as a free-standing unit rather than as a social being. In this sense, we have to prefer the visions of the Kropotkins and Goldmans over those of the (Herbert) Reads.

Social progress can move vertically to new levels and new ideas, and it can move horizontally, to spread new levels and new ideas across more and more of the social landscape. I have been at pains to illustrate why it is difficult to support the idea that "scientific progress" has facilitated or represented "social progress".

Whatever positive impact science has had on social progress has been primarily on the horizontal levels of ideas and their technological outcomes. To the extent that social progress depends on new types and new levels of knowledge about the human condition, it has been facilitated by some aspects of scientific inquiry, even within the institutional boundaries of modern science. But in order to discard the cultural heritage embodied in the term science, and to broaden the base of our methodological and theoretical resources, I prefer to work with the more general term epistemic strategy. I use the term human inquiry for the epistemic strategy or strategies consistent with the idea of social progress. This term may be considered kin to Marx's conception of "human science", his projected mode of inquiry for a communistic society and an alternative to alienated science. In the following section, I adopt a prescriptive perspective on inquiry and social progress.

Modern Science as a Social Problem

Sociologists of science do not, in general, doubt the value of modern science. They are, implicitly or explicitly, science advocates. Their research tends to affirm, imitate, and justify modern science as a progressive, well-functioning social system and the paradigmatic mode of inquiry. It is true that this view of science was challenged by way of social theory and social criticism beginning in the late 1960s. The fact is, however, that the commitment to a Grand Paradigm of science has sustained some version of the functionalist view from that period to the present. That commitment is probably stronger today than it was 30 and 40 years ago. Students of science and society need to keep in mind the arguments of C. Wright Mills, Thorstein Veblen, and other critics who have implicated modern science in problems of alienation, dehumanization, ecological deterioration, and nuclear escalation.

The characterization that sociologists of science rarely doubt or question the worth of science holds on both sides of the 1970s watershed that separates the "old" and the "new" sociology of science. On the far side of the watershed, the sociology of science is dominated by Robert Merton (1973) and "the Mertonian paradigm". On the near side, the field is part of a hybrid discipline variously referred to by such terms as "science studies", "social studies of science (and technology)", the "new sociology of science", and "sociology of scientific knowledge" (SSK). The Mertonian hegemony has been replaced by a diverse and conflictful arena of realists and relativists, strong and weak programmers, conflict theorists and neofunctionalists, and Latourians and anti-Latourians (Collins and Restivo, 1983; Restivo and Croissant, 2010). But with some notable exceptions such as Stanley Aronowitz, feminists students of science and technology studies (discussed further on), and the new political sociologists of science including Daniel Kleinman, Abby Kinchy, Scott Frickel, Kelly Moore and others, neither old nor new sociologists of science linger on the human face of science or on issues of class, gender, race, power, and ideology. Both affirm that science as it is, with all its social trappings (including elitism and competitiveness), "works". The basic goal of the old and new sociology of science is the same: to explain how science works. The old sociologists of science focused on the social system of science itself and exempted scientific knowledge from sociological scrutiny. New sociologists of science initially turned our attention to social context, social construction, and on-site studies of scientific practice (Knorr-Cetina and Mulkay, 1983). They have also made scientific knowledge an object of inquiry. These are significant, even revolutionary, departures from the Mertonian tradition in the sociology of science and from traditional philosophy and history of science. But new sociologists of science, with some notable exceptions (e.g., MacKenzie, 1986), are busy developing new accounts of science as a value system, a worldview, and a way of living and working.

There are of course, some Marxists, conflict theorists, socialists, anarchists, and radical science advocates who do carry out critical analyses of modern science (e.g., Rose and Rose, 1976; Arditti et al., 1980; and see the new political sociologists of science: Frickel and Moore, 2006, and the contributions of Daniel Lee Kleinman, Abby Kinchy, and their colleagues). These analyses tend to be generated as part of a general criticism of the modern social order. But even their criticisms are often reined in by the belief that "socialized science", science in a socialist (or communist, or anarchist) society, or some sort of unadulterated science could realize the promise of a science that would benefit humanity. These works notwithstanding, the idea that modern science is at least as much a factor in as a solution for our personal, social, and environmental ills is not defended by very many sociologists of science. C. Wright Mills' (1963: 229-230, 417) conception of modern science as a subordinate part of "the wasteful absurdities of capitalism", the military order, and the national state is not ascendant in the sociology of science.

The constructivist and relativist agendas in the new sociology of science have alarmed the guardians of the scientific community. They view them as threats to the integrity and autonomy of science, to the realist assumptions of scientific inquiry, and to the quest for truth and objective knowledge. But the leading "constructivists" and "relativists" are not antirealists in any simple sense, and many are explicit defenders of the methods and worldview of science. Bruno Latour and Steve Woolgar (1986), for example, disassociate themselves from naïve relativism; they do not deny the existence of facts or of reality. Karin Knorr-Cetina (1979: 369) also explicitly divorces her constructivist interpretation from an idealist ontology. She does not deny the existence of an independent reality. Latour's (1987: 26-27) "recantation" is even more dramatic: "in spite of our critiques – and to be fair, in spite of a few of our early claims", – the new sociologists of science, he writes, are no more "relativist" than Einstein, "and for the same reason". Latour says further that "By fighting absolute definitions of observations that do not specify the practical work and material networks that give them meaning, we take as seriously as everyone else the construction of reality – indeed, we might be the only ones to take it seriously enough."

Other sociologists of science explicitly announce that they are "for science". David Bloor (1976: 141), for example, long associated with relativism and interest theory, bases his strong programme in the sociology of knowledge on the dictum: "only proceed as the other sciences proceed and all will be well." Within this strong programme, relativism is not only not a threat to science; it is a basic condition for "good" science, that is, disinterested research (Barnes and Bloor, 1982: 44-45). Even the high priest of (empirical) relativism, Harry Collins (1979: 165-167), views his work as a defense of the authority of science ("the best institution for generating knowledge about the natural world that we have") and of the ultimate (however uncertain and fallible) expertise of scientists.

The conservative, neofunctionalist bias in the new sociology of science reflects the influence of Thomas Kuhn's *The Structure of Scientific Revolutions*. But his reception also suggests that bias was present from the beginning among the most prominent founders of the science studies movement in the 1960s and 1970s. Barry Barnes has played an important role in championing Kuhn as a significant, even radical, contributor to the new sociology of science and knowledge. Kuhn has even been hailed as a hero in the radical and feminist science studies communities. This is a great curiosity. Kuhn's work is an asociological, prescriptive defense of science, and is compatible with Merton's sociology of science, especially at the level of values, as both he and Merton have acknowledged. Michael Mulkay (1979) illustrates this point. Like most of the new sociologists of science I criticize, Mulkay can conceive an alternative interpretation of how modern science works but not an alternative to modern science. This helps to explain why he can discuss Karl Marx and the sociology of knowledge without commenting on Marx's distinction between "science" and "human science" (Marx, 1956: 110-111; 1973: 699ff.). Bloor's (1976: 144) closing remarks in Knowledge and Social Imagery make quite clear what is at stake here:

> I am more than happy to see sociology resting on the same foundations and assumptions as other sciences. This applies whatever their status and origin. Really sociology has no choice but to rest on these foundations, nor any more appropriate model to adopt. For that foundation is our culture. Science is our form of knowledge [my emphasis]. That the sociology of knowledge stands or falls with the other sciences seems to me both eminently desirable as a fate, and highly probable as a prediction.

Bloor not only understands the interdependence of science, culture, and the sociology of knowledge, he approves of it and its forms. It should be clear by now why so much of what goes by the name of sociology of science, science studies, or science criticism remains fundamentally conservative on the question of the value of science: The most influential authorities on the "sociological" nature of science, from Merton and Kuhn to Latour and Bloor, are science advocates. Advocacy in itself is not so much the problem, I want to stress, as the fact that, in the cases I refer to, it interferes with a critical sociology of science. What is missing from science criticism and from the sociology of science is the Millsian blend of structural analysis (sociology in the strong sense), social criticism, epistemological relevance, and an activist orientation toward social change – in brief, the sociological imagination.

There are two basic reasons why sociologists of science, old and new, have been unable or unwilling to follow Mills (1961: 8) in linking modern science to the "personal troubles of milieux" and the "public issues of social structure". First, the idea that science "works" and a "science fix" orientation have been amplified by runaway technological "progress". In the heady atmosphere of material plenty, people have been seduced by the icons, myths, and ideologies of modern science. Second, sociologists of science cannot afford to alienate the scientists they study by criticizing their ideas and actions, including how their social roles, organizations, and products fit into society. It is precisely this sort of criticism of "our" science, "our" culture, and "our" sociology of science and knowledge that I want to encourage.

Modern science, from such a critical perspective, is a threat to democracy, the quality of human life, and even the very capacity of our planet to support life at all (cf. Feyerabend, 1978). Moreover, modern science is a social problem because it is part of modern society which itself is a social problem. I turn next to a discussion of what I mean by the term "social problem" and why I consider modern science and modern society social problems.

There is a reluctance among students of social problems to include modern science in their analyses, criticisms, and policy studies. Social problems courses and textbooks do not, as a rule, devote space to modern science, although it may receive indirect attention in studies that deal with "technology". One reason for this is that modern science is not yet widely appreciated as a social phenomenon in the strong constructionist sense; scientific knowledge itself is a social construction. Another reason is the assumption that science (and especially "pure" science) and technology are separate, relatively independent phenomena. Other more general reasons were identified by Mills (1963: 535-536) in his 1943 paper on "The Professional Ideology of Social Pathologists". Mills criticized the situational, institutional case-by-case approach to social problems typical of most introductory textbooks. Mills proposed instead an integrated social structural, organizational, and institutional approach. This requires theories that address these interdependencies in their societal and cultural contexts.

My assertion that modern science is a social problem because modern society is a social problem is an admittedly cryptic criticism of the situational approach. By "social problem", I want to convey nothing more complicated than the Millsian notion that modern science is implicated in the personal troubles and public issues of our time. The idea that modern society is, again in the Millsian sense, a "social problem" means that concerns about personal troubles, public issues, and social change agendas should focus on a total social structure rather than one or more of its "dysfunctional" parts.

The term society, it should be stressed, poses a conceptual problem. In standard usage, it often refers to an imaginary, undifferentiated entity, and it tends to connote cooperation and "democracy". The problem can be readily identified by considering what it means to use the term state in place of society (Mills, 1963: 538-540). Our conceptions of "society" have methodological and political implications (Mills, 1963: 537).

The situational approach to the study of society and social problems has two important consequences for the study of science. First, it makes it possible to isolate science from the other institutions and classify it with the "healthy" as opposed to the "unhealthy" ones. Second, it means that, even when science is examined critically, the total social structure is unlikely to become the focus of criticism and analysis. While I cannot describe all of the ramifications of a total social structural approach to the critical sociology of modern science, I can, provide some of the conceptual resources for such an approach.

Mills' (1963: 530-31n) critique of conceptions of "social problems" in his time is still relevant. This is not only because some social problems research continues to be guided by the strategies Mills criticized. More importantly, contemporary strategies in social problems research and theory are subject to Mills' argument that they are not usable in collective actions of resistance. It is not at all clear, for example, that the fashionable "definitional" or "constructionist" (sometimes constructivist) approach avoids the pitfalls Mills identifies. I will return later to the "realistic" and "activist" implications of the sociological imagination. It is important, however, to clarify a conceptual problem that cuts across the new sociology of science and contemporary social problems research and theory: the relationship between constructivism(ionism) and relativism.

Constructivism(ionism) and Relativism

Let me first explain why I prefer "constructionism" over "constructivism". Both spellings are found in the literature without any clear rationale for preferring one over the other. I prefer "constructionism" because it seems to me to stress the "making" and "manufacturing" sense that is at the core of the concept. In what follows, I will use the "ionism/t" ending where the choice is mine and the "ivism/t" ending where that is used by the author I am discussing.

It is important to understand modern science, including scientific knowledge, as a social construction in order to appreciate it as a social problem in the Millsian sense. But there is some confusion inside and outside of science studies about what the constructionist interpretation of science means. The idea of social problems as social constructs is a key part of the framework of traditional social problems research and theory. In their critique of constructivism in social problems research, Woolgar and Pawluch (1985) assume that constructivist and definitional are synonymous and that they entail relativism as opposed to realism (but see Latour and Woolgar, 1979: 180; Latour and Woolgar, 1986: 277). The fact is, however, that the genesis of constructionsm in the new sociology of science is closely associated with if not coincident with the sociological realism of ethnographic studies of scientific laboratories. In this context, constructionism is not merely a matter of reality being constructed "by definition". It tends, rather, to be a fashionable way of talking about social structures as the day-to-day, moment-to-moment activities of scientists as they go about producing and reproducing scientific culture. There is thus no necessary connection between constructionism and relativism. Given my earlier discussion of the fact that sociologists of science such as Bloor and Knorr-Cetina are not relativist in any simple sense, and certainly not in any anti-scientific sense, it should not be assumed that constructionism in science studies and constructionism in social problems research mean the same thing.

The foregoing should alert the reader to the fact that I proceed according to constructionist principles but do not adopt any sort of naïve relativism. My approach is probably better described as "realistic" rather than "realist" or "relativist" (cf. Hooker, 1975; 1987). The wedding of constructionism and a realistic worldview does imply that there are things that are true and things that are false, and that some sort of objective knowledge is possible. But constructionism does not leave these ideas untouched; it transforms them into sociological concepts and makes sociology of objectivity both possible and necessary.

Seeing modern science as a social problem depends upon getting behind the facade of ideology and icons in science to the "science machine" and upon exposing the cultural roots of science. These are my objectives in the following sections. I begin by examining some of the important reasons for reconceptualizing science and its social relationships. I discuss Mill's notion of the Science Machine and the conceptual problems that need to be resolved in order to grasp his meaning and move beyond it to liberatory inquiry. Then, the important distinction between the autonomy of individuals and structural autonomy is introduced, followed by the rationale for dissolving the traditional boundaries that separate science, technology, and society.

The Science Machine

Mills (1961: 16) observed that a variety of troubles and issues are rooted and reflected in the relationships between modern science and other social institutions. Instead of a creative ethos and orientation to inquiry, Mills saw a set of Science Machines operated and controlled by technicians in the grip of the military-industrial complex. Within this context, science was not and could not be grasped as ethos and orientation.

There are in Mills' conception of the transformation of science into a Science Machine by "military metaphysicians" echoes of Marx's notion of modern science as alientated and of Veblen's critique of modern science as a machine-like product of our "matter-of-fact" industrial and technological era. Thinkers with this turn of mind have described modern science as an "instrument of terror", an assault on the natural world, and a tool of greed, war, and violence. In order to understand the grounds for such claims, we must distinguish clearly between isolated scientific biographies, methods, findings, experiments, and facts, equations, laws, and theories on the one hand and modern science as a social institution on the other. By focusing on modern science as a social institution, we not only can see how it is connected to other social institutions, we also transform biographies, facts, and theories into contextually situated social facts.

Scientific activity, rooted in the empirical reasoning activities of everyday human life, occurs in all societies. But modern science emerged in Western Europe after 1500, became organized around the social role of the scientist, and has grown without interruption for nearly 500 years. By the mid-nineteenth century, modern science had crystallized as a social institution. Since then it has undergone transformations in scale and power coincident with processes of professionalization and bureaucratization in the context of the increasing power of the state.

The origin and development of modern science is inextricably intertwined with the origin and development of modern society. This has been recognized in varying degrees by students of the scientific revolution. The technical utilization of science was encouraged by favorable economic conditions; arguments for the utility of science arose in a variety of institutional spheres, including religion, business, and the military; and certain key segments of society became convinced in the wake of scientific discoveries that science had an intrinisic value and were able to gain general acceptance for their view independently of any evidence for the utility of science. These ideas can be categorized as "reciprocal influences" and "utilitarian" hypotheses.

There is an alternative explanation for the scientific revolution that helps to resolve some of the difficulties of conjectures about "reciprocal influence", "utility", and "pure motives". The scientific revolution was one of an interrelated set of parallel organizational responses within the major institutional spheres of Western Europe from the fifteenth century onwards (including Protestantism in the religious sphere and modern capitalism in the economic sphere) to an underlying set of ecological, demographic, and political economic conditions. This perspective does not readily yield a conception of modern science as an autonomous social system. Modern science is autonomous in a sociological sense to the extent that it is a structurally and functionally differentiated social activity. But the "parallel responses" thesis sets modern science into the very core of the modern state and its technological foundations. This notion requires some further discussion to clarify the distinction between structural autonomy and the autonomy of individuals.

Structural Autonomy

The concept of autonomy has played a key role in research on professions and bureaucracies. In general, students of autonomy in this context tend to focus on the autonomy of individuals, and in particular of professionals in bureaucracies. Some (e.g., Scott, 1966) view professions and bureaucracies as institutions but are primarily interested in professionals in bureaucracies (cf. Freidson, 1986: 166). In some cases, the analysis may shift to the social role. But in neither case is the focus on autonomy as a structural variable, especially at the organizational and institutional levels of analysis (but see Kornhauser, 1962; on the dysfunctions of professionalization, see Restivo, 1983a: 152ff; Bledstein, 1978: 94; Friedson, 1970; and Brewer, 1971). Autonomy in this sense refers to the nature and degree to which the boundaries of social activities and systems are distinct, permeable, open, or closed. The more, for example, a system can function independently of the resources of other systems in terms of its core defining goals and interests, the more autonomous it is.

The structural sense of autonomy lends sociological meaning to the concepts "internal" and "external". The use of these concepts to refer to the two basic types of factors that can affect science and to the distinction between contextual and non-contextual analysis has been properly criticized (e.g. Johnston, 1976). But these terms can be usefully applied in the context of analyzing the interaction of social systems that vary in terms of degree of closure, that is, degree of autonomy. Thus, an "internalist" approach would be an appropriate part of the research strategy for studying a relatively autonomous social activity or system. A traditional internalist would likely consider factors such as scientific "ideas" to be independent of social forces. An internalist analysis in my sense would focus on the social structure of the system under study as a determinant of the knowledge produced in that system. Thus autonomy and the internal/external dichotomy can be rendered sociologically meaningful if we conceptualize them in terms of a structural analysis. The internal/external dichotomy is just one of a number of ideas that post-1970s sociologists of science have discarded or transformed conceptually. Another idea that has increasingly posed problems in science and technology studies is the science, technology and society triad.

Science, Technology, and Society

The boundaries between the concepts of science, technology, and society in traditional studies of science and technology have been more or less dissolved by some of the leading new sociologists of science. Harry Collins (1985: 165), for example, argues that his study of how scientific facts are established dissolves those boundaries two ways. The professional networks of science are continuous with societal networks; and cultural production in science is analogous to all other forms of innovative cultural production. The point that needs to be stressed about boundaries and networks in this context, a point relevant to the discussion of structural autonomy, is that they are to varying degrees dynamic and protean.

The relative stability of social boundaries and networks over a long period of time gives rise to systems for which we can determine degrees of autonomy. But even so, we must be alert to changes, including periodic changes, in the character of those boundaries. They may be so fixed that it makes sense to say they define an institution; but even within that framework, the boundaries may periodically break down. The system may be more closed, more autonomous, at some times than at others. Thus, Latour (1987: 174) uses two expressions to refer to two aspects of the activities of scientists and engineers. The idea, you will recall from our earlier discussion, is captured in the term *technoscience.*

Technoscience describes everything about the contents of science, all the contingencies, all the elements of the cycles of credit, all the processes of scientific production. "Science and technology" then refers to what is left of technoscience once all the negotiations have been completed, all the "trials of responsibilities" settled, all the arguments closed. His conclusion is that "the name of the game will be to leave the boundaries open and to close them only when the people we follow close them" (Latour, 1987: 175; cf. Knorr-Cetina, 1981: 88ff).

Latour's conclusion means that whether it makes sense to talk about science, or technology, or technoscience, or wider cultural spheres depends on our perspective at any given time and the details of the system we are studying. In some cases, in fact, we may find we are studying a feature of "science" that is widely diffused across and interdependent with other cultural spheres and that we will need to use a new term to describe it.

Pinch and Bijker (1984, 1986; and see Russell, 1986) propose an interesting but less radical rationale for eliminating the distinction between science and technology. They argue that technology and science should be treated within the same social construction framework. Obviously, this argument is a contribution to the more radical project Latour initially seemed to be championing. Establishing technology as a social construct is to some extent less difficult than showing that scientific knowledge is a social construct but still contributes to the groundwork necessary for seeing technoscience where we have traditionally seen science and technology. In that sense, placing technology in its social context and treating artifacts as "political", or more generally as social constructs, are relevant to the theory of the Science Machine (cf. Winner, 1977, 1985; and see Bijker, Hughes, and Pinch, 1986). But the relevance of this strategy tends to be limited because it can be carried out while implicitly or explicitly sustaining the traditional distinction between science and technology (e.g., MacKenzie and Wajcman, 1985: 2-25; Trescott, 1979).

Ruth Schwartz Cowan's (1983) work is a good example of how the contextualization of technology (in this case using the concept of "technological system") can be accomplished while implicitly treating science as a distinct phenomenon. And in the end, Cowan (1983: 215-216) misses the linkages between the work process, technological systems, and social structure, Her proposal for "neutralizing" the sexual connotation of household technology and the "senseless tyranny of spotless shirts and immaculate floors" is not a sociologically viable solution to the social problems of technology (or technology as a social problem). She fails to see the profound and far-reaching structural changes necessary to achieve the goals she sets, and this failure reflects the fact that she does not see the sorts of connections embodied in a concept such as technoscience.

There is now good reason on both empirical and conceptual grounds to argue that modern science is of a piece with modern technology and the central values, interests, and structures of the more powerful classes in modern society. As I pursue my social problem thesis, I will continue to focus on "modern science", even though I have now provided a rationale for either dispensing with the term or using it more cautiously. But that rationale needs to be developed further or developed in new directions (not only in this book but in science studies generally) before we can confidently adopt a new conception of the referent for "modern science".

By 1500, on the eve of the Scientific Revolution, Europeans were taking command of the world's oceans and beginning to subjugate the cultures of the Americas. William McNeill (1963: 569-570) identifies three "talismans of power" that enabled the Europeans to conquer oceans and cultures: (1) a deep-rooted pugnacity and recklessness operating by means of (2) a complex military technology, most notably in naval matters; and (3) a population inured to a variety of diseases which had long been endemic throughout the Old World ecumene. European militarism of the period had its roots in Bronze Age barbarian societies and the medieval military habits of the merchant classes and certain lesser aristocrats and landowners. It was in this most warlike of the major civilizations that modern science arose.

The maritime supremacy of the Europeans was the basis for the enlarged scope of their militarism beginning in the sixteenth century. Their superiority at sea was the result of deliberately blending science and practice, first in the Italian commercial cities and, ultimately, under the guidance of Prince Henry the Navigator and his successors, in Portugal (cf. Law 1986a). The Scientific Revolution institutionalized this inseparable blend of science and practice, science and technology. Modern science has been primarily a tool of the ruling elites of modern societies from the time of its origin in sixteenth- and seventeenth-century Europe (cf. Noble, 1979; Dickson, 1979).

In its earliest stages of development modern science was a part of the repertoire of "gentlemen" who were embracing capitalism and seeking to destroy the monopolies of the old landed aristocracy. But by the 1690s in England, the tie between science (and in particular Newtonian science), the culture of the ruling Whig oligarchy, and the established church (in particular the latitudinarian hierarchy) was well established: "The scientific ideology of order and harmony preached from the pulpits complemented the political stability over which [the Whig] oligarchy presided" (Jacob, 1988: 121-123).

The Scientific Revolution organized the human and cultural capacity for inquiry in ways that stressed laws over necessities, the value of quantity over quality, and strategies of domination and exploitation over strategies based on an awareness of ecological interdependencies. As a product of the commercial, mercantile, and industrial revolutions that transformed Europe and the world between 1400 and

1900, modern science emerged and developed as an alienating and alienated mode of inquiry. It arose as the mental framework of capitalism and the cognitive mode of industrialism (Berman, 1984: 37; Geller, 1964: 72). Capital accumulation and industrial products and processes became prominent features of social life and the primary factor in shaping our ways of thought, our science. We learned to think the way modern technological processes act (Veblen, 1919: 7). Modern science (including scientists and images and symbols of science) came into the world as a system of commodities and has developed in close association with the discipline of the machine (cf. Meiksins, 1982). A number of researchers from Karl Marx to David Noble have recognized this, although many of them have implicitly or explicitly distinguished "science", more or less "pure", from "modern science", science adulterated by capitalism and technology.

Given the tenacity of the myth of pure science, it is important to remember that science in every form has always been as much a part of the economic, political, and military fabric of society as modern science is. The "scientific community" did not, as Noble (1979: 4) contends for example, have to overcome "Platonic prejudices". There is some legitimate confusion about the relationship between modern science in its formative stages and modern science in its fully institutionalized form. It might be assumed that science was characterized by purity and Platonic prejudices before it became a differentiated part of European social structure through institutionalization and the crystallization of the social role of the scientist. But even if this were the case in the earliest and most diffuse stages of the history of modern science, it is clear that, once it became a major force in European culture, it "took on an immensely practical posture that moved it from an intellectual pursuit to a source for industrialization" (Jacob, 1988: 259; Musson and Robinson, 1969; cf. Carroll, 1986; and see McNeill, 1982; Postan et al., 1964).

The thesis that modern science in its earliest stages was a purely "intellectual pursuit", however, cannot survive careful scrutiny. As Jacob (1988) notes, early modern science was a tool of "gentlemen capitalists" who were not then a ruling elite but an elite on the road to ruling power. Moreover, seventeenth-century natural philosophers already expressed values of the "world politick" in their efforts to develop a mechanical description of the "world natural": "At every turn, that linkage ensured its integration into the larger culture and made its ideological formulation immediately and directly relevant to those who held, or sought to hold power in society and government" (Jacob, 1988: 38).

All of the foregoing helps us appreciate the Marxian notion that science was transformed into a productive force distinct from labor and pressed into the service of capital by modern industry. This is the starting point for David Noble's (1977: xxiv) study of science, technology, and the rise of corporate capitalism in *America By Design*. The issue of "science" aside, it is fairly clear that modern science emerged as a means of capital accumulation and thus an economic good and an article of commerce.

We can, as I hinted earlier, trace the roots of modern science to the knowledge-producing activities of earlier cultures. Those activities are everywhere inseparable from military, political, and economic interests and power (cf. Dickson, 1984: 107). The very foundations of modern science are permeated by a sense of the war-making utility of scientific knowledge, expressed by the most brilliant as well as the most ordinary scientific practitioners. Most of the texts from the formative period of modern science that recommend science also point out its utility for improving the state's capacity for waging war more effectively and destroying life and property more efficiently (Jacob, 1988: 251-252). One way to illustrate this deep-rooted relationship between science and power is to reflect on the reality that lies behind the myths of "pure" science.

The Myth of Purity

The notion of pure science has two basic referents. One is the production of ideas or knowledge through purely "mental" acts, that is, pure contemplation. The second is the pursuit of "knowledge for its own sake". The idea of pure mental or cognitive creation, of mental acts and events untouched by social facts, has been challenged by constructionist sociologists of science. They argue that all knowledge, including "scientific facts", is indexical, situational, contextual, and opportunistic (Knorr-Cetina, 1981; Latour and Woolgar, 1979; Zenzen and Restivo, 1982; Star, 1983). In my work in the sociology of mathematics, I have pressed this idea in the direction of a theory of mind and cognition as social structures (Restivo, 1992: 130-135). The fact that there are individual scientists driven by higher motives (curiosity, for example) does not mean that their social roles are not serving social interests (cf., Merton, 1968: 661-663). Similarly, we do not have to deny that individual scientists may be motivated by a desire to "understand" the world "objectively" in order to see the social functions of labeling scientific work "pure" or "objective".

The labels pure or basic, for example, can be used to demonstrate or symbolize a nation's capacity for research or its potential for generating "fundamental" discoveries that may find applications in various areas of social life. The self-applied labels pure and objective can call attention to and defend the autonomy, solidarity, and professionalism of scientists seeking access to scarce societal resources and independence from external social controls. Pure science can thus be used to intimidate competitors and enemies, project status claims, and establish territories. The scientific research centers Germany established in the early 1900s in Samoa, Argentina, and China were tools of cultural imperialism (Pyenson, 1983). The various national research camps and outposts in Antarctica labeled "pure science" mask their functions as informal territorial claims and attempts to estimate the potential value of access to Antarctica's land and resources for military, economic, and political purposes. Individual scientists may be unaware of these functions or otherwise mistaken about just what their social roles are in the Antarctica context. They may be curious about Antarctica, and they may make "fundamental" discoveries. But neither their personal views nor their motives can alter the functions of their camps and outposts in international political economy (cf. Elzinga, 1993: 138; Elzinga and Bohlin, 1989).

It should be noted that a certain amount of trained incompetence is necessary if scientists are going to exhibit ignorance or be mistaken about their social roles. Sharon Traweek's (1984, 1989) anthropological studies of the high-energy physics community illustrate some of the social mechanisms that bring about this trained incompetence. Physicists are trained to value certain emotional qualities (for example, meticulousness, patience, and persistence). As students, they go through a process of intense professional socialization focused on physics and the physics community. The social contexts of their activities are obscured and their conceptions of their social roles dramatically narrow. They are introduced to highly idealized portraits of scientists. Archimedes, Newton, Einstein, and Hawking are the principal icons of, respectively, ancient, modern, early twentieth century, and late twentieth century science. They are portrayed as men of pure contemplation who have little or no use for the vulgar aspects of science. Their interests in practical affairs are deemphasized or overlooked. They are described as "geniuses", but the development of the idea of genius in conjunctions with the concept of intellectual property under capitalism goes unnoticed (Hauser, 1974: 163; Restivo, 1989).

One of the most important social functions of the purity label is to mitigate resistance to and criticism of established interests. The state, for example, grants scientists who adopt the purity label the freedom to pursue their individual research interests so long as what they do keeps them from criticizing or resisting state actions, and especially so long as they do not interfere with the state's efforts to appropriate scientific discoveries and inventions in pursuit of military, economic, or political goals. Even in the most democratic societies, the state can enter the scientist's ivory tower with requests for secrecy and cooperation in the interest of national security and defense. If scientists resist such requests, the state can issue demands and back them up using various controls on the flow of resources for research. In extreme cases, the state can draw on its police powers and the means of violence at its disposal to control scientists.

"Basic" or "pure" science can easily end up focusing on mechanisms instead of causes. As a result, problems can be abstracted from their social context, and solutions sought that do not threaten prevailing social arrangements. The focus on basic cellular biology in cancer research, for example, assumes a solution that interrupts the carcinogen process rather than one that rearranges the social order to remove carcinogens from the environment (Ozonoff, 1979: 14-16).

To the extent that ideologies of purity stress "science for its own sake" they reinforce the scientist's alienation and obstruct the development and pursuit of interests outside of science, including the realization of the collective interests of scientists as workers. To the extent that they stress the independence of scientific knowledge from social interests, historical and social contexts, and individual subjective experiences, these ideologies help to isolate that knowledge and alienate the knowledge producers from the social processes of production and reproduction in science. To the extent that these ideologies reify the realm of purity, they function as justifications for the authority of ideas and heroic figures in the sciences as well as of texts and teachers and reinforce the principle of authority in everyday life.

The ideology of pure mathematics grows in large part out of ideologies of God and Nature as ultimate authorities. In the end, authority comes to reside in the realm of the purest of the pure sciences, logic. Classical logic, for example, as the intuitionist mathematician L.E.J. Brouwer recognized, is an abstraction from, first, the mathematics of finite sets, and then the mathematics of finite subsets. These mundane origins were forgotten when logic was elevated to a position prior to and beyond all mathematics. The substitute God logic (the Durkheimian spirit cannot be missed here) was then applied to the mathematics of infinite sets without any justification. Reified realms of purity such as logic can be functional equivalents of God, and can serve as moral imperatives and constraints that in one way or another bind us to established professional and state interests and reinforce obedience at the expense of criticism and rebellion in our relationships within established institutions.

Feminists have examined the problem of science and authority from another angle, that of male domination. In the next section, I explore the social problem of gender and science.

Gender and Science

Earlier, I discussed the role of ruling elites in the Scientific Revolution. The analysis of gender and science underscores the masculine stamp they put on modern science (Easlea, 1983). In human terms, this meant treating women (along with minorities, slaves, wage laborers, and nature) as commodities in the modern world system (Merchant, 1980: 288). As Keller (1985: 143) reminds us, "modern science evolved in, and helped to shape a particular kind of social and political context", including an ideology of gender. Arguments about science being gender neutral or value free are inevitably based on tearing individual scientific lives, sentences, or statements out of the social fabric in which they are conceived, produced, and used. Individual lives, facts, or strings of facts, are then exhibited as science. But in order to understand feminist critiques of science, science must be seen as a social activity and a social institution.

An alternative science should not be conceived in terms of alternative scientific laws or techniques but rather in terms of alternative institutions and societies. This is clear even for equity issues that may at first appear to pose no threats to science. But the achievement of equal opportunity or comparable worth for women in science depends on such factors as reducing gender stereotyping and gendered divisions of labor. It may even, as Sandra Harding (1986: 82) argues, "require the complete elimination of sexism, classism, and racism in the societies that produce science". Harding also challenges the widely held view that "the feminist charge of masculine bias" leaves physics, chemistry, and the scientific worldview "untouched (and untouchable)". She points out the apparent contradiction between building a "successor science" and deconstructing science as we know it. Her argument is that we need to pursue both goals (Harding, 1986: 246).

I have reviewed some of the features of the feminist challenge that are consistent with the perspective on modern science I advocate. There are certain limitations of the feminist challenge that are common to other arenas of science criticism. These limitations reflect the difficulty of loosening the grip of the myth of pure science. Even feminist science studies and feminist science criticism that is pursued with the greatest degree of institutional independence rely on conservative theorists for authoritative accounts of the sociology and history of science. I have already explained why neither Bloor nor Kuhn can be considered a critic of science. Bloor's approach requires adopting the "proven methods of science" and ignoring their social trappings. And Kuhn is first and foremost a traditional internalist historian of science and a firm believer in scientific progress. Latour fares no better as a resource for feminists. And yet they all are widely cited in the feminist literature as authorities on the history and sociology of science.

Harding's (1986: 250) misunderstanding of Kuhn is illustrated by the fact that she finds it ironic that his Structure of Scientific Revolutions, which she reads as undermining "the notions of science central to the Vienna Circle", was originally published as part of the International Encyclopedia of Unified Science project. But there is no irony in this association, as Kuhn himself has amply documented in the 1970 "Postscript" to his study and elsewhere (Kuhn, 1970, 1983).

Another example of the hold of traditional scientific ideology on feminist science studies is Harding's (1987: 248-250) reference to feminist scientists as "the new heirs of Archimedes as we interpret his legacy for our age". Archimedes is lauded for his "inventiveness in creating a new kind of theorizing". This is Archimedes as icon of science, not Archimedes as military engineer.

While Harding is at least willing to consider (rhetorically at least) the idea of "a radically different science", Evelyn Fox Keller (1985: 177-178) explicitly divorces herself from efforts to reject science or develop a "new" science. She refuses to follow this line of feminist inquiry because, in her own words, "I am a scientist". Her reasoning is compelling. Rejecting objectivity as a masculine ideal lends the feminists' collective voice to an "enemy chorus"; and it "dooms women to residing outside of the realpolitik modern culture" (Keller, 1982: 594). Keller (1985: 178) rejects the call for a new science on the grounds that it destroys the positive features of modern science and instead wants us to renounce the features that make it a masculine project. But renouncing the "division of emotional and intellectual labor that maintains science as a male preserve" means, from my perspective, renouncing everything associated with the culture of modern science. In practical terms, it is necessary to correct the gender inequalities in contemporary science. But, as Elizabeth Fee (1983: 24-25) argues, we also have to "push the epistemological critique of science to the point where we can begin to construct a clear vision of alternate ways of creating knowledge".

The sociological perspective, in the strong structural sense I argue for, is not a prominent feature of feminist science studies and criticism. This does not mean that the feminists do not draw attention to problems of social structure. They do not, however, do so in ways that transform epistemology from a philosophical to a sociological project. This makes it difficult for them to transcend the ideology of pure science. A sociological theory of knowledge must replace epistemology before we can begin to construct alternate ways of inquiry.

Science and Progress

To the extent that we have learned to think the way the machines around us act, so have we learned to see progress where the values of machines reign. The Scientific Revolution made modern science, rationality, and progress synonymous. By transforming "science" into a Science Machine, it turned rationality into a logic of unrelenting and unthinking machines in motion. Progress then became the label for "more and more" of whatever the Science Machine produces. As a result, the very things we take to be signs or measures of progress are coupled with the social problems that make us doubt whether there has in fact been any progress at all. Drug addiction, alcoholism, and "nervous breakdowns" are not considered signs of progress; profitable industries are, no matter what they produce. But drugs and alcohol can serve as lubricants, and mental health establishments as reservicing factories that help to keep the human machines in those profitable industries from completely breaking down (Camilleri, 1976: 42; cf. Berman, 1984: 7-8). We measure the short-term progress of our economy in terms of Gross Domestic Product. But like other measures of progress, GDP does not measure the human, social, and environmental costs and risks of producing goods and services. We "progress", then, as Theodore Roszak (1973: 426) has put it, "only toward technocratic elitism, affluent alienation, environmental blight, nuclear suicide". C. Wright Mills (1963: 238) drew attention to the "highly rational moral insensibility" of our era, raised to higher and more efficient levels by the "brisk generals and gentle scientists" who are planning the Third World War. "These actions are not necessarily sadistic; they are merely business-like; they are not emotional at all; they are efficient, rational, technically clean cut. They are inhuman acts because they are impersonal."

It may seem paradoxical to argue that modern science (allied with technology and progress) is a social problem because it is impersonal. After all, impersonal, machine-like truths and measures are supposed to guarantee that what we do is scientific and progressive. But it is precisely this notion of validation through proof-machines, logic-machines, language-machines, and number-machines that we must challenge in order to see the world of Science Machines and false

progress described by Mills and others. The sociological imagination offers us a
way out of this machine morass.

Modern Science and the Sociological Imagination

The core features of Mills' (1961) sociological imagination are: (1) the distinction
between personal troubles and public issues; (2) a focus on the intersection
between biography and history in society; and (3) a concern with questions about
social structure, the place of societies in history, and the varieties of men and
women who have prevailed and are coming to prevail in society. This perspective
draws attention to new questions for the sociology of science: what do scientists
produce, and how do they produce it; what resources do they use and use up;
what material by-products and wastes do they produce; what good is what they
produce, in what social contexts is it valued, and who values it; what are the
personal and social consequences of their work and work habits; what costs,
risks, and benefits does their work lead to for individuals, intimate relationships,
communities, classes, genders, and the ecological foundations of social life; what
is the relationship between scientists and their various publics, clients, audiences,
patrons, colleagues, and friends and acquaintances; how do they relate to their
intimates and especially to their children; what is their relationship as workers to
the owners of the means of scientific production; what are their self-images, and
how do they fit into the communities they live in; what kinds of teachers, mentors,
and educators are they; what are their goals, visions, and motives? The collective
hagiography that portrays scientists as "ingenious", "creative", and "benefactors
of humanity" does not tell us what sorts of people scientists are or what sorts of
social worlds they are helping to build.

   Normal sociologists of science in normal society have concluded that normal
science is efficient, productive, and progressive (Kuhn, 1970). But normal science
is a factor in the production and reproduction of a society burdened by widespread
environmental, social, and personal stresses. Normal sociologies of science cannot
help us see, let alone prevail in, a world of Science Machines and Cheerful Robots
(Mills, 1961). Even the sort of Millsian perspective on science, society, and
sociology of science that informs my views may prove too limited for the task of
critique and renewal. Fundamental categories of experience must be examined,
challenged, and changed to even begin to address the social problems of science
and society. The dichotomy between "nature" and "culture", for example, has
fostered a dominative, exploitative orientation to nature, women, workers, and the
underclasses in general. A fascination with spectacular discoveries, inventions,
and applications in the physical sciences and with "genius" has blinded people
to alienation in scientific work and in the lives of scientists. Inside and outside
of sociology proper (especially in the United States) there has been resistance
to unadulterated structural analysis. Individualistic and voluntaristic assumptions

and perspectives have obstructed the development and diffusion of sociological conceptions of self, mind, cognition, and knowledge.

The full implications of sociology as a Copernican revolution that has moved the group, the collectivity, and social structure to the center of the social universe have yet to be realized in much of sociology. This revolution has transformed the individual from a being of "soul" and "free will" to a set of social relations and a vehicle for thought collectives (Durkheim, 1961 [1912]; Gumplowicz, 1905; Fleck, 1979/1935). This idea does not subordinate the individual to society. Rather, by giving us a better understanding of what an individual, a person, "really is", it helps us to recognize the liberating as well as oppressive nature of the variety of social formations human beings can be socialized in.

Sociologists have generally traced their origins to ideologues of modern industrial society, notably Saint-Simon and Auguste Comte. The Marxist origins of sociological thinking have not been ignored, but (again, especially in the United States) they have not received the attention they deserve. More importantly, the working class and anarchist origins of sociology have been ignored (Thompson, 1980; Godwin, 1971; Kropotkin, 1970/1927). So have the origins of sociological thinking among women scholars and writers, and especially among feminists such as Harriet Martineau (Spender, 1983). These "oversights" have prevented the development of a sociology and a sociology of science infused with values, interests, and goals that would permit, indeed provoke, critical analyses of science and society. In particular, norms of skepticism and criticism have not been unleashed so that they could act on our deepest, our "unshakable", beliefs and assumptions. Recognizing the diverse origins of sociology depends on recognizing the distinction between the history of sociology as the history of a discipline and profession on the one hand, and as a way of looking at the world on the other. That distinction can help us to identify plural origins of science in general, and identify alternative, unrealized possibilities for the Scientific Revolution of the Galilean and Newtonian ages. That there is such an alternative in the history of science is illustrated by Merchant's (1980) study of women, ecology, and the Scientific Revolution.

The rebirth of the sociological imagination would help transform and clarify some fundamental but still cloudy issues in the sociology of science. The norm of disinterestedness, for example, is usually interpreted in psychologistic ("spiritualized") terms. To interpret it structurally means seeing its implications in terms of social interests. That is, disinterestedness means that commitments to specific social institutions are either dissolved or diffused. This is not a rarified notion. In practical terms, it means that we are in a better position to understand the world around us and ourselves to the extent that we put aside specific commitments to and interests in, for example, the national state, religions, and the bureaucracy of science. The more generalized and diffuse our interests, the more disinterested we are and, by definition, the more objective our statements about the world and ourselves are. Objectivity, then, is a social process and always a matter of degree.

Thus, the sociological imagination is not neutral or relativist (in any naïve or radical sense) on the question of truth. Mills (1963: 611) argued that the social role of the intellectual involved a politics of truth, an absorption "in the attempt to know what is real and what is unreal." But he was not a naïve realist. He argued in opposition to Hans Speier, Talcott Parsons, Robert MacIver, and Robert Merton that the sociology of knowledge was relevant for epistemology. Since our experience of nature and reality is mediated through social life, social studies have consequences for norms of "truth and validity" (Mills, 1963: 427-460). While many researchers who share Mills' political and intellectual concerns conceive of scientific objectivity in a social vacuum (e.g., Harris, 1987: 13-16), he continually stressed the social structural roots of logic and even of mind (Mills, 1963: 423-438). While he did not have the advantage of our current knowledge about the social processes of inquiry, he clearly appreciated the idea of a sociology of objectivity. The sociological imagination is not, in Mills' hands, an abstract exercise. It is implicitly and explicitly a call to arms. It is not something to exercise in a political vacuum. It is true that Mills often spoke and wrote as a reformist rather than a revolutionary. But his proposals on social problems and social change challenged and continue to challenge prevailing social arrangements in fundamental ways. What sorts of rearrangements are necessary, for example, to transform intellectuals from hired hands to peers of the powerful or, more radically, to make intellectual work and politics coincident; what sorts of changes are necessary to develop "a free and knowledgeable public"? Mills addressed these problems and sought for solutions in conventional forms of democratic reform. In fact, such changes, like the changes feminist science critics seek, require much more far-reaching social transformations than usually imagined. Anarchism lays out the foundations and programs for such a transformation.

What sorts of social formations foster disinterestedness and objectivity? That is, under what conditions can inquiry proceed unburdened as much as possible by mundane interests and commitments and within the most expansive network of information and knowledge possible? Based on the preceding conjectures, my answer is: social formations in which the person has primacy, social formations that are diversified, cooperative, egalitarian, non-authoritarian, and participatory. The person has primacy in such social formations in an anarchist sense. That is, people are neither mere parts of social systems nor isolated individuals. Their potential for developing a multitude of mental, physical, and emotional dimensions of self is recognized and nourished; it is not surrendered to the authority of one or a few parts of the self, or to external real and imagined authorities. Social formations that allow for this sort of primacy offer the most fertile environments for inquiry because they do not, by definition, demand allegiances to specific institutional interests or subordination to specific authorities. The values people rally around, for example, are very general. We are more likely to learn things that will promote individual liberty, enhance community life, and cultivate healthy environments in such social formations. There is no hope for evading the endemic conflicts, tensions, and contradictions of the human condition. The sociological imagination should not be viewed as a pathway to utopia. Rather, it should be seen as a guide to social change – and not only to social change on a grand scale, but also to marginal improvements in the conditions under which we live and inquire.

My objective so far has been to unfold the foundation for an anarcho-sociology of science. This has required me to weave in and out of the nexus of politics, values, and science while simultaneously building and connecting, allusively to some extent, sociological and anarchist agendas. In the next chapter, I discuss mathematics from the perspective of the sociology of knowledge. The better we understand the actual practices and discourses of science and mathematics, the easier it will be to make the case for an anarchistic grounding of inquiry.

Chapter 5
Math Studies
and the Anarchist Agenda

What happens in science, mathematics, and logic when we social scientists step into those arenas with our particular analytical and explanatory toolkits? What happens in science, in mathematics, in logic the moment we (scientists, intellectuals, and scholars across the full spectrum of disciplines) begin to ask questions about social responsibility, ethics, values, and social justice? We are accused, in the first instance of over-stepping our bounds, of escaping our "legal" disciplinary jurisdiction. In the second instance, we are accused by the opposition (traditional scientists, intellectuals, and even some members of the clergy) of not being rigorous, of losing our objectivity. I echo Paulo Freire here when I say that we have to defend our position as sociologists and anarchists with the passion we know pervades all knowledge, all knowing, all coming to know. We do not have to be dictators to be rigorous. We can be children at play, we can be freedom fighters. We are now on the threshold of the grounds for creativity. To be rigorous and creative and to promote social justice all at once is precisely the program of an anarchist science, in mathematics no less than in physics or sociology. To be free to inquire I do not have to try to sustain the illusion of free will, but I do have to insist on freedom from the church, the state, the KGB/FBI brotherhoods, and their everyday surrogates.

Mathematics represents and embodies human labor; and human labor is always social labor. Even when I sit and think alone, I am performing social labor because the language of my thoughts and emotions is given to me by my society and culture, and even the very self and consciousness I experience in this (as in every other) situation are social because given to me and sustained in and for me by everyday social interactions. This should sound familiar to readers of Marx's *Economic and Philosophic Manuscripts of 1844*. This principle of the pervasiveness of the social is very little understood. It is the basis for understanding mind and consciousness as socio-cultural products and processes. Even the brain is socially constructed. The significance of the social fact that minds and brains are not independent, free-standing entities and that independent, free-standing individuals are illusions has not yet reached into the social worlds of our intellectuals and educators. These ideas, so clearly stated by Marx and Durkheim almost 200 years ago have yet to find their way into the worldviews of even many of today's sociologists let alone people outside the discipline (but see Melamed, 2009).

There is a "sense of reality" that many mathematicians and educators (as well as intellectuals and wider publics) experience when they encounter mathematics.

Nonetheless, this sense of reality has been made problematic by criticisms of Platonism, a priorism, and foundationalism. This sense of reality is an illusion. Where does this illusory sense of reality come from?

One possibility is that our experience of mathematical concepts is rooted in the nature of the human nervous system. When we reason hypothetically, for example, we do so (on this neuroistic-view) by way of cognitive mechanisms that have evolved in the course of our interactions with the "real (external) world". Since the nervous system operates recursively, hypotheticals are dealt with using the logic of dealing with real world objects. This perspective readily leads to or is inevitably associated with the idea that concepts have their own internal "logic of development". This then prompts us to think in terms of individual minds, cognitive mechanisms and processes, and the central nervous system/brain as the explanatory loci for the genesis, development and communication of concepts.

How, given this perspective, are we to understand the experience of a sense of reality, a sense of objectivity, where our experiences seem to point us outside of ourselves as free-standing free-willing individuals and brains? There are two standard ways of dealing with this objectivity dilemma. One is to assume that objectivity emerges as we (qua individuals or brains) become "aware" that others share our concepts or viewpoints. The second is to rely on the related but sociologically distinct process of intersubjectivity. I showed earlier why classical (for example, Popperian) understandings of intersubjectivity fail the sociological cogito test. Sociology, and especially the form of sociology that grows out of the theories of Durkheim and Marx, can resolve the objectivity dilemma.

Consider the fuss that Roger Penrose's musings on consciousness stirred up for the neurophysiologist W.H. Calvin. Why do physicists and mathematicians feel compelled to draw on their tool kits to try to solve the consciousness problem? The "consciousness physicists", as Calvin calls them, dazzle us with mathematics and quantum mechanics thus replacing one mystery with another. They dig too deeply on grounds they are familiar with and because of a trained incompetence that nourishes explanatory arrogance. The mysteries of consciousness will not be solved in the "sub-basement of physics" but on the higher floors of neurons, synapses, and cortical layers. Let me generalize Calvin's bewilderment. Why do physicists, mathematicians, and astronomers feel they are competent to concern themselves with problems of mind, brain, consciousness, soul, the after-life, and God?

This is really quite curious, as curious as the public's readiness to turn to these scientists for answers to these questions. The situation becomes less curious when we consider how these scientists are trained and educated to be theoretically general in the broadest and most arrogant ways, and how the public understands their roles in society by way of the political ideology of science. Charitably, I am willing to accept that all of these phenomena are intimidatingly complex and require the attention of interrogators across the full spectrum of the inquiring disciplines. The problem is that the "social" floor is invariably missed, ignored, or just invisible. In the end, the problems of mind, brain, consciousness, soul, the after-life, and

God are not going to be "solved" unless we deal head on with the fact that humans come onto the evolutionary stage already, always, and everywhere social. Once we enter the social floor and familiarize ourselves with it, it will become clear that many conventional ideas and their associated paradoxes and problems become tractable. Not only that, but the social floor leads to new insights about education, teaching, and learning. I want to revisit the social construction theorem by way of some general principles based on the writings of Durkheim (1961), Saussure (1966), and Douglas (1966).

1. Social categories are the origins of the first logical categories. "In the beginning", the groupings of things and the groupings of humans (into clans and classes, for example) were to varying degrees indistinct.
2. The social relations that unite groups are the roots of our first systematization of logical relations.
3. Logical relations are domestic relations.
4. Social hierarchy gives us logical hierarchy, and the "unity of knowledge" is the unity of the group (the collectivity), a unity that extends to the universe (Douglas, 1966: 3).
5. Logical connections and divisions are grounded in domestic, social, political, economic, and other organizational forms, and are associated with the same sentiments. Note that all the principles so far ground the rationale for the claim that to be logical is to be moral; to be illogical is to be immoral.
6. Logical organization becomes differentiated from social organization as a function of the extension of social life, the enlargement of the collective horizon.
7. The collective nature of a representation is the guarantee of its objectivity. This is the origin of my claim that all communities are objectivity communities. The scientific community is then just one among many objectivity communities although one of extreme objectivity. Those aligned with me will rank objectivity communities and give the scientific community a privileged status (once we have taken account of and addressed the problem of the Cult of Science).
8. Impersonal reason is another name for collective thought.
9. The stability and impersonality of collective representations is the basis for their transformation into allegedly universal and immutable facts.
10. To think rationally is to think in accordance with lawful behavior, whether specific laws come from an emperor, the stipulations of a discipline, or the norms of a profession.
11. I would like the reader to try to grasp the sense of these principles in the most general way so that s/he might better understand Durkheim's conclusion that there is something social in every human and it is that "social" something that is the source of the "impersonal" in us. Social life encompasses representations and practices, so it follows that the

impersonality in us applies not only to acts but to thoughts. Before I offer a summary introduction on how to think sociologically about mathematics, let's review the conception of science developed within the science studies movement.

What is Science?

Scientific facts are manufactured out of locally available social, material, and symbolic interpersonally meaningful resources. These resources become facts through the social interactions of scientists in a process sometimes described as creating order out of disorder and sometimes as a new order out of an old order. In the wake of a laboratory experiment, the sequence of writings from laboratory notes to published paper moves statements through different modes, each mode more "objective" than was the previous one. That is, statements describing an experiment progressively erase the subjective, flesh and blood human experimenters from an increasingly objective, mechanistic, and technical discourse. Facts attain "universal" status first through a generalizing rhetorical strategy and then through the international activities of scientists as agents of professions and governments, and as ambassadors for the legitimacy of these facts. The field of science studies is an alternative to traditional ways of studying and understanding science. According to practitioners of science studies, not only is science a social activity, but scientific knowledge itself is socially constructed. Scientific facts and scientists themselves are social facts. Let us be clear: facts can only be known, discovered, and invented through our interactions with each other in our human-made, human-incorporated, and human-enabled environments (the contexts of human life). This is what we mean by social construction. Social construction is a realistic enterprise and does not entail or imply relativism or anti-science attitudes. To the extent that relativistic claims engage sociologists of science they do so in opposition to absolutist claims and not to realistic ones. We may be right or wrong about our facts but we do not have any alternative to social construction to get at our facts. Now let's focus this perspective on mathematics.

What is Mathematics?

Mathematics has been shrouded in mystery and halos for most of its history. The reason for this is that it has seemed impossible to account for the nature and successes of mathematics without granting it some sort of transcendental status. Classically, this is most dramatically expressed in the Platonic notion of mathematics. Consider, for example, the way some scholars have viewed the development of non-Euclidean geometries (NEGs). The mathematician Dirk Struik, for example, described that development as "remarkable" in two respects. First, he claimed, the ideas emerged independently in Göttingen, Budapest, and Kazan; second, they emerged on the periphery of the world mathematical community. And the distinguished historian of mathematics, Carl Boyer, characterized the case as one of "startling...simultaneity". These reflect classical Platonic, transcendental views of mathematics. In fact, NEGs have a history that begins already with Euclid's commentators, runs right up to Gauss and his students at Göttingen in the early 1800s, and culminates within a social network that runs through names like Saccheri, Lambert, Klügel, and Legendre with J. Bolyai, Lobachevsky and Riemann as its major nodes. Moreover, far from being independent, the latter three mathematicians were all connected to Gauss who had been working on NEGs since at least the 1820s. The appearance of mystery and genius quickly gives way to the most cursory sociologically informed historical gaze. Social networks come into view where once there was only a kind of emptiness highly susceptible to explanation by mystery and genius. The very idea of "the social" is at the heart of what we need to understand in order to grasp mathematics realistically, that is, without Platonic blinders. Within the framework of the general problem of "the social", I want to focus on boundaries and margins in mathematics and mathematics education. Exploring the purity and danger divide can help us reveal details about the intersection of logic, mathematics, and thinking with gender, race, class, and morals that we would otherwise miss.

I use the deliberately Nietzschean phrase "The Will to Mathematics" to mean the drive to see and feel in mathematics something pure, transcendent, and certain with results that approach a level of truth as high as humans can hope to achieve. The reality of mathematics lies in social practice and discourse, so mathematics is as real – and only as real – as ordinary social life. To pursue this claim, let us begin by exploring what mathematics represents.

To represent something is to construct something in symbols or images to stand for it. When we ask, "What does mathematics represent?" we are asking, "What do math symbols and images stand for?" What *might* they stand for? For simplicity, I will phrase the question as follows: "What *are* mathematical objects?"

There is an interesting mythology about mathematics and mathematicians that reinforces ideas of purity and genius, and even madness. Surely, Edmund Landau is not the only mathematician who has claimed that "Wir Mathematiker sind alle ein bi*B*chen meschugge".

Consider again the case of NEGs. Could scholars of the caliber of Struik and Boyer have been unaware of the social networks and histories of NEGs, or were they bound by some code to present the case in a rhetoric of mystery and transcendence? And consider the case of the famous number, 1729. This is the number of the taxi that the Cambridge mathematician G. Hardy rode in on his way to visit a hospitalized Ramanujan. He tells Ramanujan that the taxi had "a rather dull number". Ramanujan replies that on the contrary it is a very interesting number. It is the smallest number that can be expressed as the sum of two cubes in two different ways. Now this is as much as most people have ever read about this episode, and it is easy to come away with the notion that this genius had on the spot and virtually instantly recognized this feature of 1729. But Ramanujan's biographer, Robert Kanigel (1991: 312), makes the more plausible claim that Ramanujan had noticed or come across this quality of 1729 years earlier, recorded it, and remembered it. It is not incidental that neither Hardy nor Ramanujan mentioned any of the other ways the number 1729 is interesting. For example, an historian might have noted that 1729 was the year Edmund Burke was born, and an historian with the wits of a Ramanujan might have known that Burke was the only future British statesman born that year to a Protestant solicitor father and a Roman Catholic mother in Dublin. Or that in that same year, Leopold Joseph died and Francis III was born – a former and a future Duke of Lorraine. Newton's *Principia* was translated into English, and Emperor Yung Cheng outlawed opium smoking in China. Clara Reve, the English novelist, and Catherine the Great were born in 1729. And the Treaty of Seville was signed by France, Spain, and England. But the story that reinforces the sense of genius is a much better story for mathematics, isn't it? It is a story repeated for many instances of mathematical genius and even occurs in the cases of idiot savants. In these cases, the mystery of genius is substituted for the mundane quality of hard, even obsessive work, recording, memorizing, and remembering (Dehaene, 1997: 167-172). Why are these good stories for mathematics?

Mathematics might represent a reality, or a mathematical reality that lies "outside us", as Hardy (1967: 123-124, 130), for example, believed. Hardy was a Platonist. Michael D. Resnik (1993: 39), a contemporary Platonist, describes Platonism as the idea that mathematical objects are outside of space and time and cannot interact with ordinary spatio-temporal bodies. Platonism refers to Plato's notion that the objects of our sensory experience are reflections of ideal non-spatio-temporal "forms". Sometimes, Platonism is used to label the idea that mathematical objects are "real" (Schechter, 1998: 113).

As a sociologist I want to know the social function of labelling mathematics "transcendent". What is the consequence of defining mathematics outside of "ourselves," why do we do this? Re-read Plato with me, along with Huntington Cairns' "Introduction" to *The Collected Dialogues* (Hamilton and Cairns, 1989). "Parmenides" is interesting because it has caused scholars great difficulty: first, because the dialogue is one of the most resistant to reasoned interpretation and second, because the close scrutiny of the idea of the "forms" can leave one wondering just what Plato had, so to speak, in mind and how satisfied he was with the very idea (Hamilton and Cairns, 1989: 920). The whole idea is left in doubt at the end of Parmenides' critique. Cairns (in Hamilton and Cairns, 1989: xviii-xix), who has explored this issue with an expertise that I lack, concludes that Plato did indeed believe that the "forms" or "Ideas" exist outside of our minds. But he also suggests the concept may be more earthly than ethereal, in some ways kin to "naturalism, pragmatism, positivism, analysis, and existentialism." Could Platonism be infected with a relatively benign form of the social construction virus?

Even if one can find hints of social theory in Platonist views of mathematics, the image of something "outside" of us – something transcendent, godlike, pure, abstract – keeps mathematics ultimately separated from the social and material realms of experience. For the sociological theorist, references to realms "outside" of us are understood as pointing to social referents. Emile Durkheim and George H. Mead pioneered in the development of sociological theory as the rejection of transcendence, immanence, and psychologism.

The peripatetic mathematician known for his "open brain," the late Paul Erdos, wrote that "There's an old debate about whether you create mathematics or just discover it. In other words, are the truths already there, even if we don't yet know them? If you believe in God, the answer is obvious. Mathematical truths are there in the SF's [Supreme Fascists's] mind, and you just rediscover them…" (in Hoffman, 1998: 26).

Mathematics might also represent God or a religion. In Mesopotamia, the ratio 2/3 was deified as the god Ea the Creator. The mathematical properties of certain numbers make them candidates for representing deities. "7" was a symbol for the sacred world in Mesopotamia. The Hebrews rejected the practice of deifying numerals. Isaiah 44:6 is sometimes cited as an exception; but this is a bit tricky. In this passage, the Lord says "I am the first and I am the last" (in the closing paragraphs of the New Testament, these words appear again when the Lord says: "I am the Alpha and the Omega, the first and the last, the beginning and the end" (Rev. 22:13)). Generally, insofar as mathematics has historically been the science of the infinite it has been the science of God. There are many other examples I could point out, but the important thing is that in the case of God as in the case of the "forms", mathematics represents a transcendental realm.

In spite of the widespread support in mathematics and the philosophy of mathematics for Platonism, supporters have not been able to escape the self-contradiction, and even the absurdity, of the transcendence claim. If mathematics is outside of space and time how can we reach it from our earthly grounds? It is clear that exactly the same problem arises in the case of God when the faithful argue that God cannot be captured by our eyes, our words, or our minds. What can such claims possibly mean? Any effort to answer such a question will mangle logic, experience, and understanding. Paul Gordan expressed a similar sentiment when he replied to Hilbert during their invariant theory proof war, "*Das ist nicht Mathematik, das ist Theologie.*" One can now imagine a parallel response concerning claims about God: "*Das ist nicht Theologie, das ist Absurdität.*"

It is interesting to note that Paul Erdos, who claimed (quoting an old Hungarian saying) that "A mathematician is a machine for turning coffee into theorems", behaved in opposition to this idea as if in fact mathematics was "a social activity, a movable feast" (Schechter, 1998: 14). The idea that mathematics as a vocation is social would not be disputed by many working mathematicians. The trouble begins when the sociologist wants to draw out the more technical meanings of "social". Furthermore, the sociologist wants to press the idea of the "social" beyond its everyday meaning and to argue that mathematical objects themselves are social. The transcendental realm is a cultural creation, not a reality out of space and time. So is the supernatural, and so then are the gods. The fundamental project of the sociological sciences can indeed be viewed as locating the everyday world referents for transcendental and supernatural experiences.

What can we conclude as social constructionists, that is, as sociological and materialistic realists? The idea that mathematics is pure or transcendent is "an expression of the felt autonomy of the inner activities of the intellectual network" (Collins, 1998: 878). The certainty of mathematics is a function of how tightly the generational links across mathematical networks are interwoven. The "chain of social conventions" in mathematics is robustly repeatable. It is this robustness that accounts for the sense of certainty mathematicians and laypeople alike share about mathematics.

Neither truth, certainty, nor thought itself "arise in isolated brains or disembodied minds" (Collins, 1998: 877). They all arise in social networks. At the end of the day, sociologists are wont to ask "How could any of these phenomena arise anywhere else; what is there that is anywhere else?" It is discourse, with its "objective, obdurate quality", that produces that "strong constraint that answers the concept of truth" (Collins, 1998: 865). Even the most elementary exercise in mathematics, indeed even the most elementary understanding of an equation, engages us in a form of discourse (and more broadly, in Wittgenstein's terms, a form of life), a network of teachers and students, of researchers, inventors, and discoverers. The "universality" of mathematics, like the universality of any cultural system, trait, or representation is grounded in the universality of its social practice and discourse.

Toward an Archaeology of Mathematics

It may appear that I want to reject outright the certainty, purity, and universality of mathematics. I can be more modest and seek only to disturb the tranquility with which these notions are accepted. The point would then be to show that mathematics does not come about of itself, but that it is constructed. If it is constructed, there must be rules of construction, and these must be knowable. Consider: what are the conditions under which it is reasonable and legitimate to do, use, apply, and teach mathematics? Are there things about mathematics, including mathematics itself, that we might want to consider discarding because they are illusions, illegitimate constructions, or ill-acquired? Should we never use them, draw on them temporarily, store them for possible future use? Is it enough to simply remove mathematics from its throne of purity?

Whether we are modest or immodest in our methods and theories, as soon as we question (for whatever reasons) the unity, purity, and universality of mathematics, "it loses its self-evidence; it indicates itself, constructs, only on the basis of a complex field of discourse" (Foucault, 1972: 23-24). Foucault, of course, was not thinking of mathematics here. He treated mathematics as something of a special case, immune to the power of his archaeological method. Do numbers hide something? Are they embedded in networks of power, and are they deployed in ways that purposefully obscure the power behind their visual and oral representations? How is it then that mathematics seems to have escaped matter? How has it hidden the fact that it is a discipline that disciplines? Mathematics is an everywhere dense discourse. How do we reveal the systems of regularities that determine mathematicians by determining their situations, functions, perceptions, and practical possibilities? How do we reveal the social, cultural, and historical conditions that "dominate and even overwhelm" mathematicians? Mathematics is more than a discourse, more than a language. It is an institution embedded in a culture and assigned a more or less specific domain of control.

We need, following Foucault's method, to be able to reconceptualize the problem of mathematics not as a problem in ontology (or even in classical epistemology) but as a problem in politics and ethics (or as we will put it here, a problem in morals). Let us pursue this Nietzschean turn.

The Morality of Mathematics

Individuals do not make decisions about what is right and wrong or true and false on their own. Such decisions are settled by institutions. We are born into classifications, logical operations, languages, and metaphors. It is on the basis of such Durkheimian considerations that sociologists of knowledge of my type reach the conclusion that mathematics is a moral system. It is important to keep in mind Durkheim's remarks on the categories of space, time, and causality. These are the most general relations between things, and they dominate our intellectual and everyday lives. Communities of men and women must be in accord about these essentials at any given historico-cultural moment. Without this accord, they would not connect intellectually, emotionally, and linguistically. Humans are not free to choose or deny "the categories". Social life requires a minimum consensus without which society dissolves. This makes adherence a moral imperative, a moral necessity. Keep in mind these categories, "reality in itself", have an a priori aspect but arise and crystallize in social and cultural contexts.

What role do numbers play in grounding our ideas or experiences of abstraction, purity, and the sacred? How do numbers play into constructing and sustaining boundaries and relationships? The moral necessity of mathematics is enhanced as its professional boundaries are constructed and concretized around those thought communities and thought collectives (Fleck, 1979/1935) dedicated to these very ideas.

All institutions provide the categories of thought, set the terms for knowledge and self-knowledge, and fix identities. But more than this, they "must secure the social edifices by sacralizing the principles of justice" (Douglas, 1986: 112). In mathematics, classifications and theorems, proofs and conjectures are held together by the sacred glues of logic and reason. Given the sociological conception of the nature and functions of institutions, it should not be surprising to find that questions and issues of morals merge with questions and issues of what is real and what is illusory. As educators, to turn to practice, we are left with the following question: how does classroom practice change if we understand that problems of truth and falsity, what is right and what is wrong, are moral problems? What would it mean to address our classroom practices in this context?

The Word or the Act?

> What, "In the beginning was the Word?" Absurd. Then maybe it should say "In the beginning was the Mind?" Or better "...there was Force?" Yet something warns me as I grasp the pen, That my translation must be changed again. The spirit helps me. Now it is exact. I write: "In the beginning was the Act."

Thus did Goethe (1963: 153) have Faust speak. No one was clearer and more elegant in locating the social sources of ideas, words, and mind than Marx (1958: 104). I have quoted Marx on this point earlier, but it is worth revisiting him:

Early in this century, Emile Durkheim and Marcel Mauss (1963) demonstrated that ideas and concepts in "primitive societies" arise from and reflect social structures, networks of human beings interacting in conflict and cooperation. Here are the beginnings (in conjunction with earlier writings by Durkheim and Marx) of what we commonly refer today as social construction theory. It is important to clarify the nature of this theory before we go on, since it has generated so much confusion even among its advocates. The very idea that science and mathematics are socially constructed helped to provoke the Science Wars, and made sociologists of science targets for physical scientists and philosophers (as well as other intellectuals) who have labelled us with the philosopher Willard Quine's most pejorative epithet, "anti-science". When our anti-science image is coupled to our image as relativists, we are readily painted as dangers to the very foundations of Western civilization. But anti-science and relativism are not necessary ingredients of social constructionism. Durkheim (1961: 31-32) himself already remarked that "From the fact that the ideas of time, space, class, cause or personality are constructed out of social elements, it is not necessary to conclude that they are devoid of all objective value."

The most unsettling pseudo-deduction from social construction theory is that it eliminates the possibility of telling the truth. If postmodernism has eliminated the possibility of telling the truth, or at least made telling the truth problematic, it has done so by masking the truths of sociology and anthropology. Social construction theory must be in a sense turned on itself in order to eliminate pseudo-deductive monstrosities. For in fact, as Dorothy Smith has so elegantly pointed out, it is just social construction theory that makes telling the truth possible. Reference and representations are social activities and processes. Following Mead (1938, 1947) and Bakhtin (1981, 1986), Smith (1996: 193-195) argues that "a fully social, dialogic account of knowledge and truth holds out for systematic inquiry the possibility of telling the truth about what it finds". Truth and knowledge, as fallible and tentative achievements, are manufactured by human beings who accomplish what they know and what they can know in common (cf. Fleck, 1979, on thought collectives).

The Public Understanding of Mathematics

Ancient and esoteric debates and dialogues about the nature of mathematics have spilled over into the public domain of modern mathematics. The February 10, 1998 issue of *The New York Times* carried the following headline: "Useful Invention or Absolute Truth: What is Math?" The author, George Johnson (1998: 1), reviewing a recent book by mathematician Reuben Hersh, writes: "Dr. Hersh's book is one of several recent works contending that mathematics is not an ethereal essence but comes from people who invented, not discovered it. The sentiments presented in the books are not entirely new and the mathematical puzzle has hardly been solved. But the idea of a human-centered mathematics may be gaining force and respect."

The authors Johnson cites in sketching the idea of a "human-centered mathematics" are all "working mathematicians and scientists, not postmodern critics viewing the territory from afar". They emphatically reject, Johnson writes, those who try to dismiss mathematics and science as arbitrary constructions, or white male Eurocentric folklore; but they are just as adamant in rejecting what most mathematicians and many scientists have come to take for granted: the Platonic creed. A boxed insert announces that "Some scholars say mathematics emerged from the inferior parietal cortex, not a Platonic ether."

Let's review these excerpts and tease out what the author has accomplished in this article. First, it looks like he has advanced the public's understanding of mathematics in terms science studies researchers would all advocate to one extent or another: mathematics is invented, not discovered; it is human-centered. The distinction between "invention" and "discovery" is not as transparent as dictionary definitions might suggest, so that issue requires more sustained attention. On the other hand, the idea that mathematics is human-centered is sociologically unproblematic. But in fact the author has reinforced the pernicious idea that physical and natural scientists and mathematicians are the ultimate authorities on how the world works, and even on how the human-centered world works. The human, social, and cultural sciences and humanities are summarily dismissed under the rubric of postmodern scholarship which can only study science and mathematics from "afar". Not one sociologist's or anthropologist's name appears in the article, even though it is easy enough to find such names in the writings of mathematicians like Reuben Hersh (who cites, for example, both David Bloor and Sal Restivo).

If articles like this advance in some way the public's understanding of mathematics, they do so in a way that masks the public's understanding of just those scholarly endeavors that have facilitated human-centered ways of thinking about mathematics. In the end, articles like this promote the authority of a traditional hierarchy of inquiry that legitimates the physical and natural sciences and delegitimizes the social sciences and humanities. That authority extends not only to reflections on the social nature of science and mathematics, but to the very heart of the subject matter of the social sciences and humanities – including the study of religion, God and gods, the soul, consciousness, mind, and thought.

Furthermore, it is clear that programs to advance the public understanding of mathematics (along with science more generally) are not about the technical content of mathematics. Mathematicians, public officials, and already understanding publics want people to be able to do the mathematics they need to be able to do in order to achieve the objectives of their governments and immediate employers. They want people to participate in the social and moral orders of educated publics. They want women and minorities to share in the mathematical skills needed to keep society running (without much consideration for the differential benefits that accrue to members of that society). And at some level they would like the public to appreciate mathematics and mathematicians. The social sciences and humanities enter this public understanding project primarily in the aborted, truncated and crippled forms internalized by mathematicians and philosophers. The result is that the actual voices of the social scientists and humanities scholars are silenced and the alleged dangers of legitimizing their inquiries are not interrogated. Public understanding of mathematics with a human face then comes to be about demonstrating the limits of mathematics and science, the ease of learning these traditionally esoteric subjects, and the all too human qualities of their practitioners.

The point of the public understanding programs should be to go beyond understanding and appreciating mathematics and mathematicians to encompass their social grounds, roots, forms, and functions. This is not a call for eliminating the voices of the mathematicians and philosophers in advancing the public understanding of mathematics in the broader context of my discussion. It is important, however, to open up opportunities for social scientists and humanities scholars to play a more visible role in advancing the public understanding of mathematics.

"There Is No There, There": A Manifesto in Defiance of *Der Kulte der Reine Vernünft* – Mathematics Revisited

Paulo Freire (1970: 183) wrote that in order to oppress, the oppressor needs a theory of oppressive action. It follows, he continues, that in order to be free, the oppressed too need a theory of action. The dream of establishing secure foundations for mathematics has never recovered from Gödel's attack. His findings, however, have not been construed as a reason to abandon all hope of extracting meaning from mathematical inquiry. Gödel himself seemed to hold the view that Platonic realism provided the clearest definition of mathematical truth. There is as much reason to assume that mathematical objects exist as there is to assume that physical bodies exist. If Platonism has been vanquished in public it continues to be observed secretly and almost spiritually by some individual mathematicians, philosophers, and logicians.

In 1870, Friedrich Max Müller gave a lecture at the Royal Institution in London on "the science of religion". He reminded his audience of Goethe's remark about language: "He who knows one, knows none". Müller was in effect arguing for multicultural religious studies, a comparative religion. Adolf von Harnack, the leading historian of Christianity at the time, opposed Müller's views and approach. Harnack claimed that Christianity was all that mattered: "Whoever does not know this religion knows none, and whoever knows it and its history knows all." There was no point to looking to the Indians, the Chinese, the Negroes, and the Papuans, for it was Christian civilization that was destined to endure. This is the context in which the math wars, along with the science wars and the culture wars have been carried out.

The West's encounter with the East, the North, the South, and the Other has provoked a series of cultural identity crises and put all of our traditional institutions on alert. Terrorism has brought the world's political realities to America's front doorstep. Science studies and the science wars have brought the Other's knowledge into the laboratory in at least two respects. First, social scientists have entered scientific laboratories – (social) scientists studying science and scientists. This has upset a routine in which scientists told their own stories and controlled and protected their own spaces or territories; philosophers reduced those stories to logically coherent narratives and served as a secondary line of defense of the territory of science. Second, feminists and other postmodern researchers have found science lurking in the most unexpected places, from the kitchen to the garage to the culture of bodybuilding. The math wars put Americans on notice, not that there are "alternative mathematics" but rather that there are other/Other and differently valenced mathematics. And let us not lose sight of how the laboratory as an icon and vanguard of the sciences has moved into the world. These differences clearly exist across cultures; they also exist within our own industrialized culture. And most importantly for understanding the math wars, they exist within mathematics themselves (sic). This view of mathematics is a product of the so-called "new" (post-Mertonian) sociology of science and, more broadly, the diversity of intellectual trends in the twentieth century loosely labeled postmodernism.

In its simplest guise, postmodernism was a response to the naïve worldviews that had grown out of an ontological and epistemological arrogance and complacency among nineteenth century scientists and science watchers. We can think of postmodernism and poststructuralism as bringing to the center of our attention space the idea of multiple narratives and a variety of more or less fragmented discourses. "Things fall apart, the centre cannot hold," wrote Yeats, long before Derrida made decentering and deconstruction watchwords of twentieth century theory. This, perhaps more than the true convictions of their authors, made Einstein (relativity theory), Gödel (the incompleteness theorems) and Heisenberg (the uncertainty principle) among the most prominent co-authors of the myth of objectivity. Clearly, however, Einstein and Gödel at least never lost their commitment to the idea of an objective reality. Neither did that paragon of paradigmatic postmodernist science, Thomas Kuhn, ever lose his commitment to the ideas of scientific progress, objectivity, and truth.

We are left, Einstein, Gödel, and Kuhn notwithstanding, with the problem of how to tell the truth after postmodernism. Dorothy Smith, as we saw earlier, has cut through all the relativistic conclusions of the postmodern extremists to show us how postmodernism has in fact taught us *how* to tell the truth.

This lesson depends on doing a lot of technical work to figure out how to represent and express the nature of the social. There is no understanding the math (and science) wars without understanding the fundamentally social nature of mathematics, the social construction of mathematics. Even this depends on the more difficult notion that our very selves are social things. The ability of a sociology (and anthropology) of mathematics to "tell the truth" depends on entering it into a dialogue with everyday activities, on recognizing our relations to others and how we are coupled, with, linked into social relations. As a social constructionist (and as a Smithian sociologist of knowledge) I am resistant to substituting a single objective hegemony for the multiple and divergent realities of our everyday/everynight world. Here I stand shoulder to shoulder with the postmodernists. The social and cultural constructionist approach to mathematics develops out of active inquiry and not out of empty theorizing or philosophical speculation. We must locate ourselves in our social relations, we must contextualize everything.

I must emphasize again that this does not mean we must become relativists or anti-science. Like Feyerabend's anarchist who walks out the front door when s/he leaves a building (as opposed to Lakatos' "anarchist" who might climb out a window instead), we anarcho-sociologists use the door and look both ways when we cross the street. The multiple and divergent realities we want to support are not castles in the sky, they are not fantasy worlds; they are off-shoots of the world of walking out doors and crossing streets safely. In New York City, I look both ways before I cross the street; in London, I would do well to look down at the painted directions off the curb which remind me that traffic rules are different here; crossing streets in Rome and Paris often requires a limber neck to capture cars travelling fast and in a variety of directions at complex intersections. These different cultural configurations do not violate the principle that you must look before you cross to avoid getting injured or killed.

We must wonder about the resistance of Platonic and transcendental thinking to the lessons of modernity and postmodernity. These lessons, admittedly, are buried beneath the rubble of the wars, holocausts, political economic failures, and ecological disasters of the twentieth century. The brilliant flare-up of the very idea of "the social" between 1840 and 1912-1920 and the discovery sciences it gave form to has remained virtually invisible on the intellectual landscape formed over the last 150 years. Until and unless we uncover that revolution, we will continue to be haunted by the ghosts of Plato, Descartes, and God. These ghosts cannot be banished by materialism *per se*. What is required is a sociological materialism, a cultural materialism, and in the end an anarcho-sociology. It is no simple ideological or political victory I champion but an adaptation, an evolutionary matter of life and death. So long as these ghosts haunt us, we will be unable as a species to take advantage of whatever small opportunities are left to us to make something worthwhile flourish on this planet for even a little while. The issues here are that big.

We must chase these ghosts down at every opportunity. Every time a critic of social and cultural thinking about science raises the banner of the "brute fact" he or she raises the banner of God. We can have a critically robust realism sans Plato, Descartes, and God that is consistent with a social and cultural theory of science, mathematics, and logic. So long as we allow ourselves to be deluded by the "transparent" claim that Gödel, Einstein, and Heisenberg have given us the three most important insights into who and what we are, a claim made by the philosopher and novelist Rebecca Goldstein (2006), we will be stuck on a path of almost daily and almost universal suffering, and face a future that can only promise more of the same without relief. In fact it is to Darwin, Marx, and Durkheim that we must turn for the most important insights. We do great harm to ourselves and our planet if we rely on Gödel, Einstein, and Heisenberg for our self-image as persons and as a species. We are, indeed, thermodynamic systems and we run at some level according to the laws of physics, biology, and chemistry. But what we are above all is a social and a cultural thing, a society, social beings, cultural entities sui generis. We are, individually and collectively, social facts. I will acknowledge the gendered danger of standing on the shoulders of these six giants but remind you that they and I stand on the shoulders of so many other giants that gender, race, and class does not matter. If I contradict myself, if I fail to stand apart from my own gender, race, and class I can remain silent or carry on. I choose to carry on. I have not forgotten the Madame de Staels, the Rosa Luxembourgs, the Harriet Martineaus, and the Emma Goldmans who hold up half the world of these insights.

I have laid out a pathway to rejecting transcendentalism and supernaturalism. I have also shown why God is a formidable barrier to ending the hegemony of pure reason. Without the end of God, there is no end to pure reason, no end to pure mathematics, no end to hegemonic views of what mathematics is. By following this path, we risk ending mathematics itself, science itself. But if we keep in mind that we are opposed to absolutisms and not to realisms, we can avoid this consequence. There are battles and struggles, conflicts and controversies on all of the paths before us. I have not sought here to offer practical politically viable solutions to the problems of the math wars. Rather, I have tried to shed some light on these paths in order to facilitate such solutions. There is no better way to conclude this part of our excursion than by recalling Spengler's insight that there is no Mathematic, only mathematics.

The mysteries of intuitions, geniuses, and eternal truths outside space and time nourished by books like Dr. Goldstein's are no mere exercises in pure reason for the sake of pure reason. They sustain a worldview that is more medieval than modern. We social ones must take our stand again and again against those who, however well intentioned, continue to support knowingly and unknowingly, the One Logic, the One God, and the separation of the realm of faith and belief from the realm of science and knowledge. The most pernicious dogmas flourish in this atmosphere. For example, undergraduates are fond of repeating this "truism" learned from their masters: "You can't prove or disprove God." And what leg do you stand on when public intellectuals of unimpeachable brilliance like the late Stephen Jay Gould argue for the separation of science and religion? Claims such as these can only make sense in a world of science that excludes social science. Once we admit social science to the halls of verifiable, validated, discovery sciences and proof communities such claims evaporate. Proofs, I must stress, are social constructions, social institutions, indexical. Within a framework that includes the social sciences we can determine what God (in any and all cultural and historical guises, disguises, singles, and plurals) is, that is, the referent for whatever we mean by "God". That referent is always going to be a sociocultural one, rooted in the material earth and its human populations and not in some transcendental or supernatural realm.

Even the strongest opponents and upholders of this claim tremble as they make it. They tend to leave openings for believers, including themselves in some cases, because the barriers to banging the last nails into the coffin of religious faith and belief are, let us admit, formidable. They are formidable, as both Marx and Durkheim recognized, because they have something to do with keeping society and individuals from becoming unglued. It is not religions and belief in the gods that are universal but rather moral orders. All societies, all humans, require a moral order to survive, to move through the world and their lives. That is, they require, to put it simply, rules about what is good and bad, right and wrong. Religion is just one way to systematize these rules. There are other ways to do this. We can organize moral orders around almost any human interest from politics (as Michael Harrington has demonstrated) to physical fitness (as the life of fitness guru Jack LaLanne demonstrates). There are ways to construct moral orders that do not depend on unreferred entities.

Society is symbolically useful in thinking sociologically but does not convey the central idea I want to emphasize, that our selves are structured and re-structured, produced and re-produced, in moment-to-moment social interactions during the course of our everyday, everynight lives. These interactions are, in fact, ritualized and linked (in what Randall Collins has called "interaction ritual chains" or IRCs), and these rituals and ritual chains are the crucibles in which we make and re-make our selves and our cultures. We could, then, say that mathematics, like language, and like any cultural system, represents the product(s) of networks of interaction ritual chains.

We need to help ourselves and others understand the power – the critical and subversive power – of theory, and to help eliminate the idea of theory implied in such statements as "it's only (or merely) theory", "it's fine in theory, but not necessarily in reality", and the idea that somehow theories worth the label are constructed in vacuums out of nothing, without any grounding. Theories are only theories if they are constructed referentially in terms of concrete or more generally material elements. Every thing or event we experience is indeed referentially constructed. The problem is to try to get the referent right. If we try to locate our referents in non-material realms we will generate transcendentals. The classic example here is God. If we tie the word "God" to an invisible entity, we make a mistake in reference. The experience of God is real but the referent for the experience is the social group. God is a symbol of that group. I will explore this idea further in the final chapter.

When we say that something is "conventional", we should mean that something is based on collective behavior and not that it is arbitrary. This is true of every means of expression. Symbols are often considered arbitrary, but they are not in fact empty forms that you can fill in any way you please – there is some form of bond between the signifier and the signified rooted in cultural significance and meanings. Every term's or expression's meaning or value is formed by its sociocultural and material environment. This is true of symbols, words, sentences, grammar, and language; and it is therefore true of scientific terms and mathematics. This may seem to be too sudden or radical a leap for some readers, but it will seem less so the more they become comfortable with the principles laid out above.

Our collective truths – whether in the traditions that link generations of shamans or the facts that help constitute scientific communities – are achieved in and through social processes. Where, then, our critics say, is "nature", or "reality"? Again, a review of the general principles provides a basis for the insight that nature and reality are themselves collective achievements that become stabilized by way of our use of language. We social constructionists do not want to deny nature or reality, but we do need to problematize (or "deconstruct") them in the light of the social construction conjecture. For Durkheim (1961: 31-32), "the social realm is a natural realm". And if our ideas about these realms are socially constructed, it does not necessarily follow that they are not objective.

Critics of social constructionism err in equating it with "reductionism", assuming it is a synonym for religious, political, economic, and military causes, and assuming it means "false", "arbitrary", and "not objective". Sometimes they mean that it is reductionist because it reduces a phenomenon to social causes. They make these errors because (1) they cannot accept the idea of social causes, (2) they do not understand that all knowledge, like all culture, is grounded in the social interactions of human beings at every organizational level from small groups, families and social networks to professions, communities, and societies, (3) they fail to realize that the only way we can invent or discover is through social practice and discourse, and (4) they don't understand that individuals are themselves social beings.

It is no accident that a particularly recalcitrant blindness to the "social basis of essential categories" is characteristic of capitalist culture (Taussig, 1980: 4). The reason is that commodification reifies abstractions. Things are set apart from life, from social relations. And as "thingification" (or commodification) proceeds, it more and more obscures social relations in general. This process also encompasses human bodies and social relationships. One of the "bewildering manifestations" of this process is the denial of the social construction of reality. I must leave the further details of this argument to Taussig (not to mention Marx). We must now confront perhaps the most powerful pseudo-deduction from the social construction conjecture: that this intellectual "monstrosity" eliminates the possibility of telling the truth. This pseudo-deduction can be made by social constructionists who don't fully understand the conjecture as well as by anti-social constructionists.

The way to confront and get rid of this monstrosity is to turn the social construction conjecture, in a way, on itself. Postmodernism, of course, has made telling the truth problematic, if not impossible. But it has done this in part by skirting around sociology and anthropology. I have already alluded to Dorothy Smith's (1996: 193-194) solution. The objective is to find and recognize our position in relation to others, to grasp how what we are doing and what is happening is linked to those relations. We should not, however, seek to pre-empt multiple and diverse perspectives by putting in place a hegemony of thought and consciousness.

Smith's sociological perspectives moves us away from thinking and seeing in terms of hierarchies instead of social networks. It also suggests that we should remain vigilant about not restricting our network thinking to cyberspace. It is possible that the "powerful computational contexts" Kathryn Crawford (1998) draws attention to are simply underlining something that is true of the best forms of human learning; that "networked environments", in the most general sense, are more constructive than hierarchical ones. By continuing to try to construct computers that "think" like humans, we miss the point that computers herald a new level of network thinking. Beyond sequential thinking and logics and their associated hierarchical foundations lies a realm without numbers, a realm of pictures and patterns, a reality of "intermaths" (cellular automata, neural networks, genetic algorithms, artificial life, and classifier systems; see, for example, Bailey (1996)).

The Sociology of the Mind: A Preview

The idea that the mind is a social construction is crucial to reforming our understanding of mathematics education in the light of the sociological perspective. I come to the sociology of mind by way of the sociology of science, mathematics, and knowledge. In particular, I have been concerned over a major part of my research career in bringing mathematics down to earth. To bring mathematics out of the Platonic clouds, out of transcendental realms, is equivalent to negating the idea of "pure mind" and indeed of mind itself.

When, and to the extent that, mathematics becomes a functionally differentiated, institutionally autonomous social activity in any given social formation, it will begin to generate mathematics out of mathematics. The vulgar notion that "mathematics causes mathematics" (pure mathematics) arises out of a failure to (and to be able to) recognize that in a generationally extended mathematical community (or social network) of mathematicians, mathematicians use the results of earlier generations of mathematical workers and mathematicians as the (material) resources for their mathematical labors. Systematization, rationalization, generalization, and abstraction in mathematics are dependent on organizing mathematical workers in a certain way. In general, this means specialized networks and sustained generational continuity. The significance of iteration produced by generational continuity has been widely recognized in a variety of ways by working mathematicians and philosophers.

At the moment in which you say, "Look, but now I invite you to be responsible!", immediately the opposition thinks that your hypotheses are not rigorous. This is where the fight begins, and our weapons have to be love, passion, and freedom. I understand with Paulo Freire that rigor *lives* with and needs freedom. By perpetuating the school as an instrument for social control and by dichotomizing teaching from learning, educators forget Marx's fundamental warning in his third thesis on Feuerbach:

> The educator should also be educated. (Freire, 1985: 105)

> Just as there is no such thing as an isolated human being there is no such thing as isolated thinking. (Freire, 1967: 134)

My conception of theory reflects my anarchist objectives. The craft or practice of theory is widely misunderstood. It is, properly practiced, a subversive activity; indeed, it may be the most subversive activity humans are capable of. From an anarchist perspective (and here I follow Brian Martin (1997: 33)), "Ideas are central to social struggles. Most of the intellectual work in government, corporations and universities is too technical or obscure to be of any value for popular use, or else, like advertising, it is manipulative. Are there ideas and methods of thinking that are specially suited for developing insights and strategies to challenge hierarchical systems? How can 'theory', thinking systematically, become a popular pastime rather than an elite pursuit?" The sociologist Charles Lemert (2004: 3) has in fact argued that "Everyone can do [theory]. Everyone should do more of it. Responsible lay members of society presumably would live better – with more power, perhaps more pleasure – if they could produce more social theories." We need to help ourselves and others understand the power – the critical and subversive power – of theory, and to help eliminate the idea of theory implied in such statements as "it's only (or merely) theory", "it's fine in theory, but not necessarily in reality", and the idea that somehow theories worth the label are groundless.

> Dialogue in any situation (whether it involves scientific and technical knowledge, or experiential knowledge) demands the problematic confrontation of that very knowledge in its unquestionable relationship with the concrete reality in which it is engendered, and on which it acts, in order to better understand, explain, and transform that reality. (Freire 1974: 111)

Paradigm for an Anarchist Theory of Education and Inquiry

Anarchists have always paid special attention to education. One reason for this is that education is a local arena of potential social change that we can work in while waiting and working for more general social changes. For the most part, what is taught in a given community's schools is not the knowledge or the ways of thought of "the unshackled and unprejudiced members" of the same community (Godwin [1793], in Woodcock, 1977: 266-277). The anarchist goal in education is to help keep minds alive. The path to this goal is not and cannot be paved with creeds or catechisms. Anarchists are opposed to any form of national education to the extent that it is allied with a national government's ideological agendas, a relationship that is more formidable and dangerous than the old alliance of church and state. At the same time, we do not want schools to be at the mercy of local school boards. What is to be done?

We teachers should not be so eager to educate that we forget the aims of education. Perhaps the easiest way to remove the barriers to education would be to set ourselves the task as educators of exciting ourselves and our students with the desire to know. If we can bring up this desire, then a good deal of what we do will not involve authoritative instruction but more often clearing paths for our students and for ourselves so that they and we can exercise and direct their and our desire to know. This would also blur the boundary between teacher/student and teaching/learning, and create an atmosphere more consistent with the social realities of what minds, thinking, and learning are as social constructions.

Classroom teachers do not have to be anarchists to realize that there is something wrong with schools. But they do not always have the cultural resources (including the power and authority) needed to challenge the status quo, to break the inertia of institutions. Let's not put the burden, then, on individual educators and students, or on particular classrooms but rather on school organization, on the very institution of education.

What does an anarchist theory of education have to offer the classroom teacher? Of course, we have our ideals and visions. Ideals and visions are very vulnerable to the charge that they are unrealistic and utopian. But social change cannot be carried forward if we allow ourselves to be turned away from our ideals and visions by appeals to our rationality and logic. This does not mean we should be guided by irrational and illogical standards. Let me explain under the guidance of Paul Goodman (1962).

First, we could introduce a few "no school" and "no school building" classes during the day, or during the week. Students would work in groups in or, in some cases, out of the school building on their own with or without specific directions, and with or without teachers present. The degree of "no school" would depend on a number of factors, including the age of the children, their social backgrounds, the character of the immediate school environment, and so on. Here the objective would be to take advantage of the community's streets, stores, museums, parks, factories, and churches and temples, including the public in action. Classicists will recognize this as the Athenian model of education, and social workers will see in it elements of the youth gang organized to pursue education and inquiry instead of delinquency.

Second, draw on the resources of unlicensed citizen-teachers in the community, from doctors and druggists to plumbers, mechanics, lawyers, and priests. They can work hand in hand with sympathetic licensed teachers. Third, attendance should be voluntary. There are many viable variations on this idea (see, for example, A.S. Neill's *Summerhill*). Fourth, decentralize large urban schools into storefronts, clubhouses, church basements, and even private homes. These units would be arenas of "play, socializing, discussion, and formal teaching." Bring back The Little Red Schoolhouse for short or longer term runs, combining age and grade groups in one relatively small building that can hold 20-30 students. Five, try to revitalize rural and factory culture by allowing groups of six to seven students to volunteer to observe and (if they desire) work on farms and in factories for a couple of days or a week or more. And six, provide for *moratoria* (as Eric Erickson has suggested) in people's educational and career lines.

My preference for anarchism is based on its capacity for decapitalizing the terms of thinking and reasoning without decapitating them. This is why anarchism is our best hope for giving free but disciplined rein to criticism, skepticism, and humor. The very idea of Truth forestalls the discovery of any truth (Nietzsche, 1968: 171). It is the name for "insane passions for the truth", passions that we can only break by laughing at truth and making truth laugh (Eco, 1983: 291). Logic and rationality are Gibraltars, but vulnerable to those of us who wish to go on living (Kafka, 1964: 286). I hold these views not because I am a "relativist" but because I appreciate the dialectical complexities of social structures. It is not all those good terms, such as truth, objectivity, logic, and science that I criticize but their cults and their cults' faith in those terms.

This is where the concept of anarchism as one of the modern sociological sciences (Kropotkin, 1970/1927: 191) becomes all important. When we talk about those good terms, we are always talking about social relations. Just as Marx claimed that a "human science" would flourish under communism, I claim that a "human inquiry" would flourish under anarchism. I make this claim as a social theorist, not as a utopian or post-modern dope.

Education must be voluntary. Intrinsic motivations are the key to greater freedom. This is good anarchist rhetoric, but it must be tempered and qualified by social theory. In particular, we must understand words like "voluntary" and "freedom" in a political sense. These are not spiritual, social, or philosophical realities, let alone absolutes, universals, or transcendental.

> Our aim must be to make a great number of citizens at home in a technological environment, not alienated from the machines we use, not ignorant as consumers who can somewhat judge government scientific policy, who can enjoy the humanistic beauty of the sciences, and above all, who can understand the morality of a scientific way of life. (Goodman 1962: 62).

In *The Grass Roots of Art* (1955), Herbert Read wrote about the place of art in society. Based on my claim that good art and good science are twin goods, I take the liberty here of substituting *scientist* for *artist* in Read's (in Woodcock, 1977: 279-286) description of children as artists.

Children are *scientists* in the same way that they are walkers, singers, talkers, and players of games. If, incidentally, children are artists, they are also theorists. For what is theory if not "The appreciation of good form, the perception of rhythm and harmony, the instinct to make things shapely and efficient..." Theorizing is an exercise in aesthetics. I would not claim, as Read does, that these characteristics are innately human; but we wouldn't be able to survive culturally or individually if we weren't capable of a social life that drew out these potentials. How, then, do we socialize, educate, program to bring out these characteristics of the artist/theorist? Here is how Read (in Woodcock, 1977: 283) puts it:

> The bad results [of education] are always produced by a method which is too conscious and deliberate, by a discipline which is imposed from without, which is the command of a drill-sergeant. The good results are produced apparently by no method at all, or by a system of hints and suggestions, and the discipline which undoubtedly exists and must exist, arises out of the activity itself, is in fact a kind of concentration on tools and materials, an absorption in concrete things.

This is another way of recognizing that good education, and additionally and integrally good science, good theory, and good art are promoted by an anarchist agenda. I would add too that the discipline Read remarks on arises out of an absorption in symbolic things, for symbolic things are just another type of concrete thing. I will return to the issue of mathematics and education in Chapter 8 from a different angle.

In the first five chapters I have drawn attention to the widespread impact of open systems and dialectical thinking, the research on creativity and innovation in organizations, and the dysfunctions of certain widespread forms of social organization and values that impact upon science. Open-systems thinking in general is a provocation for exploring the anarchist agenda as a sociological agenda. Against that background, I am now ready to focus more closely on anarchism and modern science.

Chapter 6
Anarchism and Modern Science

Prelude: Technoscience or Tyrannoscience Rex?

"Science Imitates Art Imitating Science." So goes the title for a box in a *Science* magazine Research News report on molecular paleontology (Morrell, 1992). Against the explicit backdrop of Michael Crichton's 1990 "sci-fi thriller", the real excitement of scientific discovery and the development of techniques for amplification of prehistoric DNA are dulled by the shadow of terror in the speculative fiction of *Jurassic Park*. The real connections between University of California entomologist George Poinar and Crichton are part of the novel, and part of the news report. The potential (fictional or not) reconstruction of organisms might be chilling to an imaginative reader: "So if a big green flesh-eater goes cruising past your bedroom window one of these dark nights, you'll know just who to blame: Michael Crichton and George Poinar."

But the potential for critique is "safely enclosed" in a box, just as the fictional characters assume their re-created dinosaurs will remain "safely enclosed" in their cages. And the questions of responsibility are, in the *Science* review, separated from the contexts of power and the cultural significations that drive research. Alan Grant, the paleontologist in Crichton's novel, is asked as the novel closes (with the animal cages open): "Please, señor, who is in charge?" He replies, "Nobody."

Dinosaurs, their evolutionary biology and paleontology, whether macroscopic or molecular, hold great fascination as teratological versions of human origin/ apocalypse myths. The dinosaur has served as a kitsch icon, an allegory of our history, and a disaster metaphor. The dinosaur might also be read like the cyborg (Glass, 1989); as a cultural transitional object, making a narrative space for multiple readings by a heterogeneous audience. These multiple readings do not, however, come together into a vision for social change. They serve, like Crichton's novel, as examples of speculative or science fiction (SF), "where possible worlds are constantly reinvented in the contest for very real, present worlds" (Haraway, 1989: 5). Like debates in primate studies, the debate in paleontology is about what has been, what is, and what might be. Jurassic Park conjures up a potential future and a science fiction lesson in the social relations of science.

The dinosaurs that roamed the earth 235 to 65 million years ago emerged without the help of human beings. In fact, humans would not come into the planetary picture until long after the age of the dinosaurs. Now, in Jurassic Park, the human dynamics of science, technology, money, and greed have given new meaning to the old zoological park and circus imperative of Bring Them Back Alive. The dinosaurs have been brought back alive and put on display in Jurassic Park. The

Dr. Frankenstein behind this Mesozoic Disney Land is John Hammond. Hammond is elderly, eccentric, very rich, and madly enthusiastic about dinosaurs. Under the auspices of his Hammond Foundation, and International Genetic Technologies, Inc., of Palo Alto, Hammond leases an island from the government of Costa Rica. The island is perpetually enshrouded in clouds; thus its name, Isla Nublar, Cloud Island. Hammond then brings together a team of scientists and advisors to exploit dinosaurs from Velociraptor mongoliensis to Tyrannosaurus rex. Hammond wants to provide the children of the world with a novel piece of education and entertainment. But his overriding intention, revealed to his chief bioengineer, Dr. Wu, is to make money – "A lot of money." Using science and technology "to help mankind" is a terrible idea, Hammond points out; it drags too many bothersome institutions and regulations into the picture. The idea, Hammond says, is to go after money free of government intervention – any government, anywhere.

Given the existence of the appropriate DNA and a cloning technique, Hammond thinks he can realize what he views as a simple idea. But he fails to reckon with the fact that butterflies are more powerful than millionaires, scientists, and even that greatest of land predators, T. rex. At least, mathematical butterflies are. A mathematical butterfly can stir the air in Brazil today by flapping its wings, and this can lead to a storm in Boston next month. This butterfly, the Butterfly Effect, has become the metaphor and image for the currently fashionable mathematics of fractals and chaos theory.

Crichton organizes his story into seven main "iterations", each one prefaced by the prophetic words of his character, mathematician Ian Malcolm. The story unfolds in correspondence with Malcolm's seven fractal phrases: from 1, "At the earliest drawings of the fractal curve, few clues to the underlying mathematical structure will be seen", to 4, "Inevitably, underlying instabilities will begin to appear", to the penultimate fractal nightmare, 6, "System recovery may prove impossible". Fractals – a way of seeing and studying shapes, dimensions, and geometry grounded in the claim that the degree of irregularity in an object remains constant over different viewing scales – were once described as monstrosities. And this is one of the reasons the fractal metaphor works here. For the dinosaurs of Jurassic Park are true monstrosities, living things out of their own time.

The Butterfly Effect in Jurassic Park begins with some little flaps on Cloud Island. As we proceed through the story at high-tech thriller speed, we follow the little flaps as they move toward more global effects. Dinosaurs escape their pens on the island and some people die. But almost from the first page, the reader is aware that the Butterfly Effect has already caused the beginnings of a storm beyond the island. In the end, we are left to speculate on just how big the storm will be and how far it will spread.

Crichton carries us along fractal step after fractal step through this tale of suspense, thrills, gore, and geometry with a prose that is as compelling and uncomplicated as the bite of the velociraptor. But this book is much more than a clever goulash of fashionable popularized science and technology and best-seller seasonings, just as the movie, however diluted its cautionary tale about science, is more than a record-setting summer thriller.

While a few reviewers and associates have remarked on the cautions about science in Jurassic Park, the movie and book are inadequate as science criticism. They illustrate, perhaps, like Robocop and other science fiction films, a genre in the politics of despair (Glass, 1989). Here we find consumerist criticism, kitsch (Montgomery, 1991), and recycled sentiment from prior generations of science horror films. These films presume a helplessness and a distance between those who might actually be able to do something, the scientist-expert-corporate agent and the viewer-citizen. The result is a critique of "bad science" or bad scientists rather than a critique of the system as technocratic and unresponsive. The "new bad future" films may result in lowered expectations and a resignation or passivity toward a future full of violence, corruption, and inhumanity. But "we cannot expect simplistic bourgeois closure on a narrative that cannot yet be closed" (Glass, 1989: 47-48). These science fiction futures are being contested now, in laboratories and marketplaces, and on a number of literal battlefields across the globe.

Modern science is, like all of the other institutions of contemporary (post) industrial societies, a social problem. Crichton captures the everyday minutiae of this still widely resisted social reality. But even Crichton is not immune to the myth of pure science. He seems to believe in a Golden Past, where pure scientists shunned business and money. This is what he tells us as narrator in an introduction that sets the documentary tone for the tale ahead. The Golden Past idea emerges again in the middle of the story's climax when the mathematician Ian Malcolm recalls the basic idea of science – an objective, rational view of reality that was new and appropriate 500 years ago. But science, like all forms of knowledge, is everywhere and always a product of and guardian of ruling powers and ideas. Jurassic Park is thus a story for all forms of science, not just modern science. There are lessons here not only for the scientists and engineers driven to do something because it can be done, but also for politicians and citizens. Jurassic Park may be in the Middle East, the Balkan republics, Bosnia; and it may be in your own back yard.

Anarchism and Modern Science

In this chapter, I explore the anarchist tradition as an alternative origin for the sociological perspective and the sociological theory of science. Even as an opposition, the anarchists have lacked the intellectual and academic power of the marxists in sociology and the sociology of science. I want to avoid a long dialogue with anarchists, anarchist traditions and schools, and the history of anarchism. I begin and end (but do not end absolutely) with Kropotkin's view of anarchism as one of the social sciences. I operate with a minimalist definition of the anarchist: the anarchist is the greatest champion of the integrity, primacy, and political autonomy of the person; the anarchist is the greatest foe of the state, of government, and of God; and the anarchist understands better than all other progressives and the opponents of progressives that humans are the most social of the animals, social always, already, and everywhere; social, rhythmic, musical, driven to imitate, belong, and communicate.

I begin with an observation on the relationship between anarchism and science made by the sociologist Irving Louis Horowitz in the early 1960s. He argued that in modern society, the polarization of social life (individual spontaneity and risk taking versus collective responses in line and staff organizations driven by values of order and precision) has provided a context for two converging social roles: the intellectual, "anti-political by social training and personal habit"; and the anarchist, "anti-political by intellectual conviction". Anarchism's efforts to remain grounded in the methods of science have, according to Horowitz, put it on a track of convergence with general trends in late twentieth century intellectual activity.

What, then, is the role of science in the anarchist tradition, and what are the anarchists' contributions to the social theory of science? This book is an episode in a continuing effort to link progressive social theory and the social process of inquiry. It is thus a contribution to my efforts over many years to develop and defend a critical, normative, emancipatory sociology of objective inquiry. More specifically, my goal here is to bring together materials that collectively argue for anarchy as the preferred form of life, social organization, and value system for facilitating inquiry in general and socially and politically progressive inquiry in particular.

Peter Kropotkin (1842-1921) recognized the "eminently social" quality of intellect. The intellect is social, he argued, because it is a product of communication. Kropotkin might be considered scientistic given his seemingly uncritical commitment to science and to applying science to the study of society. In *Mutual Aid*, he related his doctrines to (and in the process modified) evolutionary theory. And he argued for the construction of a political economy modeled on the natural sciences. More generally, his project as a revolutionary anarchist trained and expert in the physical and natural sciences was to establish anarchism on a scientific foundation. As we explore Kropotkin's views, it is important to keep in mind that while the charge of "scientism" is not out of place, his view of the laws of nature suggest a more open and dynamic, even Bohmian, understanding of science (Kropotkin, 1908: 74-80; cf. de Acosta, 2009: 33-34).

In the context of the rejection of transcendence, immanence, and psychologism it is important to note Kropotkin's efforts to eliminate metaphysics as a mode of inquiry. We must consider that since he views society as something that is neither complete nor rigid, he must view science in this same way, "ever striving for new forms, and even changing these forms in accordance with the needs of the time". As scientists, he tells us, we are not engaged in a world of Laws and fatalistic constraints. If gravity "compels" bodies to fall, it also "compels" balloons to rise.

Kropotkin was an authority on geodetic mathematics and Siberian geography, and he brought a commitment to scientific methods to his struggle for mutual aid and individual liberty. Anarchism has a universal relevance that embraces all of nature and is grounded in an explanatory framework that is mechanical at worst and materialist at best. Everything in nature, including human societies and their economies, polities, and moral orders, must be subjected to and understood in terms of the methods of the physical and natural sciences. Every conclusion must be verified in the manner common to these sciences.

By "scientific method", Kropotkin understood "the inductive method of natural sciences". And he understood "natural law" to mean that under certain natural conditions certain things will follow. Kropotkin's brand of anarchism was one of many attempts in the nineteenth century to construct a "science of society" (for example, in the works of Comte, Durkheim, and Marx). Anarchism is for Kropotkin, then, an attempt to apply the inductive method of the sciences to the study of human society. Moreover, this would provide a basis for predicting the future as we march on the road to liberty with the objective of improving the level of happiness to the highest point possible for every social unit.

Kropotkin was concerned with bringing the social and humanitarian sciences under the umbrella of the scientific method. He had some appreciation for the limitations of using natural scientists as role models for anarchists. Most men of science, he claimed, come from and share the prejudices of the propertied classes or else serve these classes and their governments. But he did not consider that the relationship between science and the state might be so intimate that there could be no convergence between science and anarchism. Consider, for example, Kropotkin's claim that the State and capitalism are inseparable. This implies that all institutions – for example, the justice system, the church, and the army – are state institutions. The State is in fact a mutual insurance society for landlords, warriors, judges, and priests, grounding the social order in which these representatives of the State assert and implement their authority and exploit the laboring classes.

Kropotkin might well have added state-science to his list of the basic ingredients of the State. And to the list that includes the landlord, warrior, judge, and priest, he might well have added "the scientist and the scholar". These omissions may reflect the fact that the institution of science was still in the early stages of its development and not yet as powerful an overt contributor to state power as it would become by the middle of the twentieth century. Still, a hegemonic ideology of science based on the successes of the mechanistic Newtonian sciences was already infiltrating the emerging social sciences, including Marxism and anarchism.

At the same time that the social sciences were being modeled by the social practices, ideologies, and mythologies of the natural sciences, they were paving the way for a social theory of science. Thus both Kropotkin and Karl Marx recognized that science was the social product of a social process, Max Weber had an excellent understanding of the cultural context of science and the roles of material resources and social processes in the development of science, and Emile Durkheim actually pioneered a sociology of the intellect. The tension caused by simultaneously conceiving science as the paradigmatic mode of inquiry and as social relations produced an ambivalence about science, especially among marxists (discussed at length in the writings of the sociologist Stanley Aronowitz, 1988) and anarchists.

The ambivalence about science in the anarchist tradition is nowhere more explicit than in the writings of Michael Bakunin (1814-1876). He preached the revolt of life against not science *per se* but rather against the government of science. His goal was not to destroy science, a treasonous act against humanity, but rather to settle it where it belonged at the top of the pantheon of reasoned modes of human thought. Further evidence of Bakunin's ambivalence is revealed in his opposition to what he understood to be the perils of a Marxist state. The danger was the development of science and the placing of scientific intelligence at the center of the State. He considered science (state-science in Kropotkin's terms) to be a despotic and arrogant regime, scornful and aristocratic. It promised a new class system, an ignorant population ruled by a scientifically driven minority.

And yet, liberty can be grounded in and only grounded in a reasoned relationship to natural laws without any possibility of rebelling against the law of two plus two equals four and its kin. He echoed Pierre Proudhon who argued that social order must be grounded in science (which unified all of humanity), not in religion or authority. For these anarchists science on an ever expanding scale was the foundation of liberty. But this is not an easy relationship, and Bakunin is suspicious of the socialists who arrive at their convictions only by way of science and thinking. This is the same anarchist who is clear about his intention not to underestimate science and thinking as the guiding tracks of human progress and prosperity. Suspicions linger because science gives off a cold light that leads to sterile and powerless truths. Science can only be trusted when it rests upon the truth of life. In our own era, George Woodcock represents the view that anarchism is more detached from profit and power than any other intellectual current and is thus by definition in the position of offering the most objective view of humans in the context of nature.

There is more to the anarchists' commitment to science, ambivalence notwithstanding, than simple Newtonian confidence. Modern science was viewed as having discarded the God hypothesis. God and the State stand together as the major symbols and sources of the Authority universally opposed by the anarchists. At the same time, the religious fervor characteristic of at least some anarchists should not be ignored. Thus in some cases anarchism might be best viewed as a religious transform with science or the anarchist community as a new god.

In general, the commitment to a natural science model for politics, political economy, and morals outweighs ambivalence about science among the anarchists, and to such a degree that it is reasonable to characterize anarchists as men and women of science. But ambivalence is not the whole story about science and the anarchists. Nikolai Berdyaev (1874-1948), for example, radically separated the anarchists' concern with the primacy of the person from the scientific method and its real objects of inquiry. The world of science, objectivization, and determinism is a world of alienation, hostility and law. The world of personality is, for Berdyaev, a separate world of spirituality, freedom, love, and kinship.

Modern anarchists continue to express ambivalence about science. Paul Goodman, Herbert Read, and Alex Comfort followed Kropotkin in insisting on scientific observation. But Goodman also associated modern scientific research with the markup of drug prices. Others cautioned anarchists not to dismiss the principle of the science-government-morality nexus announced by Gandhi. Gandhi pointed to the need to examine the lack of responsibility associated with science in the West. We fill, he claimed, the minds of our young with the fantasies, the nonsense, of science and technology without preparing them for their unintended consequences which we encounter too late.

Anarchists in the tradition of Gandhi (1869-1948) and Thoreau (1817-1862) have argued that we need to slow technological and scientific progress, otherwise industrialization will become our only option as a way of life. Thoreau's stand on the effort to connect Maine and Texas by magnetic telegraph is typical of this view. Perhaps, he mused, Texas and Maine have nothing important to share. Communication should not, he urged, be indiscriminately promoted. The police, the industrialists, and the diplomats will, in the end, control the lines of communication linking Texas and Maine. Is this what we would now call an example of trying to implement the precautionary principle? Or is it a know-nothing or conspiracy theory philosophy that is at work here? These questions can be raised again in the case of Tolstoy (1828-1910) who wrote that the intellectual class had traded food for things useful to intellectuals, to science and art, but completely useless to those who labor to produce the goods and services that support the activities of this thinking class. Our duty, Tolstoy argued, is to serve the laboring classes not to study and describe them. This is, of course, considered a dangerously unscientific form of anarchism by those anarchists who have a more favorable view of the role of the thinking classes. The ambivalence about science in the anarchist tradition is reflected on a larger scale in the debates about the cultural meaning of science. This is the focus of the following section.

The Cultural Meaning of Science: Daedalus and Icarus

The cultural meaning of modern science has always been an issue. From Rousseau to Roszak there have been science watchers who saw danger and alienation where others, from Bacon to Bronowski saw civilization and progress.

In 1923, the biochemist J.B.S. Haldane published an essay titled *Daedalus, or Science and the Future*. Haldane painted a glowing portrait of a future society created by applying science to the problem of promoting human happiness. Bertrand Russell replied to Haldane in an essay titled *Icarus, or the Future of Science*. Russell wrote that much as he would like to agree with Haldane's forecast, his experience with statesmen and governments forced him to predict that science would be used to promote power and privilege rather than to improve the human condition. Daedalus taught his son Icarus to fly, but warned him not to stray too close to the sun. Icarus ignored the warning and plunged to his death. Russell warned that a similar fate awaited those whom modern scientists had taught to fly.

Modern science has been described as a machine-like product of our matter-of-fact industrial and technological era, an instrument of terror, an assault on the natural world, and a tool of greed, war, and violence by some of our most prominent social critics. C. Wright Mill's conception of the transformation of science into a Science Machine echoed Marx's critique of modern science as alienated, bourgeois science. And nowhere is this association more strongly asserted than among certain contemporary Third World scholars and intellectuals who argue that violence lies at the very core of the worldview of modern science. This must sound like madness to scientists and science lovers. The idea that science "works" and a "science fix" orientation have been founded on and enhanced by a runaway technological growth masquerading as "progress". In an exuberant (and restricted) atmosphere of material plenty, uncritical admirers of science have been seduced by icons, myths, and ideologies. But in the light of a new awareness and understanding of science as a cultural phenomenon, and of scientific knowledge as a social construction, a rationale for heresy has emerged.

The foundation of the scientific revolution was a society built by, in the words of historian William McNeill, pugnacious, reckless, and militaristic Europeans. The scientific revolution itself integrated the natural world and the political world. It is no great leap once these facts are understood to see that modern science emerged and developed as an alienating and alienated mode of inquiry, the mental framework of capitalism and the mode of knowing of industrial society. Capital accumulation and industrial products and processes became prominent features of social life and the primary factors in shaping our ways of thought, our science.

Modern science (including scientists and images and symbols of science) came into the world as a commodity and has developed in close association with the discipline of the machine. It should not seem too heretical now to claim for scientific action what Bourdieu and Passeron claim for pedagogic action, that it is symbolic violence, a consequence of the impositions by an arbitrary power of arbitrary cultural formations. And what else is the myth of pure science but a prime example of symbolic violence, a power that imposes meanings, gives them legitimacy, and yet hides the power that is the basis of its actions and the force of its reason.

Pure Science?

The basic modes of pure science, pure contemplation and knowledge for its own sake, are increasingly difficult to sustain in the light of developments in sociology, the sociology of science, and postmodern political economy. The strong sociological dimension in contemporary science studies is not merely a matter of disciplinary politics, but part of a Copernican revolution in the social sciences and in intellectual life in general. I introduced this idea in Chapter 3. This revolution, rooted in the works of such social theorists as Godwin, Marx, Weber, Martineau, Durkheim, Kropotkin, Bakunun, Neitzsche, Spengler, Gumplowicz,

Emma Goldman, Fleck, and Mead has shifted the individual from the center of the social universe and replaced it with the collectivity. Durkheim, for example, argued that social conditions penetrate to the very core of the thinking process itself. Gumplowicz expressed this argument in a particularly strong form, claiming that it is the social community that actually thinks, not the individual. The source of thinking is in the social environment, an ever present influence that structures the mind of the thinker so that s/he can only think in one (however complex and diversified) way. The complexity and diversity of one's thoughts will vary with the complexity and diversity of the social environment. As we learn more about the plasticity of the brain, it becomes increasingly evident empirically and conjecturally that the brain itself is socially constructed. I will have more to say about the sociology of mind and brain in later chapters.

Building on the ideas about collective representations and collective elaborations developed by Durkheim, Gumplowicz and others, Fleck introduced the concepts "thought collective" and "thought style" in a pioneering study of the genesis and development of the concept of syphilis and the procedure known as the Wasserman reaction. Thought collectives are communities of individuals engaged in the mutual exchange of ideas and sustained intellectual intercourse. These exchanges and interactions carry fields of thought and stocks of knowledge within a certain level of cultural development, giving rise to an historically and culturally grounded thought style.

Earlier, Marx had already understood that the self is a social structure and that this implied that scientific thinking itself was a social phenomenon. He was one of the first social thinkers to fully recognize the radical socialness of the self, mind and consciousness, language, and thought.

The empirically and in particular ethnographically grounded sociology of science that emerged in the 1970s has given substance to the foregoing ideas. Sociologists of science have actually studied thinking as a social process in the scientific laboratory using ethnographic methods. As the various threads of the sociology of science and knowledge become linked, the conception of self and mind as social structures becomes more substantial. As this revolution continues, it will build on Durkheimian views of "individual" and "community", and recondition our ideas about the nature of liberty and freedom. This worldview shift does not support the subordination of individuals to communities or societies, or to the collective power of church, state, or military. Rather, it provides a sturdier foundation for understanding and realizing the value of the person and the ecological and community bases for individual liberty and freedom, and the social conditions for creativity.

The origins of established sociology in the works and lives of apologists for and ideologists of industrial society and the Christian west such as Saint Simon and Auguste Comte may account for and reflect a collectivist orientation to social order. The preeminence of "society", "social structure", "culture", and "social role" in this context is based on their roles as stand-ins for the power and legitimacy of those persons who are collectively the state. But there is an alternative sociology that developed in the works of the anarchists. Drawing on this tradition sustains the worldview shift that gives us a social theory of self and mind, but grounds that shift in assumptions about the value of individual liberty and the need to resist all forms of unbridled Authority. It will also become easier to understand the significance of cooperation and nonviolence for survival and growth in individuals and societies through the vehicle of what I call "anarcho-sociology".

The fact that there are individual scientists apparently driven by the "higher motives" (curiosity, for example) does not mean that their social roles are not serving social interests. And we do not have to deny that individual scientists may be motivated by a desire to "understand" the world "objectively" in order to see the social functions of labeling scientific work "pure" or "objective". The labels "pure" or "basic", for example, can be used to demonstrate or symbolize a nation's capacity for research or its potential for generating "fundamental" discoveries that may find applications in various areas of social life.

The Sociology of Science

I showed earlier how the labels "pure" and "objective" can call attention to and defend the autonomy, solidarity, and professionalism of scientists seeking access to scarce societal resources and independence from external social controls. I also pointed out that a certain amount of trained incompetence is necessary to shield scientists from their latent social roles. The social contexts and social problems of modern science are marked by key icons of science: Archimedes drawing pretty figures in the dust, Newton searching for shapely pebbles at the beach, Einstein riding light beams in his mind, and Hawking coming close to realizing the Platonic dream of pure intellect connected directly to or become one with the world of spirit. The myth of pure science is a cornerstone of modern science as a house of worship. What realities lie behind the icons?

Let's consider how sociologists think about the relationship between individual motives and social structures. One of the most significant moments in the history of science as an exercise in sociological realism was the Marxist claim that Newton's *Principia* was rooted in the social and economic issues of his time and not a simple product of pure intellectual motives. There were, of course, defenders of the purity of science and of the portrait of Newton as a saintly scientist who came to his defense. From a sociological perspective, however, it is crucial to distinguish personal attitudes and motives from social roles. It is in fact readily demonstrated that the social structure of seventeenth-century England determined the basic themes of science during that period. It is also important in this context to question the idea that science and technology were almost completely divorced in the seventeenth century. If this were true, then we could demarcate "science" and "technology" and blame technology rather than science for our social and environmental ills. But science and technology have never been so separated except in the ideologies of science and technology.

Consider, following Robert K. Merton's analysis, that Newton's astronomical observations were based on Flamsteed's work at the Greenwich Observatory. The observatory was built by order of Charles II to support the Royal Navy. Moreover, Newton was strongly influenced by some of the most practically oriented scientists of his time (e.g., Halley, Hooke, Wren, Huyghens, and Boyle). Any conjecture about pure motives must be measured against the fact that many of the scientists of this period were explicitly aware of the practical roots and implications of their research. It was more the rule than the exception to find the most notable scientists of this period at some point and with respect to some of their research working on practical problems.

Archimedes, like Newton, played down his role in practical affairs; at least that is the report we get from Plutarch. According to Plutarch, writing nearly 300 years after Archimedes' death, Archimedes was completely immersed in issues of beauty and subtlety uncontaminated by the common problems of everyday life. Indeed, Archimedes appears to have written only one "mechanical" treatise, *On Sphere Making*. In order to challenge Plutarch's views and those of some historians of Greek science, we would have to equate "mechanical" with "construction" yet somehow save "pure" contemplation. But Archimedes deals with many practical matters including the calendar, optics, centers of gravity, balances, and levers. The fact that he was a great inventor, and that some of his inventions were designed for political and military purposes, cannot be ignored as "incidental". It is unreasonable to suppose that Archimedes could completely detach his mechanical interests and talents from his interests and talents in so-called pure mathematics. The coexistence of these talents and interests, amply documented, is sufficient grounds for arguing that Archimedes' mathematics was not a product of "pure contemplation". In his book *Method*, discovered in 1906, Archimedes outlines the mechanical bases of his formal ("pure") geometric proofs. His tendency to suppress or separate the "vulgar" roots of the results he presented in a logical format for public consumption is not an unusual strategy in the history of mathematics. Biography may offer some clues to this strategy. Archimedes was the son of an astronomer (Pheidias), and an intimate (perhaps even relative) of King Hieron. His *achieved* social position, at least, and the fact that he was in a position to generalize the generalizations of earlier mathematical workers, and then generalize his own generalizations (thus producing relatively high levels of "abstraction"), could easily have lead admiring biographers (ulterior motives aside) to emphasize that his inquires were not prompted by "vulgar" considerations. And whatever Archimedes' motives in any particular situation, they cannot alter the fact of his relationship to the political and military authorities of his city, a relationship that tells us something about the ties between knowledge and power.

The case of Albert Einstein, the most prominent icon in twentieth-century science, is more complicated than the cases of Archimedes and Newton with respect to the relationship between individual motives and social roles. Einstein worked in an era of professionalized science. Twentieth-century science is more highly professionalized and bureaucratized than earlier forms of science or inquiry. I have been using the word "science" rather loosely when referring to pre-nineteenth century philosophers and natural philosophers; the terms science and scientist are late nineteenth-century inventions. Whewell introduced the term "scientist" in 1833 and this term fed back in time to give "science" its modern sense. In the era of professionalized science it is easier for individual scientists to work in apparent dissociation from the practical concerns of everyday life and vulgar political economic interests because they are shielded by complex institutional relationships. It is therefore crucial to examine the scientific community's relationship to the wider society, and to the state, in order to understand the social role of any individual scientist.

Einstein's activities illustrate how the scientific community – through its own internal social structure and its ties to state interests – can protect and provide for its members, and even provide niches within which one can engage in the sort of so-called private thinking sometimes labeled "pure contemplation". Einstein said that he was at one with Schopenhauer in believing that "men" are motivated to go into the sciences and the arts in order to escape the crude hopeless dreariness of everyday life and the burden of their desires and emotions.

But Einstein's social role – and more generally the relationship between science and society – is revealed in the public relations of Albert Einstein. There is no need to impugn Einstein's motives or his humanitarian spirit to recognize that there is something sinister in all of those photographs showing Einstein posing with kings, queens, prime ministers and presidents. The shadow of Adolf Hitler that darkens these photographs should not lead us to make the mistake of viewing the states represented in them as benevolent; it should not keep us from seeing that what is sinister about these photographs is not what they tell us about Einstein and King Albert or Einstein and President Harding, but rather what they tell us about science and the state. One can see similar symbols of the relationship between state and science in the life of Stephen Hawking; meeting with President Obama in the Blue Room and presented with the Presidential Medal of Freedom; being awarded the Order of the British Empire; and becoming linked to popular cultural icons through appearances on, for example, *Star Trek: The Next Generation, The Simpsons*, and the TV series *Dark Angel*. I don't want to make of these connections and relationships that they reveal some dark, conspiratorial connections to the Evil One. My point is that there is meaning to be found in the relationships – however superficially benign – between icons of science, the state, and the public. Let me pursue this further by turning to a brief exploration of the more general relationships between so-called "pure" science and society.

The iconography of science is rooted in the myth of pure science. The idea that pure science is a purely intellectual or cognitive creation untouched by social facts has been undermined if not yet demolished by sociologists and social theorists from Durkheim and Fleck to contemporary researchers in science studies. How, then, are we to understand what it is that pure science – so often personified in Archimedes, Newton, Einstein, and Hawking ("…in my mind I am free") –

represents? Let us consider this question in terms of the purest of the pure sciences, pure mathematics.

Pure mathematics is the activity of doing mathematics because one is interested in the mathematics-in-itself, not as a tool for pursuing other interests or as a tool for solving problems outside of mathematics *per se*. The word "interests" here already begins to shift our focus from the experience of the individual mathematician to the politics of pure mathematics. In his *A Mathematician's Apology*, G.H. Hardy (1940) famously wrote that he'd never done anything useful or contributed in any way, for good or ill, to humanity. The noted chemist Soddy considered Hardy's views scandalous. The world is sickened, he said, by such "cloistered clowning". But Hardy's statement must be measured against for example the importance to humanity of Hardy's Law which applies to the study of Ph-blood groups and the treatment of hemolytic disease in newborns. His work on Reimann's zeta function, for another example, has been used in studying furnace temperatures. Hardy's radical defense of purity must be understood as an intellectual strategy. The fact is that Hardy hated war and the application of mathematics to problems in ballistics and aerodynamics. Thus, one aspect of the politics of pure mathematics is that it is an intellectual strategy for responding to and distancing oneself from social problems, issues, and conflicts.

Within mathematics, the argument that there is a politics of pure mathematics is supported by the perennial rift between pure and applied mathematicians on university faculties. Peano's conflicts with Volterra and other members of the mathematics faculty at the University of Turin are one example of this rift from the early history of professionalized mathematics. The social dynamics of contemporary mathematics are often revealed in these conflicts, which reflect disagreements about how mathematical knowledge should be used and struggles for scarce resources within the university system and in the larger funding arena.

Because of its generality, pure mathematics plays an important role in establishing the purity of scientific disciplines. One of the few political leaders to acknowledge the political function of pure mathematics was the mathematically inclined Napoleon I, who recognized the relationship between mathematical progress and national prosperity.

Purism, then, is an intellectual strategy that has multiple roots and functions. As a political strategy, it can demarcate and defend the pursuit of knowledge from military, economic, and political interests one is opposed to; it can be used by ruling elites to establish territorial claims indirectly; and it can help political leaders maintain control over creative and innovative researchers – pure scientists are granted "academic freedom" so long as what they do keeps them from becoming active critics of government and from actively interfering with their government's efforts to put their discoveries and inventions to use in the interests of military, economic, or political advances.

Religion and science are often mated in psychological purism and its variations. This is especially the case in mathematics and mathematized sciences. Consistency and completeness, hallmarks of pure mathematics, are central features of the Holy. Pure mathematics and religion were, for example, closely linked in the lives and works of George Boole and W.R. Hamilton. The religious imperative is widely recognized as a feature of early modern science, but its manifestations in contemporary mathematics is not so apparent. Gauss still held to an idea common to his peers and predecessors, that pure science exposes the immortal nucleus of the human soul. Already with Gauss, however, we find a transition from worship of God to worship of Nature as the object of human reason. Gauss still believed in an eternal, just, omniscient, omnipresent God. He was always trying to harmonize mathematical principles with his meditations on the future of the human soul. Cantor believed in the Platonic reality of infinite sets because their reality had, he claimed, been revealed to him by God. And Bourbaki (the pseudonym for an influential group of early twentieth-century mathematicians) claimed mathematical problems evoke aesthetic and religious emotions.

The development of pure mathematics can be portrayed in one of its aspects as a transition from an orientation to and a belief in God, to an orientation to and belief in Nature and then Logic (recall Brouwer's analysis of the reification of logic discussed earlier).

The association of modern science with the discipline of the machine (an extension and intensification of the traditional relationship between science and technology) makes any easy assumptions or assertions about modern science as a force for social progress unwarranted. For the very signs we take to mark material or technological process, whether in weaponry or medicine, are often indicators of social problems. This helps to explain the highly critical judgements some scientists and science observers have leveled at science. G.H. Hardy, as we saw earlier, defended pure mathematics as strongly as he did as a way of drawing attention to and resisting the fact, as he saw it, that the perceived utility of a science is a function of its capacity for increasing inequality and promoting the destruction of life.

Hardy wrote his apology in 1940. J.D. Bernal, as we saw earlier, did not see the signs of progress others saw. More recently, writers such as Theodore Roszak, Morris Berman, Eugene Schwartz, and David Dickson have echoed Hardy and Bernal in their criticisms of science as a worldview and a way of life. The common message of these observers is that the association of science with profits, war, and the rape of nature is driving humanity and its planet toward destruction. Indeed, the association of modern science, violence, and warfare has ancient roots. From its origins in the ancient world, science has been linked to military power and military goals and interests. The modern era has witnessed an escalation in this relationship or conjunction, and two world wars have created a foundation on which to develop and apply advanced science and technology to weapons of mass destruction. It is hard not to conclude that the preeminence of science in the world's societies has been in great part due to its contributions as a confederate of technology to contribute to the development of military systems. Feminist theorists such as Carolyn Merchant, Evelyn Fox Keller, Sandra Harding, and Elizabeth Fee have added a new dimension to the critique of modern science by linking it to issues of gender and power. They have not strayed far from what are easily recognized as anarchist agendas.

Gender, Science, and Anarchism

In the post-1970 era of science studies science as a social institution and social construction has been linked to gender, race, and class. Most of the research in this area has focused on gender, in great part because of the contextually driven strengths of feminist science studies. Some feminists have argued that equity issues might require the elimination of sexism, racism, and classism altogether. More realistically, some feminists argue that it is important to keep our eyes on the target, the masculinities of science, and to continue to pursue the goal of de-sexing and de-gendering science. Others want to create a "successor science". And of course many of those feminists originally trained and educated in the sciences are trying to stay clear of relativism and maintain some version of the science they lived and learned to love. Is it possible to get rid of the "bad" (masculine) parts of science and retain what's left? Amidst all these and other positions and arguments among the feminists in science studies, there is a fairly clear imperative to move the agenda in the direction of new ways of knowing and new forms of inquiry.

The contest between the extremes of masculine objectivities and feminist "relativisms" can be resolved, perhaps, by a commitment to constructing best or better accounts of the world. Anarchism in the traditions of Kropotkin and Goldman is compatible with this view of things by virtue of its commitment to doing away with wrong and foolish things. Anarchism, like Marxism, socialism, and feminism does not give us a neutral, detached science. Science in an anarchist social order, or anarcho-science, gives us an explicit moral order, a form of life, a worldview; that is, it offers us a best or better way to live our lives critically, realistically, and humanely.

The Problem of Rationality

To be rational can mean to have the faculty of reasoning, or to be endowed with reason. This notion can be coupled, as it was in fourteenth century Europe, to the idea of exercising or being able to exercise one's reason properly. In other words, to be rational can mean and has meant to have sound judgment, to be sensible and sane. Rational was deployed against empirical. Two classes of ancient physicians were opposed here. The rational physicians relied on deduction, observation, and experiment rather than "theory". The empirical physicians were pragmatists; they adopted a practice if it worked, whether they understood why or not. Later, unscientific physicians or quacks were painted with the label empirical or better empiricist.

As an organized scientific community began to emerge in seventeenth century Europe, the idea of being rational retained many of its traditional associations with the reasonable and sane life. The more we explore the lexicography of "rational" the more it becomes apparent – certainly to the sociological eye – that we are dealing with community standards. Again and again we encounter words such as "proper", "sound", "sensible", "sane", "acceptability", and "orderly". Once we associate the state of being rational with community standards, we can expose the source of recurring arguments for and against rationality as conflicts between competing community standards, that is, conflicts between communities defending different moral orders. There is a labeling dimension in these conflicts. To be rational is to be superior, to have a privileged status or position, and to justify one's or a group's right or power to define what is proper, sound, sensible, and sane. The "Rational" Christians, for example, claimed that their standards of rationality were superior to those of other Christians. It should be clear by now even from this brief and general overview that to be rational does not have the same sense as to be scientific, at least if we do not dig too deeply here (recall the idea of objectivity communities). Every community and sub-community establishes what is to count as reasonable and sane behavior and labels these "rational". This helps account for the adjectivization of rationality that gives us scientific rationality, legal rationality, theological rationality, and so on. There are overlapping communities of rationality. Demarcationists who wish to establish scientific rationality as somehow superior to other forms of rationality must claim it as the only truly or really rational mode of thought and knowing. I will have more to say about the issues discussed here later on. For the moment, it is enough to begin to associate standards of rationality with cultural standards.

In this chapter I have explored the sociology of science and mathematics while at the same time unfolding key ingredients of anarchist thinking. I have also continued to stress the idea of social construction. It is important to keep returning to this problem because one of my objectives is to demonstrate that the more we learn about science as a practice the more apparent it becomes that this practice is best characterized in terms of the principles of anarchism. My plan here is to have the anarchist idea emerge out of the evolving narrative that is this book. But it will help the reader to have some guidelines concerning what to expect "at the end".

It is imperative that anarchists and non-anarchists alike keep firmly in mind that I follow Peter Kropotkin's conception of anarchism as one of the sociological sciences. Here then is an initial schematic of the anarchist agenda (acknowledging that I have benefitted from a wide reading in the anarchist literature for this particular adaptation).

The Anarchist Agenda

The zeroth order condition for implementing an anarchist agenda is a robust universal system of education designed for critical and creative thinking.

1. Focus on understanding and improving the nexus of human and ecological contexts in the interest of human survival with dignity and integrity.
2. Theorize the self, personhood, as a social structure, community dependent and inter-connected.
3. Promote diversity in selves and communities.
4. Transform bureaucracies into worker organized and operated organizations.
5. Strengthen popular involvement in and control over mass media.
6. Demarchy: local networks of volunteer based functional groups, dealing with various community functions including education.
7. Anarcha-feminism: bringing the anarchist movement to bear on male domination and the oppression and suppression of women.
8. Intersectional anarchism: bringing the anarchist movement to bear on all forms of oppression and suppression.
9. Search for and implement alternatives to state-market political economies.
10. Develop networking into a strategy for social action.
11. Challenge taken-for-granted ideas about material and intellectual property, and promote non-ownership and collective usage; the rejection of propertyism, consumerism, and commodification.
12. Facilitate organized nonviolent action in and by communities.
13. Promote science and technology for the people, alternative technosciences, science and technology (technoscience) shops.
14. Nourish theory as a subversive activity.
15. Intellectually and theoretically, reject transcendence, immanence, and psychologism.
16. The complexity of the world requires that anarchists avoid becoming enclavists, and instead work in consort with other activists for social change to the extent that this is possible. Do not shy away from the reality that you cannot work in consort with Nazis or religious dopes.
17. The anarchist tool kit should be part of a larger variegated toolkit of strategies, skills, tactics, and technologies for social change.
18. Anarchists should practice heterodox borrowing of ideas, perspectives, strategies, theories, and technologies.
19. Anarchists should avoid drama and dogma in theory and practice.
20. Promote anarchism as a form of life.

The big question here is how to organize the world community. The answer is not to aim at organizing the world community, but rather to focus on local communities and agendas. One of the common features of the progressive traditions in this respect is the reliance on decentralized federations. We start by organizing local councils, cooperatives, or assemblies. At the regional level we organize a federation of the local communal entities, and at the world level we organize a federation of the regional entities; in the end, our aim is to organize a federation of communes of different scale (Schwitzbuëbel, 1908, in Guérin, 2005: 235; de Acosta, 2009: 33; Restivo, 1991: 186-196). In the next section I consider two perspectives on science that contribute to the anarcho-science worldview.

Nietzsche and Feyerabend: Preludes to Anarchy and Inquiry

I take a backward step in this chapter, to my original concern with science and the anarchist tradition. I bring together two profound students of inquiry in whom I find important anarchistic commonalities. By bringing Nietzsche and Feyerabend into the picture at this point, I make the original portrait more complete but at the same time press forward to some constructive comments about the anarchistic perspective on inquiry. Why Nietzsche and Feyerabend? Simply put, I learned profound lessons about inquiry from these two philosophers. And I learned as much too about interrogative honesty and courage.

Nietzsche was, to put it mildly, not fond of the anarchists. But his opposition to the state and his defense of the individual, the "single one", make him an anarchist in the sense I intend in this book. Nietzsche criticizes modern science as a reflection of the same motives underlying religion, in particular Christianity, even through modern science has helped to "kill" – anthropologize – God. Nietzsche's critique is balanced by a defense of a demystified science, and furthermore of an alternative "joyous wisdom".

Science, Nietzsche argues, has been promoted owing to three errors. The Newtons promoted it as a means to understanding the goodness and wisdom of God – the first error. The Voltaires pursued it out of a belief in its absolute utility and its intimate association with morality and happiness – the second error. And the Spinozas because they believed that evil impulses play no part in science – the third error (Neitzsche, 1887/1974: 105-106). Explanations are suspect because we begin by transforming the objects of our inquiries into images of our selves. Explanations thus turn out on close examination to be descriptions – and it is our descriptions that have improved, not our explanations where we do no better than our predecessors (Nietzsche, 1887/1974: 172). I think it is fair to read this notion of explanations (especially in the light of Nietzsche's other writings on science) as in line with Kropotkin and Marx on the social construction of knowledge.

Speaking philosophically, our faith in science is ultimately a metaphysical faith. In his philosophy and in his life, Nietzsche demonstrates how difficult it is to escape the faith in something Christian, something Platonic, some truth in Godhead, some divine truth. It takes a leap of faith to consider that all of this – Christianity, Platonism, religion, God itself – could become increasingly incredible. Everything divine an error, a mistake caused by blindness, a lie; and then, God, what? The lie that has endured and been nourished even by the most skeptical minds? Science is dangerous to the extent that it is pursued with a passion for certainty, and in ways that strip life of its ambiguities and reduce it to calculations and mathematical diversions. To count, calculate, weigh, see, and touch, and to do nothing more brings us to the edge of mental illness and opens up a world for idiots. What Nietzsche is concerned with in using this kind of language when cautioning us about science is that it might be revealing only the most superficial and external features of our lives, of our experiences. Could it then be giving us the "most stupid" of all the ways we might interpret these lives and experiences?

The alternative to science, in particular modern science as a Science Machine, is joyous wisdom. The emphasis here is on *thinking* – and thinking for Nietzsche is grounded in inclinations that are "strong", "evil", "defiant", "nasty", and "malicious". We do not succeed or fail in our experiments; we only get answers. Thus, in order to find pleasure in wisdom, we must be capable of finding pleasure in folly – the *hero* and the *fool* must be discovered in our passionate pursuit of knowledge. I see this as a way to escape metaphysics and faith.

Nature confronts us with *necessities*, not *laws* – no one commands, no one obeys, and no one trespasses. We should value mathematics, for example, because it helps us to learn about ourselves. Here, as elsewhere in his writings, just when Nietzsche seems to be embracing something we value, it turns out that he values it for different reasons, or holds it to its own ideals. But keep in mind here Nietzsche's slogan, "long live physics"; for he wants us to become the best learners and discoverers of everything lawful and necessary. Knowledge must be grounded in hyper-realistic inquiries about what we really experience, about the contexts of our inquiring moments, about the brightness and boldness of our reasons and our willful opposition to all deceptions and all the seductions of the fantastic. There cannot be a moment when we are not scrutinizing ourselves and our experiences with a severe scientific attitude, when we are not ourselves our own experiments. To be a scientist, an inquirer, a thinker is to be above all honest. In the end we must value not mathematics or physics but that which compels us to turn to these disciplines, and that is our honesty.

Imagine a scientist, an inquirer with no convictions, with faith and presuppositions, driven by the will to truth, committed to resisting deceptions from all corners, even from within oneself. When Nietzsche affirms the love and passion within inquiry he comes very close to an anticipation of contemporary feminist epistemologies. Solving problems requires the great love of secure inquirers, inquirers who tie their problems to their personal fates. Cold curiosity may hold some significance for certain periods of time in the life of inquiry but it cannot and must not prevail. The notion of impersonal science, of disinterestedness, has been the traditional hallmark of the scientific attitude. For Nietzsche, the idea is absurd in the extreme. It *should mean* that the scientist commands his pros and cons and chooses when to use them.

That the grounds for Nietzsche's view of "good thinking", of science, and of inquiry in general are in a social theory of knowledge can be variously illustrated. The faith we have in a proof is nothing more, he argues, than an understanding of the "good workmanship" known in all hard-working families. The idiosyncrasy we can identify in every scholarly act will always be a reflection of family, occupation, and craft. There is also a sociology of logic in Nietzsche. Accepting the high regard for logic attributed to Jews, he locates this not in any racial characteristic but rather in the social roles of Jewish scholars. This is, in fact, a theory of logic as the product of marginal urban groups who have a high regard for the force of reason. The contrast is with the sons of Protestant ministers who, as scholars, rely on being believed because they prove their arguments through the vigor and warmth with which they state them. The significant thing to attend to here is the effort to locate ideas and concepts in social roles and institutions. Nietzsche's theory is consistent with the thesis that logic was born out of commercial interests in rational calculation, and in the thoughts of the ancient Ionian philosopher-merchants represented initially by Thales.

Finally, to cap his claim to being a founder of the sociology of mind, he grasped the idea that consciousness is a network of social relationships. Nietzsche also recognized, sometimes crudely and sometimes profoundly, the social functions of science and knowledge. His thoughts on logic are an important illustration of this recognition. Logic is democratic, it calms us, and it gives us confidence. One has to be careful here not to miss the fact that logic is associated with the rationalizations of the powerful, the materially and culturally successful – and it benefits from their hegemonic dynamic.

Nietzsche spares nothing in warning against the myth of pure science, and recognizes the social reasons that tell against the myth. At the same time, he sketches the conditions for good inquiry. We must bring a diversity of perspectives and interpretations to our inquiries, but we must know how to do this so that inquiry is served well. We must eliminate the language of purity and absoluteness from our lexicons of thinking and inquiry. It is worth reiterating here points I made in an earlier chapter. Traditional ideas about pure science depend on an impossible eye, an eye with no direction, no powers of action and interpretation. It is precisely these powers that allow to see "something". Seeing and knowing are about perspective, and we foster objectivity by bringing as many eyes and emotions to a given matter of inquiry as possible. It is no mere aside to note that Nietzsche finds our first encounter with the concepts of "pure" and "impure" in the rise of spiritual supremacy associated with the establishment of a political supremacy. They are originally "signs of class".

Laughter is very important for Nietzsche. He is highly critical of the "ethical teachers," the "teachers of a purpose". These teachers of morals and ethics that we are forbidden to laugh at are all eventually defeated by laughter, reason, and nature's necessities. For this reason it is important to interrogate science on whether it fosters human joys or transforms us into cold stoic statues. Is science a dispenser of pain, perhaps "the greatest dispenser of pain"; or is science about unfolding "new galaxies of joy"? The will to power operates in science as everywhere else. Here it manifests itself as a lust for new knowledge, a passion for possessing new knowledge. One may, indeed, speak of the "will to truth".

Paul Feyerabend, Anarchism, and Science

I want to be very careful here about how I characterize Feyerabend's contribution to the anarchy and science dialogue. On the one hand, he is a persuasive defender of something very much like the gay science or joyous wisdom. On the other, he tries with all his might not to stray too far from a conservative – yes, even Popperian – model of science. Let us see how these contradictions manifest themselves, and what, in fact, Feyerabend means by an "anarchistic theory of knowledge". The subtitle of his first and best known book, *Against Method*, is "Outline of an Anarchistic Theory of Knowledge".

Against Method, published in 1975, was dedicated to Imre Lakatos, "friend and fellow-anarchist". The main argument of the book is summarized in the analytical index on pages 10-15; here, Feyerabend asserts that science is at its core a theoretically anarchistic practice. This theoretical anarchism is characteristically humanitarian and stands apart from law and order paradigms of science. But the word "anarchistic" in the subtitle is asterisked. The reason for the asterisk is that Feyerabend wants to disassociate himself from the self-styled "anarchists" of the 1960s (Cohn-Bendit is among the "exquisite exceptions", he writes). The term had, in his view, become associated with people who care little for the lives and happiness of human beings outside their small core of believers and adherents. This is a Puritanical view that Feyerabend adamantly opposes. So already by page 21 he is ready to throw the term overboard, the term that appears in his subtitle and in his dedication. Now he prefers the term "Dadaist" – because a Dadaist would never hurt a living thing. Feyerabend's description of the Dadaist reminds me of Nietzsche's image of the seriousness of a child playing. A worthwhile life requires taking things lightly, removing the kinds of passions that guide the search for truth or the defense of justice, passions that have a volatile potential for promoting law and order and at the extremes fascist (my words, not Feyerabend's) agendas. Better to be a "flippant Dadaist" than a "serious anarchist". Dada was not a program and was opposed to all programmers. Feyerabend has no interest in movements or slogans. He is interested in the problem of whether there is a principle for guiding science that will not inhibit progress. His case studies of science suggest the only viable principle is "anything goes". His critics, of course, wasted no time in picking away at "anything goes".

It is worth noting that in *Farewell to Reason*, Feyerabend (1988: 283) claims that the slogan "anything goes" is not his and was not meant to summarize his case studies. But the phrase appears in the analytical index of *Against Method*, and it is repeated as the epigraph for Chapter 1. "Anything Goes" is also the title of Chapter 4 in Part One of *Science in a Free Society*. And that book has seven entries in the index for "Anything Goes". The explanation for the disclaimer must be that Feyerabend did not mean by "anything goes" the principle of chaos it seems to have meant to his critics. Given what science is in fact rather than in myth and ideology, Feyerabend argues "reason cannot be universal and unreason cannot be excluded."

This is the grounds – that is, scientific practice in contrast to philosophical and other forms of reconstruction – for "anything goes" (Feyerabend, 1974: 180).

Feyerabend sometimes seems to threaten his readers in a way remindful of Nietzsche and Spengler. These are thinkers who have no need for gods. And they understand, in a profound way, that Reason, along with Obligation, Duty, Morality, Truth, and the Gods are all "abstract monsters" that have been used singly and together "to intimidate man and restrict his free and happy development". Under an anarchistic imperative, they – like the State they represent – wither away, if not literally then at least as internalized controls on our thinking.

In order to appreciate that what can appear to be an assault on science (not only in the present context but in the science wars of the 1990s) we must recognize what is in fact an assault on the Cult of Science. And in order to further appreciate what is at stake here, we must recognize that when we talk about science, truth, logic, and related ideas we are always talking about social relations, social constructions, social institutions, and moral orders. This way of seeing sensitizes us to the progressive and regressive aspects and potentials of words, concepts, and ideas.

The Limits of Epistemological Anarchism

We have already seen that Feyerabend prefers to be thought of as a "flippant Dadaist" rather than as a "serious anarchist". He is very careful to point out that he is urging epistemological anarchism, not political anarchism – and certainly not religious or eschatological anarchism. He eschews violence, and violence – he claims – "whether political or spiritual, plays an important role in almost all forms of anarchism". The debate then is not about whole social structures but about – and only about – methodological rules. The objective is to remove – and only remove – methodological constraints on the scientist (Feyerabend, 1974: 187):

> The scientist is still restricted by the properties of his instruments, the amount of money available, the intelligence of his assistants, the attitude of his colleagues, his playmates – he or she is restricted by innumerable physical, physiological, sociological, historical constraints.

No method is considered "indispensable". The epistemological anarchist opposes positively and absolutely one thing only: "universal standards, universal laws, universal ideas such as 'Truth', 'Reason', 'Justice', 'Love', and the behavior they bring along..." But this is not to deny that "it is often good policy to act as if such laws (such standards, such ideas) existed, and as if he believed in them". He may approach the religious anarchist in his opposition to science and the material world, he may outdo any Nobel Prize winner in his vigorous defense of scientific purity (Feyerabend, 1974: 189). Thus, the fundamental theorem of epistemological anarchism (Feyerabend, 1974: 195): "given any objective, even the most narrowly scientific one, the anarchistic non method has a greater chance of succeeding than any well-defined methodology". Lakatos challenges Feyerabend by arguing that no epistemological anarchist is so contrary that s/he will skip the lift in a tall building and walk out a window. Feyerabend replies that, in the first place, anarchists generally behave predictably; and in the second place, choosing the lift does not mean that one is being guided by a theory of rationality, it does not mean that one decides on a behavioral path based on their knowledge of the most advanced research programme. Nothing requires the epistemological anarchist to go against custom.

The scientist must have complete freedom when he or she is trying to solve a problem. Nothing the logician or philosopher worked out in his/her rocking chair with paper and pencil, no matter how plausible it seems, should ever restrict the actions of the scientist. History, culture, and biography are inescapable constraints on human behavior. Therefore, what we seek as anarchists, in my terms, is unfettered and courageous interrogation of anything and everything that comes into our view. The entire universe is, in this sense, profane. What this means in practice is freedom from the constraints of real politicians, priests, and soldiers, freedom from threats, prisons, torture, and death for any act of inquiry.

We have already seen that Feyerabend defends a highly specific and restricted form of anarchism, epistemological anarchism, and even then this seems to mean in practice some sort of *methodological* anarchism. But even this restriction is diluted in his reply to Joseph Agassi (Feyerabend, 1982 : 127):

> I do not say that epistemology should become anarchic, or that the philosophy of science should become anarchic. Epistemology is sick, it must be cured, and the medicine is anarchy. Now medicine is not something one takes all the time. Ones takes it for a certain period of time, *and then one stops*…Anarchism, I say will heal epistemology and *then* we may return to a more enlightened and more liberal form of rationality.

In the end, (though, I must return to *Against Method* here) Feyerabend (1974: 214) *embraces* Lakatos: "I shall join Lakatos rather than continuing to beat the drum of *explicit* anarchism." This is because under present conditions in philosophy ("at the present stage of philosophical consciousness"), an irrational theory falsely interpreted as a new account of Reason will be a better instrument for freeing the mind than an out-and-out anarchism that is liable to paralyse the brains of almost everyone.

In fact, "anything goes" is compatible with Reason as defined by Lakatos (Feyerabend, 1974: 186). Lakatos' standards neither prescribe nor forbid any particular action. But the epistemological anarchist rightly regards them as "mere embroideries". Yet, "they…give content to the actions of individuals and institutions who have decided to adopt a conservative attitude towards them". The point is not to recommend "anything goes" as the principle of a new methodology or to defend "anything goes" as a principle (Feyerabend, 1974: 39, 197, 284):

146 *Red, Black, and Objective*

...it is a "principle" forced upon a rationalist who loves principles but who also takes history seriously. Besides, and more importantly, an absence of "objective" standards does not mean less work.

Foundations for an Anarcho-Sociology of Science

Contemporary science studies has done much since the late 1960s to reveal the wisdom of the Nietzsches and Feyerabends on the nature of good inquiry. And they have done this within the boundaries of current and historical scientific practices. They have focused attention on the tinkering aspect of knowledge production in science, the common place rationalities that guide scientific inquiry, the ways in which choosing particular technical assumptions can (to use Brian Martin's phrase) "push an argument", and the nature and significance of selecting, interpreting, and using evidence. We have learned that in a specialized form of intellectual labor such as science, presuppositions seem to be missing because they have become embodied in scientific instruments and scientific practices. And we have learned more about the institutional and intellectual linkages between scientific research and theory and the power centers of modern industrial technological societies.

Unlike the view from the perspective of functionalist and related sociologies of science, the view of modern science from the anarcho-sociology of science perspective reveals a mode of knowing that is neither well-functioning nor progressive. The rationalization of the scientific worldview has proceeded hand in hand with the modernization and bureaucratization of the industrial and technological states. The source of Reason, like the old source of God, continues to be located in the power centers of these societies. This key process of the modern period is the source of the separation of rationality and science from ethics and values. This separation is a core feature of the ideology of science.

To say that there is an ideology of modern science means in part that there is a dogmatic support for modern science as a way of life, false consciousness about the intellectual, social, and cultural grounds and consequences of scientific activities and products, and false consciousness about the social role of the scientist. The ideology of modern science sustains struggles for power and status, and for institutional survival. And it promotes the use of science (to the extent that it overemphasizes quantification, rigor, control, and prediction) as a resource for reducing personal anxieties and fears.

The process of rationalization that Max Weber wrote and worried about now underlies the mechanization of individuals, and increasingly manifests itself as a routinization of rationality. One consequence of sustaining the routinization of rationality is that the range of the schema of criticism in our culture will be increasingly narrowed and our individual capacities for critical thinking will slowly wither away. If all of this sounds vaguely familiar, it is because it should remind us of the most recent crisis in economics and economies, that of 2008, and the depressing studies of what Americans don't know about how the world works.

Chapter 7
What's Mind Got To Do With It?

In 1939, C. Wright Mills (1963) argued that without a sociological theory of mind, the sociology of knowledge would be in danger of becoming a set of "historical enumerations and a calling of names". Without such a theory, knowledge will tend, in spite of all efforts, to continue to be thought of as some sort of stuff "inside" brains, minds, or individuals; and the social will tend to be thought of as something "outside" brains, minds, or individuals. Theories of mind have traditionally come from philosophy and psychology. Such theories have tended to causally tie mental phenomena to or make them identical with brain processes. Given such a framework, John Searle (1984) could argue that pain and mental phenomena in general are nothing more than features of the brain and perhaps of the central nervous system. But the way people feel pain, express those feelings, and respond to the pain of others are all cultural products. This follows from Durkheim's analysis of the different degrees of social solidarity and the social construction of individuality. A form of the conjecture that pain is culturally constructed was already formulated by Nietzsche in *The Genealogy of Morals*. And Wittgenstein raised all sorts of questions about the nature of pain in *Philosophical Investigations* that cleared a path for an anthropology of pain. Nietzsche also already conjectured that "consciousness is really only a net of communication between human beings" and thus provided one of the bases for an anthropology of pain.

For centuries, it has seemed obvious that the study of mind should be under the jurisdiction of philosophers and psychologists (in their pre-modern as well as modern roles). As the matrix of mind studies became increasingly interdisciplinary in the latter part of the twentieth century, sociology and anthropology were, with some notable exceptions, left out in the cold. It may be that it is just these modes of inquiry that have any hope of making sense out of the tortured efforts in contemporary physics, astronomy, biology, artificial intelligence, and the neurosciences to "explain" mind and brain.

In 1943, Warren McCulloch and Walter Pitts helped set the agenda for an immanentist approach to mind. They claimed that the discipline we should charge with explaining the brain and mentality is logic. Their reasoning was that logic guides the operation of neurons. Durkheim had already rejected immanence along with transcendence in *The Elementary Forms of Religious Life*. That is, he rejected in the first instance the notion that ideas such as Aristotle's categorical imperatives and Kant's categories are either (a) logically prior to experience, immanent in the human mind, or otherwise a priori; or (b) crafted by isolated individuals. In the second instance, he rejected the idea that there are transcendental referents (for terms, for example, such as "soul", "God", and "heaven"). The crystallization of the rejection of immanence and transcendence is one of the great on-going achievements in the history of thought. The project arguably begins as early as Socrates. Cicero said that Socrates brought philosophy down to earth. A more recent example of this imperative is Dirk Struik's (1986: 280) conception of the goal of the sociology of mathematics: to haul the lofty domains of mathematics "from the Olympian heights of pure mind to the common pastures where human beings toil and sweat".

John Searle (1992: 128), in spite of a continuing failure to see "the social" in any profound sense, helps to open the door for sociologists of mind:

> I am convinced that the category of "other people" plays a special role in the structure of our conscious experiences, a role unlike that of objects and states of affairs...But I do not yet know how to demonstrate these claims, nor how to analyze the structure of the social element in individual consciousness.

A similar door opener comes from the neurosciences; Antonio Damasio (1994: 260) writes:

> To understand in a satisfactory manner the brain that fabricates human mind and human behavior, it is necessary to take into account its social and cultural content. And that makes the endeavor truly daunting.

And even in artificial intelligence research, projects from Rodney Brooks' COG (the baby robot) to the view of mentality as "physically and environmentally embedded" (Torrance, 1994), and the idea of cognition as embodied action (Varela, Thompson, and Rosch, 1991), paths are being opened for social and cultural studies of mentality.

I began my efforts in the sociology of the mind by making a simplifying assumption (following Randall Collins) that thinking is internal conversation. This poses an immediate problem. That is, given everything I have written so far, and given Wittgenstein's writings on mind and thinking, I do not want to claim that thinking (as conversation, for example) is something that happens inside heads or brains. There are efforts abroad to develop an explanation of cognition as embodied action. A theory of embodied action that is properly sociological dissolves the inner/outer dilemma and the chicken/egg problem. The chicken point of view is that there is a world "out there" with pre-given properties. These exist before and independently of the images they cast on the cognitive system. The role of cognition is to recover the external properties appropriately (Realism). From an egg perspective, we project our own world, and "reality" is a reflection of internal cognitive laws (Idealism). But a theory of embodied action explains cognition/ mentality in terms that depend on having a body with a variety of sensori-motor capacities embedded in more encompassing biological, psychological, and cultural contexts. Cognition is lived; sensory and motor processes, perception, and action are not independent. This approach promises to dissolve the inner/outer dilemma, and to eliminate representational paradoxes in the theory of mind. Details on how such a perspective bears on our understanding of how we learn mathematics can be found in Stephen Lerman's (1998) work.

For the moment, I want to focus on the "phenomenology" of a certain kind of thinking experience. A sociological theory of mind must account, one way or another and sooner or later, for the experience of "inner thought". And it must do so without the assumption or claim that this experience is universal across humans and cultures.

Conversation is the prototype for a certain kind and level of thinking, the kind of thinking we, initially at least, have in mind (so to speak) when we set out to construct an artificial intelligence, develop a theory of mind, or think about our own thinking. We must learn to speak out loud before we can think "silently", "in our heads". "External" speech already contains all the crucial elements of thought: significant symbols, capacity to take the stance of one's interlocutor or listener, and the ability to take the role of the other and orient to the generalized other (explained a few paragraphs on).

Internal conversations do not necessarily have the same structure as external conversations. Short-cuts, shunts, and short-circuits in our thinking are possible when we (as adults) are thinking smoothly. We may know almost immediately where a thought is going and whether to pursue it or switch over to another thought-track. Because we can monitor multiple thought-tracks (the dispatcher function) we can rapidly switch between alternatives, elaborations, objections, and conclusions. Thought-tracks and trains of thought connect syntactically and pragmatically in Hesse-type networks (Hesse, 1974). And words invoke other words, ideas invoke ideas, concepts invoke concepts (because of similar meanings, sounds, and/or associations). Generally, these switches, invokings, and associations occur smoothly and without the exercise of "will"; and they can produce what I call thought cascades. If the process is disrupted in any way, however, our attention will shift, the process will slow, and we will proceed with awareness. This contributes to the illusion that we think "willfully".

If we treat thinking as internal conversation, then thinking must be constructed out of past, anticipated, and hypothetical conversations. In other words, what we think is connected to our social networks (including reference groups). Then the greater the attraction to given parts of the network, the more we will "be motivated" to think the ideas circulating in those parts.

The connections among ideas are emotional as well associative and grammatical. Words, ideas, and images have valences. And consciousness itself is a type of emotion, attentiveness. Normally this attentiveness is very mild and attached to certain sign-relations. The level of attentiveness presumably changes as social situations (real and imagined) change. Only when the smooth and easy inference (or "next move") is blocked, or contradicted by something in the situation, does the emotion erupt into awareness. So emotional weightings (valences) affect what a person thinks about at a particular time. These ideas are consistent with neuroscientific and sociological research that suggests the existence of a baseline emotional state.

The Generalized Other Revisited

The generalized other is the core concept in George Herbert Mead's social theory of mind. Mead introduced the idea of the generalized other to describe that component of the self constructed out of the variety of messages we receive from the people we come into contact with. The generalized other is the source of our ability to take the roles of others, and also the source of our understanding of the "rules of the game" in everyday interaction. It is the locus of what Freud called the super-ego, which gives us "conscience". And it is the locus of what I call "moralogics". When we reason, generalized others are with us all the way, approving and/or disapproving our every move. We always reason from a standpoint. There are many standpoints, and each is guarded by a generalized other. Operating logically means operating in terms of standard and standardized critical and reasoning apparatuses. *Individuals* cannot be logical or illogical. They can only be in agreement or disagreement with a community of discourse, an objectivity community, a thought collective. And patrolling standpoints is therefore a moral act. If, then, reasoning is always grounded in a standpoint, there can be no General Abstract Reasoner, no eternal, universal logic.

If, furthermore, patriarchy has constructed Platonism, and relativity theory, and truth-seeking Diogenes and the propagandist Goebbels, the podiums of rationality and objectivity and the arenas of emotion, then there is good reason (from a certain standpoint, now!) to conjecture that mentality or mind is "man-made". Thinking is, therefore, on these principles, gendered. Logic is the morality of the thought collective, and carries the weight of how gender, race, class, and power are distributed therein.

Neither "laws of logic" nor "laws of thought" (as imagined by the mathematician George Boole) are intuitive, innate, or a priori. Generalized others carry socially derived logical systems that restrict, govern, filter, direct, and cue logical speech acts. Inside every word, inside every vocabulary, inside every sentence, and inside every grammar we find discourse communities. It follows that our thoughts, insofar as they draw on the resources of languages, are socially textured. Here Goffman's (1974) frame analysis provides another ordering apparatus. And the distinction he attends to between conversational talk and informal talk has an analogy in thought. Just as informal talk holds the individual together across parsing moments and breaks in continuity in social projects, and just as much of what we say in the presence of others is related to creating and sustaining social solidarity, so informal thought is also about self-solidarity. Speaking, Goffman points out, "tends to be loosely geared to the world". Talk is looser. I conjecture that thinking is even looser, and more vulnerable to the processes Goffman calls keying and fabricating.

Now let us think again about moralogics. Mathematics communities are in part crucibles for refining the idea of God through exercises with infinity(ies). The most abstract efforts then turn out to be tied more or less explicitly to the God project. Boole's goal was to reduce mathematical and logical systems to one pervasive law. This is not a simple metaphor, for Boole was set on establishing the existence of God and a universal morality. So too Cantor's transfinite numbers are implicated in the search for a proof of the existence of God. I cannot pursue this further here, but see the appendix on mathematics and God in Restivo (1992).

Where is Thinking?

The introduction to the social construction theorem should make it easier to understand what I mean when I say that minds and thinking are social constructions. This conception carries with it the notion that thinking is a networked and dialogic process, a series of social acts rather than something that goes on inside isolated, independent heads and/or brains. This does not mean that heads and brains are dispensable, nor that neuroscientists and psychologists have nothing to teach us about minds and thinking. But it is social relations that give rise to consciousness and thinking; the genesis of consciousness and thinking is in society not in the brain. Free standing brains do not and cannot "become" conscious, and do not and cannot generate consciousness in some sort of evolutionary or developmental "brains in a vat" process. Consciousness, thought, and language cannot be explained or understood independently of the understanding that human beings are through and through social beings.

Individualized thoughts must be tied to their social bases if we are to understand their genesis and nature. Communicable thoughts are, by definition, shareable and shared (Durkheim, 1961: 485). All concepts are collective representations and collective elaborations – conceived, developed, sustained, and changed through social networks of intellectuals that cause particular ideas to come into being and develop or die out. This line of thinking leads to the conclusion that it is social worlds, or communities that think and generate ideas and concepts, not individuals. Social worlds do not, of course, literally think in some superorganic sense. But individuals don't think either. Rather, individuals are vehicles for expressing the thoughts of social worlds or "thought collectives". Or, to put it another way, minds are social structures (Gumplowicz, 1905; Fleck, 1979: 39). Mentality is not a human invariant. And even vision is an *activity* and not a neurological event (Davidson and Noble, 1989; and see Heelan, 1983 on the social construction of perception).

In order to grasp the idea that thinking is radically social, and to keep it from slipping into some spiritual or mystical realm, or becoming an empty philosophical or theological concept, one must keep firmly focused on and fully comprehend the idea that humans are social beings and that the self is a social structure. It is also crucial that we do not project our modern post-literate experience of mentality and mind-body duality on all humans in all times and places. "Mind" is not a cultural or human universal (cf., Olson, 1986, and Davidson and Noble, 1989).

Ritual and Cognition

Cognition arises situationally out of the natural rituals of everyday interactions and conversations. These rituals form a chain, and as we move through this chain, we come across and use more or less successively blends of cultural capital and emotional energies (Collins, 1988: 357ff.). The concept of ritual developed in the work of Emile Durkheim can be generalized and conceived as a type of framing (following Goffman, 1974). This leads to the idea that the theory of ritual can be developed in terms of the different types of framings and reframings which constitute our movement through interaction ritual chains. From this perspective, solidarity rituals take place in a social market that is variously stratified. Language is a product of pervasive natural rituals (words, grammatical structures, speech acts, and framings are collective representations loaded with moral significance). The ingredients of language refer outside conversations, and their sense is their symbolic connection to social solidarity and their histories in interaction ritual chains. All thoughts take place in several modalities – visual, aural, emotional, sensual – simultaneously. Indeed, it is the socially constructed, gendered, cultured body-in-society that thinks, not the individual head, brain, or mind.

We are now ready to enter the world of the sociology of mathematics once again, but from a different entryway. But I must stress that if we enter without at least some preliminary comprehension of the ideas that self and mentality are social, the sociology of mathematics will seem like a voyage through the Looking Glass – without any of the charm of Lewis Carroll's guidance. Entering the world of the sociology of mathematics again, we now find ourselves prepared to engage it as a window on the mind and brain.

The Sociology of Mathematics

If we now enter the realm of mathematics with our social constructionist toolkit, we enter a world that mathematicians will not readily recognize. For the social constructionist, this is a world of social relations, social interaction, social networks; it is a world of human beings communicating in arenas of conflict and cooperation, domination and subordination, a world of social practice and discourse. And all the ingredients of this world – from the mathematicians themselves to their marks on paper and the ideas "in their heads" – appear to us as social forms. I will concede that, in fact, many mathematicians will think they recognize in what I have just written their own sense of the social nature of mathematical work. But this is because they, like all human beings, possess a certain sociological competence

(Lemert, 1997) or folk sociology, not because they have a deep understanding of the nature and pervasiveness of the social.

I wrote earlier about those mathematical thinkers and others who experience a "sense of reality" about mathematics. We are likely to find among these persons a sense that mathematics, like morality, cannot be "localized". That is, they are likely to find it self-evident that there are not culture-bound answers to questions of whether children should be tortured or given mathematical propositions are true or false. This juxtaposition of morality and mathematics (which we actually find in the work of the philosopher of science Ian Jarvie, 1975) is of great interest to sociologists and anthropologists of mathematics. Let us begin by considering what it means for something to be self-evident.

Quine (1960) is a locus classicus for the discussion of self-evidence. Self-evident statements carry their evidence within themselves; that is, they are true by virtue of what their words mean (Douglas, 1975: 277). If such statements are denied, their supporters react the way they do to foreign sentences they do not grasp. "All bachelors are unmarried men", and "2+2=4" are classic examples of self-evident statements. Quine (1960: 66-67) wrote eloquently about the bewildered reaction to the person who denies such statements. But it took an anthropologist to improve Quine's account of self-evidence.

Mary Douglas (1975: 277-280) went beyond the psychology of the individual and the public use of language to add a social dimension to the analysis of self-evidence. The bewilderment Quine pointed out turns out to be a function of the logic of social experiences – class experiences, the emotional power of social relations, the investments some people make in sustaining social structures and others in overturning them. The reason people can become so furious in identifying and opposing the "illogical" is that it is a threat to *moral* order. "Moral" here must be understood in sociological terms – that is, as the "glue" that holds social relationships together. In this sense, moral order is as much a necessary ingredient of social relationships as the heart is of the human organism. The reader will miss the point here if s/he thinks of morality in theological, ethical, or philosophical terms. There are many ways to ground moral orders. Religion is the most widely recognized source of moral order. But other systems – for example, politics or science (or sociology, for that matter) – can ground moral orders. Moral orders reflect and systematize the logics of social and emotional relationships, and that is why reactions to illogical behavior or reasoning can produce such volatile and even violent reactions.

Early on in the twentieth century, the self-evidence of mathematics (aside from any damage done to this idea between Hilbert and Gödel) was undermined by the appearance of two opposing (and independent) viewpoints. For the mathematics teacher and polymath Oswald Spengler (1926), mathematics was a cultural phenomenon. The first substantive chapter in his *The Decline of the West* not only sets up mathematics as a key to understanding culture and history, but provides for a sociology and anthropology of mathematics. This aspect of his work did not make a difference to the sociology of science until David Bloor publicized its significance. On the other hand, Karl Mannheim (1936), a major influence on the sociology of knowledge and science, argued that mathematics was outside history and culture and that there could never be a sociology of 2+2=4. That tension has been resolved in the eyes of today's handful of sociologists and anthropologists of mathematics, who stand for the most part in Spengler's camp. So the issue before me at this moment is not whether a sociology of mathematics is possible but of what interest and use it could be to mathematicians and mathematics educators. In other words, I am not going to defend the very idea of a sociology of mathematics but rather (having set the foundations) assume it. Let us look, then, at what it is ,sociologists of mathematics have to say and why it might be interesting and useful to mathematicians and mathematics educators.

This task is facilitated by three facts. First, some mathematicians and mathematics educators have achieved a certain reflexive social awareness within their everyday practice that has made them open to the sociological perspective on mathematics (e.g., Stephen Lerman, the late Leone Burton, Jean Paul Van Bendegem, Roland Fischer, Ole Skovmose, Chandler Davis, Paul Ernest, Ubiratan D'Ambrosio, the late Thomas Tymoczko, and Nel Noddings). Second, the sociology of mathematics has become a visible and practical input into mathematics education. An outstanding example of this is the work on social constructionism in mathematics by David Bloor and myself. And third, the philosophy of mathematics, and what we can refer to more generally as math studies, has come increasingly to be grounded, at least in principle, in the actual everyday practices of mathematicians. Math studies still operates under the shadow of Platonism (e.g., Resnik, 1993), but increasingly the focus is on what mathematicians as real people in the real world *can* do, and what they in ethnographic fact *do* do. Some philosophers of mathematics now argue that mathematical practice should be *the* focus of their research (e.g., Tymoczko, 1991, 1993). This is the drift of the current literature in math studies, but in the wider sea of inquiry this movement is in the direction of naturalisitic rather than sociological accounts. But by undermining foundationalism, Platonism, and apriorism, naturalism does tend to make math studies more, and increasingly more, open to sociological accounts.

What, then, are the practical implications of the sociological theory of mind and thinking for the mathematics classroom? This question can be posed in another way: does it make any difference for the activities and processes in mathematics classrooms if (a) the brain is not a free-standing, independent and autonomous agent or entity, (b) the individual is not a free-standing, independent, and autonomous agent or entity, (c) the brain does not possess an immanent logic, and does not evolve according to an immanent program toward some form of logical or rational maturity, (d) cognition does not evolve or develop in a series of universal and inevitable stages, and (e) there are no transcendental referents or authorities? Suppose individuals are not empty vessels which if put into the proper attentive orientation are capable of absorbing a teacher's messages more or less directly and thus "learning"? Now when I put the question in this multi-faceted form, some educators will probably agree with most of what I say in principle. But it is unlikely that they will be able to readily and expertly translate this agreement into actual classroom practices; for the most part, they are likely to adopt teaching and learning methods that are grounded in psychologistic assumptions about learning and cognition. The reason for this is the pervasive Western bias, especially in the United States, in favor of individual entitivity, agency, and responsibility and against anything that hints at the power of the collectivity or social group. Therefore it is necessary to provide some guidelines for educators who would like to take the ideas in this chapter seriously and apply them in the classroom.

For all of my confidence on this matter, I am not prepared to be as helpful as some mathematics educators might wish me to be at this point. First, other contributors to the field will do some of this work for me (e.g., Lerman, 1998) as will authors and contributors to the literature on the social construction of mathematics and mathematics education (e.g., Ernest, 1994). Second, my objective in this chapter has been to outline and clarify the social construction theorem that is abroad (in a more conjectural and philosophical form) in mathematics education today in order to provide a grounding for the less formal treatments of this conjecture one comes across in the educational and philosophical literature. Having said that, I am prepared to offer some guidelines for mathematics educators that are relevant to educators in other fields as well.

1. Take seriously the fact that you and your students are a collectivity, and that your communication is based on collective representations. Whether you stand at the front of the room facing your students, or sit amongst them, you are not dealing with a set of individuals but a collectivity.

2. Because language is constructed out of collective representations, communication is not a straightforward logico-rational process. There are many social and cultural factors that affect communication linkages in a classroom, and both teachers and students need to be aware of this (cf. Janet Kaahwa, 1998).

3. From a sociological perspective, there are no individuals. But this does not mean that there are no persons. And if agency, free will and responsibility are eliminated by a radically sociologized view of persons, they come back to life in a political framework. Persons are real, and they are not simple cogs in the collective machine; but they are through and through social. This fundamental fact must be kept in mind whenever teachers and students interact one-on-one, face-to-face.

4. The classroom is "a site of socio-cultural negotiation" (Burton, 1996). But so is the person. It is time to fully jettison whatever remains of hierarchical conceptions of learning "objective mathematics", and of "Piagetan" models of fixed developmental patterns.

5. Mathematics is not the product of individual mental acts, and should not be taught as if it is. And knowledge is not obtained by way of individual acts; nor is it obtained by linking two individual actors or agents (Noddings, 1993; Skovsmose, 1993).

6. The advantage of the Piagetan approach has been its emphasis on activity. This is also true of constructionism. The disadvantage of these approaches is that they do not fully appropriate a thoroughly social understanding of brain, mind, and person.

7. Mathematics educators should question the idea that the child's intellectual development should be the focus of primary education (following a Piagetan model); and that pedagogy can be planned outside the classroom, as if classroom goals are fixed by the formalities and logic of mathematics (Skovsmose, 1993).

8. Give up the idea that the basic relationship in the classroom is between textbook and learner, or teacher and learner, or textbook/teacher and learner. Instead, take seriously the epistemological potentials extant in the collectivity – between and among students (including the teacher). And learn to seek the genesis of learning and knowledge, thinking and reasoning, in interpersonal relationships In adopting this approach, consider the dialectics of people and technologies (Crawford, 1998) but without letting it obscure the fundamental emotional coupling that ties people together in social networks.

9. Challenge the hierarchy and authority of teachers, texts, and facts; challenge the idea that there are coherent sources of knowledge; and challenge the concept of knowledge as a homogenous body of "stuff" (Skovsmose, 1993: 178).

One can now say, to echo Nietzsche, that "Science is dead", and "Mathematics is dead". This does not mean the end of truth, as I pointed out earlier. It does mean that new conceptions of teaching and learning are abroad and ready to be brought into the classroom. There is at least an implicit anarchist sociology that grounds these conceptions and the principles that should guide classroom activities.

What About the Brain?

It seems to me that a sociologist, unlike a philosopher, a psychologist, or a cognitivist, has to offer some rationale or justification for taking on problems of the brain, mind, consciousness, and thought. I will begin, therefore, with a brief genealogy, a genealogy that is the root of a multi-pronged provocation for a sociology of mind and brain. The classical provocation comes from the writings of the classical social theorists, notably in my case, Emile Durkheim, Friedrich Nietzsche, and Karl Marx.

There is then what might be called a neo-classical provocation rooted in the works of George Herbert Mead, Lev Vgotsky, Ludwik Fleck, and John Dewey. Their work leads to a second-order neo-classical provocation, from Mead in particular to C. Wright Mills and Randall Collins and from Vygotsky to James Wertsch among others and the social cognitionists. These provocations are direct and lead more or less explicitly and transparently to the sociology of mind. For the beginnings of the sociology of brain, we can look to the writings of the anthropologist Clifford Geertz (1973: 74):

> The synchronic emergence in primates of an expanded forebrain, developed forms of social organization, and, at least after Australopithecines got their hands on tools, institutionalized patterns of culture indicates that the standard procedure of treating biological, social, and cultural parameters serially – the first being taken as primary to the second, and the second to the third – is ill-advised. On the contrary, these so-called levels should be seen as reciprocally interrelated and considered conjointly.

If we think of the brain and central nervous system as logically and genetically prior to society and culture then we will be prompted to focus our attention on genes and brains in accounting for human behavior. If Geertz is right, then we may be asking too much of the brain, or at least perhaps asking the wrong questions about the brain. This has already occurred to some neuroscientists and life scientists. Their "social accounts" tend to be limited in two ways. One of the most sophisticated social theorists among the neuroscientists, Leslie Brothers (2001), tended at least initially to see the social in terms of a network of brains rather than a network of persons. And the biologist Alva Noë (2009) uses a virtually sociological vocabulary and perspective to criticize the isolated brain assumption but curiously identifies biology as the science of the social. He treats life in the context of the environment and where I would use the words social and cultural he thinks in terms of "the world" and the "environment". As a result, he reinvents ideas formulated much earlier by sociological theorists from Durkheim to Mead and from C. Wright Mills to Randall Collins and Sal Restivo.

The Anarchy of the Brain

In philosophy, the *brain in a vat* is any of a variety of thought experiments intended to draw out certain features of our ideas of knowledge, reality, truth, mind, and meaning. It reflects the idea, common to many science fiction stories, that a (mad?) scientist might remove a person's brain from the body, suspend it in a vat of life-sustaining liquid, and connect its neurons by wires to a supercomputer which would provide it with electrical impulses identical to those the brain normally receives. According to such stories, the computer would then be simulating a reality (including appropriate responses to the brain's own output) and the "disembodied" brain would continue to have perfectly normal conscious experiences without these being related to objects or events in the real world. The brain in a vat idea shows up in the 1999 movie *The Matrix*. The reality humans perceive in this movie is simulated by sentient machines.

The simplest use of brain-in-a-vat scenarios is as an argument for philosophical skepticism and solipsism. A simple version of this runs as follows: Since the brain in a vat gives and receives the exact same impulses as it would if it were in a skull, and since these are its only way of interacting with its environment, then it is not possible to tell, *from the perspective of that brain*, whether it is in a skull or a vat. Yet in the first case most of the person's beliefs may be true (if s/he believes, say, that s/he is walking down the street, or eating ice-cream); in the latter case they are false. Since, the argument says, you cannot know whether you are a brain in a vat, then you cannot know whether most of your beliefs might be completely false. Since, in principle, it is impossible to rule out your being a brain in a vat, you cannot have good grounds for believing any of the things you believe; you certainly cannot *know* them.

This argument is a contemporary version of the argument given by Descartes in *Meditations on First Philosophy* (which he eventually rejects) that he could not trust his perceptions on the grounds that an evil demon might, conceivably, be controlling his every experience. It is also more distantly related to Descartes' argument that he cannot trust his perceptions because he might be dreaming. Descartes' dream argument is anticipated by Zhuangzi (369-286 bce) in "Chuang Chou dreamed he was a butterfly". In this argument the worry about active deception is removed.

Such puzzles have been worked over in many variations by philosophers in recent decades. Some, including Barry Stroud, continue to insist that such puzzles constitute an unanswerable objection to any knowledge claims. Others have argued against them, most notably Hilary Putnam. In the first chapter of his *Reason, Truth, and History*, Putnam claims that the thought experiment is inconsistent on the grounds that a brain in a vat could not have the sort of history and interaction with the world that would allow its thoughts or words to be *about* the vat that it is in. In other words, if a brain in a vat stated "I am a brain in a vat", it would always be stating a falsehood. If the brain making this statement lives in the "real" world, then it is not a brain in a vat. On the other hand, if the brain making this statement is really just a brain in the vat then by stating "I am a brain in a vat" what the brain is really stating is "I am what nerve stimuli have convinced me is a 'brain', and I reside in an image that I have been convinced is called a 'vat'." That is, a brain in a vat would never be thinking about real brains or real vats, but rather about images sent into it that resemble real brains or real vats. This of course makes our definition of "real" even more muddled. This refutation of the vat theory is a consequence of his endorsement, at that time, of the causal theory of reference. Roughly, in this case: if you've never experienced the real world, then you can't have thoughts about it, whether to deny or affirm them. Putnam contends that by "brain" and "vat" the brain in a vat must be referring not to things in the "outside" world but to elements of its own "virtual world"; and it is clearly not a brain in a vat in that sense.

Many writers, however, have found Putnam's proposed solution unsatisfying, as it appears, in this regard at least, to depend on a shaky theory of meaning:

that we cannot meaningfully talk or think about the "external" world because we cannot experience it; this sounds like a version of the outmoded verification principle. Consider the following: for a brain in a vat, language is connected by a program to sensory inputs that do not represent anything "external". How can this lead to representations and language in use that refer to any external thing? Putnam here argues from the lack of sensory inputs representing (real world) trees to our inability to meaningfully think about trees. But it is not clear why the referents of our terms must be accessible to us in experience. One cannot, for example, have direct experience of other people's internal states of consciousness; does this imply that one cannot meaningfully ascribe mental states to others?

Subsequent writers on the topic, especially among those who agree with Putnam's claim, have been particularly interested in the problems it presents for *content*: that is, how – if at all – can the brain's thoughts be *about* a person or place with whom it has never interacted and which perhaps does not exist?

To the extent that a culture such as America values individualism it is predisposed to psychological, biological, and genetic explanations of human behavior. These sorts of explanations have a volatile potential for supporting racist, classist, and sexist value systems. Explanations like this place responsibility for human behavior squarely on the shoulders of individuals. At the same time, such explanations undermine efforts to bring social forces such as education and social welfare to bear on solving human and social problems. Another consequence of this way of thinking is that it looks to individuals for the springs of creativity, and not just to individual persons but to individual brains. Consider the obsession with Einstein's brain. This obsession must somehow reflect the assumption that Einstein *was* his brain. Imagine now that we could have transplanted Einstein's brain at his death into another healthy human being. Would that person have become Einstein? You are invited to consider various Frankensteinian scenarios: Einstein dies in his 70s. His brain is then transplanted into a 20-year-old male, a 20 year old female, an older male or female, a male or female Einstein's age. The idea that we would get Einstein back in this way falls apart as soon as we begin to think about who and what Einstein was. The same sort of thinking is behind the science fiction scenario of downloading our brain into a computer in order to achieve machine immortality.

Einstein's Brain has become a metaphor and a point of entry for a participant's journey through virtual landscapes. The figure of Einstein embodies a variety of references from the comic figure of the mad professor, to the socially conscious scientist and humanist. His name is synonymous with genius. His body seems feeble beside the awesome, mechanical power of his brain. He is, as Roland Barthes has written, "at once magician and machine". His name invokes the human quest for the secrets of the universe. His brain has passed into the world of myth, cut up and minutely examined but revealing little. He has become a link between science and mythology, between the machine and its capacity to offer a key to the unknown and the continual re-presentation of familiar structures and myths. Even the brain is sometimes hard to pin down ontologically and referentially. This research frontier in sociology promises more than I can capture here outside of pointers and eye openers.

The basic problem with individualistic explanations of human behavior is that they start out by ignoring the most important thing about us: we are social animals in the most profound sense. If we can show that psychological explanations do not adequately account for creative discovery and invention in science, we can begin to understand the nature and limits of genetic, neurological, and biological explanations in general. It is in part at least the cultural predisposition to individualism that generates absurdities disguised as philosophies such as brains-in-a-vat ideas.

The 1990 song "The Emperor's New Clothes" by recording artist Sinéad O'Connor has the same general message as the original fairytale. The song ends with the lines, "through their own words/they will be exposed/they've got a severe case of/the emperor's new clothes."

The Copernican Trauma: Ask Einstein's Brain

Some brainists might suppose that a post-mortem study of Einstein's brain would provide clues as to the cerebral processes underlying genius. After many studies over many years, it was determined that there was significant enlargement of the gyri comprising the parietal association cortices, suggesting variation at some early stage of cerebral ontogeny. The brainist could then conclude that this reflects an extraordinarily large expanse of highly integrated cortex within a functional network – a notion consistent with the speculation that variation in axonal connectivity may be a neuronal correlate of intelligence.

Consider now the question raised by Mary Thomas Crane (2000) at the very beginning of her book, *Shakepeare's Brain*: Did Shakespeare have a brain? She echoes Foucault when she writes that this "odd question" requires an explanation. Foucault was considering the question "what is an author?" in an essay that redefines an author as "a complex and variable function of discourse." He is so successful, Crane remarks, that his question no longer seems odd; her question, however, does appear odd. Shakespeare scholars have always assumed that Shakespeare had a *mind*. Searching for a referent for mind tends to be a wild goose chase for the reason, as I claim, that the mind is a secular transform of the soul and without an ontological status. What Crane wants to do is treat Shakespeare's brain as one material site for the production of his dramatic works. After about 14 pages, Crane says that Shakespeare must have had a brain.

In recent years, there have been notable convergences between research in the brain sciences and social sciences that are beginning to give us an outline of the brain as a social thing. In brain research as in other areas of science, classically useful categories and classifications are proving increasingly obstructive. Neuroscientists and social scientists alike have begun to challenge the idea that their researches can sustain the brain-body, mind-brain, mind-body dichotomies. What is new about this is not the challenge itself but the ways in which research is demonstrating the need to eliminate these dichotomies in favor of a new set of categories and classifications and a new integrative or at least interdisciplinary model of brain and behavior. Recent results in the neurosciences recommend greater cooperation between neuroscientists and social scientists, and promise the possibility of cobbling together a new sociology of the brain.

MIT's Evelyn Fox Keller has called the language of molecular biology "historical baggage". And the Broad Institute's Eric S. Lander said that he is not worried about any confusion that may arise in references to "genes". We can say the same things, respectively, about the languages of the brain sciences and references to "brains".

I speak about brains at the intersection of the Age of the Social and the End of Locality. This is a place where many have lost their sociological innocence and gone on to seek new modes and levels of inquiry, following a path to the End of the Social. But in the way psychology was Freud's Schillerian tyrant, sociology has been and is my tyrant. I am, to paraphrase Freud, tormented by the goal of examining what shape brain science takes if one introduces sociological considerations.

Now we take a step back and ask if there is a way to model each of the ingredients of the classical dualisms using the same model. We already have metrical models of the brain and neurons. We therefore have by extension metrical models of neural nets. Metrical models are simultaneously fractal, chaotic, and non-linear. This general idea has been expressed in terms of "transforming vector arrays". If we could extend the metrical modeling of brain, neuron, and neural nets to bodies and IRCs (iteraction ritual chains) we would have the foundation for a metrical model of the body as the locus of IRCs. Some social roboticists have been modeling behavior based on the morphological self-similarity of the mini-micro, micro-meso, and macro domains. All of this is very promising in terms of the idea of a single metrical model of the body-as-locus-of-IRCs. I recommend this approach only as an initial step in the direction of an integrated model and theory that eliminates the various perplexing dualisms. There is some momentum behind this approach and that is why I recommend moving in this direction. All of the preceding is the foundation for a strong programme in the sociology of thinking and consciousness. I offer the following "strong programme" in the sociology of the brain as a heuristic plan to further future research and theory in this area.

The tenets of the strong programme in the sociology of thinking and consciousness (where "body" is short for "body-as-locus-of-IRCs"):

1. The brain is a subsystem of the body.
2. It is the body that thinks, the body that is aware.
3. The body is programmed for thought, emotions, and consciousness.
4. The programming process involves three sets of input systems:
   a. social inputs from interaction rituals and interaction ritual chains;
   b. systemic inputs from within the system, conditioned by (a);
   c. general environmental stimuli.
5. Inputs and outputs can be described in terms of information flows.
6. The body is a receiver and a transmitter.

7. IRs and IRCs are transmitters and receivers.
8. Why privilege the body? The answer is axiomatic – always privilege the material alternative.
9. Cherchez le chair et le sexe.
10. Eschew the pursuit of secure locations.
11. Our aim should be, in the contemporary context, to develop a model and a theory of the brain-CNS-body-IRC unit as a circulation of information.

In these early stages of developing this solution to the dualisms problem, I will necessarily be carrying over some old terms and their meanings even as my efforts and those of sympathetic colleagues across the disciplinary and interdisciplinary landscape are transforming what those terms mean and how they refer. The metrical model we are looking for will reflect the general move across the intellectual world to think in terms of networks rather than hierarchies; it will embody plasticity and complexity; it will develop into a circulation of information model. Thoughts and consciousness will come to be seen as consequences of the circulation of information throughout a network we can identify phenomenologically as the body and sets of bodies, and at another level as the consequence of the circulation of information throughout IRC networks. In other words, as a first approximation it is the body as a network of circulating information that thinks; in the end, however, it is social networks and bodies as the loci of IRCs that are the loci of thought and consciousness. This theory follows classically from Émile Durkheim and George Herbert Mead and is nowhere better expressed than in Randall Collins' (1998) sociology of philosophies.

The type of fully sociological theory of mind one finds in the work of Randall Collins and myself builds on the contributions of Durkheim (1995/1912) and G.H. Mead (1934). The most prominent social theories of mind in contemporary research draw more on the works of L. Vygotsky. Vygotsky is not as radically social as Mead, and thus appeals to the more psychologically minded researchers in AI, robotics, and social cognition. The Meadian approach will eventually have to prevail over Vygotsky in order to construct a robustly sociological theory of thinking, consciousness, mind, and brain.

These remarks serve as an introduction to the more thorough treatment I am developing in my book-in-progress, *The Social Life of the Brain*.

Chapter 8

Science, Religion, and Anarchism: The End of God and The Beginning of Inquiry

The God question and the science question are intimately intertwined. The God question is simply "Is there a God?" Adopting the form of anarchism that I have adopted here, anarchism as one of the sociological sciences, answers this question. And it answers the question once and for all in the same way and to the same degree that Copernicus, Galileo, and Newton answered once and for all questions about the basic shape of the physical world. This form of "once and for all" is realistic and not absolutist. If Copernicus, Galileo, and Newton give us the universe once and for all, they do it in a way that does not preclude Einstein or post-Einsteinian physics.

Religion and God have had a free pass for escaping critical scrutiny for centuries, and that free pass remains in force even today. We are all, whatever our color, creed, nationality, class, gender, or race encouraged to tolerate religious differences and the very idea of religion. There are various ways in which religion and God are placed beyond the pall of intelligent curious and critical interrogation. Perhaps the most pernicious is the idea that even seduced the sometime Marxist evolutionary biologist S.J. Gould – the idea of non-overlapping magisteria. Not only does this idea completely segregate science and religion, it leaves room for other modes of "inquiry" such as art. As soon, however, as we allow the social sciences to enter the marketplace or arena of the sciences, this idea and all other efforts at segregation evaporate. The social sciences – and sociology and anthropology in particular – make religion and God subjects and objects of scientific inquiry. Notice the dangerous idea still held in a sort of medieval abeyance by many members of the "real" (read "physical" or "natural") sciences that the social sciences are not really sciences. The entry of the social sciences into the religion and God sweepstakes is based on the unequivocal corralling of these two phenomena into the realm of human behaviors and social institutions.

Religion is a social institution, God is a social fact. The end of the transcendental, a project finally crystallized in the works of Émile Durkheim but hardly noticed even by his most adoring acolytes and less fervent admirers, means the end of God as an entity outside human society and culture. This is the great discovery – hinted at and intuited for millennia by the most insightful and fearless men and women among the host of fearful and cringing humanity that has desecrated this planet and human reason almost instinctually – that crystallized among the nineteenth century social theorists and social philosophers and critics.

In Defiance of der Reine Vernünft
Some orienting quotations: Why the death of the gods, the spiritual, religionism, and the rejection of the transcendental and supernatural matter for anarchist social studies of science.

POINT: I was sitting by the ocean one late summer afternoon, watching the waves rolling in and feeling the rhythm of my breathing, when I suddenly became aware of my whole environment as being engaged in a gigantic cosmic dance...I "saw" the atoms of the elements and those of my body participating in this cosmic dance of energy; I felt its rhythm and I "heard" its sound, and at that moment I knew that this was the Dance of Shiva, the Lord of Dancers. *Physicist Fritjof Capra*

COUNTERPOINT 1: Bread and meat would have robbed the ecstatic of many an angel visit: the opening of the refectory door must many a time have closed the gates of heaven to his gaze. *Anthropologist E.B. Tylor*

COUNTERPOINT 2: Physicists, according to Capra, "have made a leap towards the worldview of the Eastern mystics"...Even if Capra is, in some sense, correct, it is neither intuitively obvious nor logically necessary that the next step (or steps) must be in this same direction. We must also entertain the possibility that the "great step" was, from the point of view of the future of physics, a step in the wrong direction. Of course, Capra's approach is entirely, anthropologically speaking, wrongheaded. *Sociologist Sal Restivo*

COUNTERPOINT 3: Culture is developed and evaluated in particular historical situations. It cannot be studied apart from its use; its use is how we know it. Differentiated kinds of culture, such as we perceive "science" or "ideology" to be, are not concrete embodiments of different kinds of interest; rather they are single sets of resources more or less commonly used and evaluated in particular kinds of context with regard to particular kinds of interest. *Historian Steve Shapin*

COUNTERPOINT 4: ...the rationality of our society depends on its social structure. We witness in recent centuries a great progress called "secularization," which "disenchants" the world of superstitious ideas, substitutes scientific explanation, displaces religious authority, and substitutes legal-rational institutions...Precisely because society is integrated by the reciprocal dependencies of the division of labor, it does not require fanatical adherence to religious beliefs to hold together; therefore rational ideas can prevail. If the Valkyries (maidens of Odin) who choose the heroes to be slain in battle and conduct them to Valhalla (the Hall of Odin) are not to return, therefore, we must hope to see a healthful continuance of organic integration. But what in fact happens to organic solidarity in our time?* *Social theorist Daniel O'Keefe*

The integration concept here is based on Durkheim"s 1893 work The Division of Labor in Society. *Mechanical and organic solidarity are the two basic ways in which social solidarity is fostered.*

This great discovery – which dwarfs all others in our history except the discovery of how to discover – was echoed in the loss of faith among the nineteenth century intelligentsia as one historical or archaeological find after another piled up into an imposing ensemble of probabilities or consiliencies of evidences that buried faith and belief – or began to. For, while this era of discovery should have been enough to kill off this delusion once and for all, it lived on. And if we don't understand why it lived on, we will never understand what is at stake in aligning ourselves with the death of godders. God is a symbol, not a material or transmaterial entity (whatever that could possibly mean); consider the limitations of apohatic theology which continually verges on a degree of divorce from reality that borders on insanity. All gods symbolize the societies that generate them. There are many forms and types of gods but they are all symbolic projections of social realities.

What are the consequences for the view of history as the divine unfolding of God's plan and God's voice if we adopt a view of history as a human narrative and moreover as a social and cultural narrative? What is the significance of death of God narratives in theology and philosophy for our understanding of history and time? Physical and natural scientists have had a great deal to say about such issues in dialogue with theologians and believers, both as participants in dialogues of harmony, convergence, and détente (reflected in the contemporary writings and lectures of Tenzin Gyatso and Karen Armstrong) and as conflictful skeptics (notably through the efforts of aggressive opponents such as Dennett, Dawkins, Harris, Hitchens, and other so-called "new atheists" under a banner of the logic of anger).

Students often ask me, "If sociologists have discovered God, why isn't this more widely known and taught?" My colleagues themselves are very tentative, ambivalent, and uncertain about this issue. One of them said to me, "I agree with you that we have discovered God, but I don't think you should be revealing that sociological truth in your lectures or writings". Some are suspicious of my use of the term "proof" because they think even though they agree with me the phenomenon is too complex to be captured in a proof, sociological or otherwise. Some of them write textbooks that demonstrate this discovery, but in the interest of a kind of misguided tolerance often start or end with the ill-fitting caveat that their findings should not disrupt your beliefs. Science – systematic inquiry – is nothing if not a continuing process of upsetting and resetting our beliefs. At some point, those of us who are in a position to communicate mundane and revolutionary findings to our students and the reading public need to reveal the nature of our convictions. We need to do this without any intention of imposing our views on others, or with the goal of forcing others to take up our intellectual causes. We do, however, have an obligation as scholars and intellectuals to let people know what we are up to. This is – education is – a dangerous enterprise because it propagates new ideas that may eventually take hold in the future. There is no neutral position here. The very idea, the very practice of education has a politics of knowledge, a preference for a certain form of life. We are the children who will speak up when we see that the emperor has no clothes, even while all the adults claim that he does so as not to appear foolish or, what amounts to the same thing, out of step with the mob.

Secularization is just one sign that the old religions are dead or dying. The web of doubt that spread among nineteenth century thinkers was an early sign of this process – the novelist Thomas Hardy writing a poem titled "God's Funeral", Nietzsche infamously proclaiming "the death of God"; H.L. Mencken making a list of immortal gods who had died; the disappearance of colleges with religious affiliations; and the very disappearance of God.

I do indeed plan to stress the phenomenological reality of people's experiences with religion and God and the positive value of these experiences. At the same time, I have to raise the question of who benefits and in what ways from those experiences (in behavioral and social micro, meso, and macro contexts). And I have to raise the problem of reference – *this* is the Durkheimian problem. People need (in a fundamentally sociological sense) moral order and social solidarity, but these come in a variety of forms and from a variety of places. My claim is twofold: first, it *matters* where they come from and in what form they come in; and second, believing in things that don't exist, when sustained over long periods of time institutionally and culturally, can indeed lead to a form of institutional or collective insanity. At this juncture of history, culture, and global ecological geopolitics, our survival as a species depends on eliminating delusionary takes on how the world works.

Truth, of course, is a social construction and a creation of truth communities. There are good reasons why diverse contemporary truths and truth communities that are at odds will continue to stand tall and firm. In the end game, however, the choice will go like this; those who stand with Copernicus, Galileo, and Newton against Ptolemy, who stand with Darwin against the creationists, who stand with the germ theorists against those who believe in demon possession – those people, those communities, who stand with Durkheim, Marx, and Nietzsche – will have the best chance to solve the developing problems of survival we face as a species.

The Hegemonic Rule of the Physical and Life Sciences over the Realms of Soul, Spirit, Consciousness, Mind, and God

Here is the scientist Francis Collins, M.D., Ph.D., Director of the Human Genome Institute at the National Institutes of Health in Washington D.C. in an interview with Discover magazine (February 2007: 76):

> Is there any dogma more unsupported by the facts than from the scientist who stands up and says, "I know there is no God"? Science is woefully unsuited to ask the question of God in the first place. So give the religious folks a

break. They are seeking the kind of spiritual truths that have always interested humankind but that science cannot really address.

Now line up Richard Dawkins, Daniel Dennett, and Sam Harris. Harris studied philosophy at Stanford and is at this writing completing a doctorate in neuroscience. Richard Dawkins is an ethologist and evolutionary biologist, and Daniel Dennett is a philosopher in the analytic tradition and a self-styled autodidact informally tutored in a variety of sciences by leading scientists. They are all proponents of what Collins might call the atheist's creed. Contrast Collins' claim with the arguments made by Victor J. Stenger, physicist, astronomer, philosopher, in *God: The Failed Hypothesis – How Science Shows that God Does Not Exist* (2007). If we were asked to be tolerant and respectful of people who believed that 2+2=5, and if indeed there were significant numbers of such people, we would consider it irresponsible and in fact argue that that belief constituted a clear and present danger to our way of life and our capacity for survival. My caveat here is only that we understand 2+2=5 more as an Orwellian belief (as in *Nineteen Eighty-Four*) and less as a Dostoevskian act of creativity and rebellion that leaves 2+2=4 honored and untouched (as in his *Notes from the Underground*).

There are two other considerations here. First, I want to speak from a ground on which 2+2=4 interprets or symbolizes a world in which if I collect two apples, and then collect two other apples, and then group them together, I will have four apples. Second, I want to protect 2+2=4 and its form from being applied willy, nilly to such situations as, for example, mapping the movement in which one cloud is moving east, another is moving west on the same line and in the same plane, they meet, and they coalesce. Symbolizing this physical event using mundane arithmetic gives us a pseudo-equality 1+1=1. Thus, while there are in a sense multiple realities (and indeed working algebras based on 1+1=1), they all rest on the ground of what I shall call Reality I, the world in which two apples and two apples give four apples, the world in which survival depends on looking both ways when you cross the street. It is irresponsible to be tolerant and respectful of people, groups, and cultures who believe in God, gods, spirits, etc. because it is transparently clear that these beliefs are wrong in the same way that 2+2=5 is wrong and that these beliefs pose a clear and present danger to our species' ways of life, capacity for survival, and potential for creative and critical cultural development. I propose the following strong programme in the sociology of proof, a step we need in other to demonstrate the fallacy of the idea that you can't prove or disprove God.

The classical proofs for the existence of God and their modern mathematical imitations are tautological in extremis and border on schizophrenic constructions. They resolve to "God exists, therefore God exists". Consider, in evaluating the nature of proofs, that the classical syllogism is itself a tautology in extremis. If A is B and B is C then A is C. But if A is B, then B is A. If B is C then C is A. So here is what the syllogism states: If A is A, and A is A, then A is A. Perhaps there is some

Proofs are not transparent. They have to rest on background assumptions and specific knowledge about symbols, relations between and among symbols, syntax, grammar, and semantics. The proof for 1+1=2 takes on very different forms over time. For Plato the proof seems transparent; it is necessarily true because it is independent of any preliminary act of construction. Leibniz takes a few lines to carry out the proof which is based on the axiom that if we replace equals by equals in an equation the equality continues to hold. From a later period, we can construct a somewhat more complicated proof based on Peano's postulates that takes a little more space than the proof Leibniz proposed. The postulates define the number series as the series of successors to the number zero. Informally they are: (i) zero is a number; (ii) zero is not the successor of any number; (iii) the successor of any number is a number; (iv) no two numbers have the same successor; and (v) if zero has a property, and if whenever a number has a property its successor has the property, then all numbers have the property. And Whitehead and Russell spend all of the first volume of their *Principia Mathematica* (1910-1913; 1927) and about one hundred pages into volume two before they can establish that 1+1=2 (Theorem #110.643). Note incidentally that the sociologist of knowledge Karl Mannheim considered arithmetic equalities such as 1+1=2 and 2+2=4 outside the realms of history, culture, and society. Oswald Spengler, by contrast, offered perhaps the earliest argument for a sociology of such equalities. Science studies pioneers Bloor and Restivo independently constructed sociologies of 2+2=4.

Applied mathematicians seem readier than pure mathematicians to accept proofs involving large amounts of computer time (as in the case of the proof for the 4-color theorem). When I claim that we can prove there is no God, I do so based on sociological resources and the sociological cogito, resources not available to proof communities which adhere to the idea that you can't prove or disprove God, or that you can prove or disprove God using physical or natural science. In order to begin to grasp why it is in fact possible to prove that there is no God the following statements about proofs must be kept in mind:

PROOFS ARE SITUATED
PROOFS ARE CONTEXTUAL
PROOFS ARE INDEXICAL
PROOFS ARE SOCIAL INSTITUTIONS
PROOFS ARE SOCIAL CONSTRUCTIONS
PROOFS ARE PRODUCED BY, IN, AND FOR PROOF COMMUNITIES

logical sleight of hand here, so I don't want to lose sight of the fact that proving is a complex social activity. But proofs are, at the end of the day, communal technologies for reinforcing social solidarities and moral orders. See the dialogue on the syllogism in the Appendix.

A Lecture On Religion And God For The Twenty-First Century Mind

As long as the belief in God or Plato's forms is nourished, purity in mathematics, logic, and science will be sustained. As long as purity is sustained the human capacity for problem solving on the evolutionary stage will be compromised. Sal Restivo.

Grundlagen

I use the German word here because if I write "the fundamentals" I lay myself open to charges of being an epistemological fundamentalist. If I write "foundations", I might be charged with being ignorant of the arguments against foundationalism.

Some things are clearly true, and some things are clearly false. Postmodernism has demonstrated that truth and falsity are complicated, contextual, and contingent not that we cannot tell true from false. It's true we humans will all die sooner or later; it's false that there are humans who can fly without the aid of apparatuses. It's true that bullets will hurt, maim, or kill unprotected humans. It's false that humans can survive without oxygen for an hour. Truisms, perhaps, but truisms are the shadows of a realm of truths. If you wish to add the caveat that even the most self-evident truths deserve our skeptical scrutiny, I will agree with you. Clearly, however, truths and falsities come to us with different degrees of uncertainty, different warrants for skepticism, and different degrees of hesitations concerning practical applications. I grant all this but note that I am attracted to the recalcitrance of certain features of the world represented in truth statements that come to us with high degrees of closure.

Some people know more than other people. Knowledge is always fallible, corrigible, and indexical. This means people know things and know them in ways that have practical and demonstrable consequences. My doctor does not have to be perfect to know more than I do about how bodies work and to be able to put this knowledge to practical use in, for example, removing my appendix with a high probability of success. Applying the Grundlagen to religion and the gods, we get the following propositions:

1. There are things that are demonstrably true and false about religion and the gods.
2. Some people know more about religion and the gods than others. The people who know more are not necessarily the most religious or those with the greatest faith.

   2a. Those people who know the most about religion and the gods don't have to be religious or have faith but they do have to have a religious sensibility.
3. Don't be intimidated or seduced by the Socratic and Cartesian aporia. Bringing their level of doubt into your worldview requires a highly educated intelligence. Even for those with such an education my advice is the same: build your life around material, demonstrable certainties. Make these the grounds for living your life and nourishing your worldview. Even your

dreams, fantasies, and imaginings should find their ground in the social and material certainties of our everyday world. But be careful; certainties are plentiful but they contain many traps for the unwary. Perhaps the rule should be: build on your certainties but keep all of them under aporial surveillance.

4. There are certain fallacies that follow from a comprehensive interdisciplinary knowledge of and understanding of how the world and human beings work. I have identified the following fallacies:

The Fallacies

These fallacies are the raw materials for a set of theorems about how our world works.

The Transcendental Fallacy (also known as the theologian's fallacy) is that there is a world or that there are worlds beyond our own – transcendental worlds, supernatural worlds, worlds of souls, spirits and ghosts, gods, devils, and angels, heavens and hells. *There are no such worlds.* They are symbolic of social categories and classifications in our earthly societies and cultures. There is nothing beyond our material, organic, and social world. Death is final; there is no soul, there is no life after death. It is also possible that the so-called "many worlds interpretation" in quantum mechanics is contaminated by this fallacy as the result of mathegrammatical illusions. The world, the universe, may be more complex than we can know or imagine, but that complexity does not include transcendental or supernatural features. Stated positively, this is Durkheim's Law.

The Subscendental Fallacy (also known as the logician's fallacy or eponymously as the Chomsky fallacy) is that there are "deep structures" or "immanent structures" that are the locus of explanations for language, thought, and human behavior in general. *Such "structures" are as ephemeral and ethereal as transcendental and supernatural worlds.* They lead to conceptions of logic, mathematics, and language as "free standing," "independent," "history, culture, and value free" sets of statements. And they support misguided sociobiological, genetic, and brain-centered explanatory strategies. Restivo's Law.

The Private Worlds Fallacy (also known as the philosopher's fallacy) is that individual human beings harbor intrinsically private experiences. The profoundly social nature of humans, of symbols, and of language argues against intrinsically private experiences (as Wittgenstein, Goffman, and others have amply demonstrated). Goffman's Law.

The Internal Life Fallacy is that when we engage in discourses about surrogate counters, imitation, and artificial creatures that mimic us, we need to remind ourselves that we are working in an arena of symbolic and materialized analogies and metaphors. Such efforts carry a high emotional charge because they take place at the boundaries of our skins. Analogy and generalization, if they can be shown to have constructive scientific outcomes, need not obligate us to embrace identity. Consider, for example, the case of building robots. Robots will not have to have "gut feelings" in the identical sense humans have gut feelings because they are organic machines. Even this "fact" needs to be scrutinized. What we "feel" is given to us by our language, our conversations, our forms of talking, our cultures and social institutions. At the end of the day, feelings are not straightforward matters of bio-electro-chemical processes. Electro-mechanical creatures will turn out to be just as susceptible to internal life experiences as humans once they have developed language, conversation, and forms of talk. They will have electo-mechanical "gut feelings". This implies a social life and awareness. Roboticists may already have made some moves in this direction with the development of signal schemas and subsumption-based hormonal control (Arkin, 1998: 434ff). The development of cyborgs and cybrids may make this point moot.

The Psychologistic Fallacy (or neuroistic fallacy) is that the human being and/or the human brain is/are free standing and independent, that they can be studied on their own terms independently of social and cultural contexts, influences, and forces. This is also known as the neuroistic error. It encompasses the idea that mind and consciousness are brain phenomena. *Human beings and human brains are in fact constitutively social.* This is the most radical formulation of the response to this fallacy. A more charitable formulation would give disciplinary credibility to neuroscience and cognitive approaches to brain studies. These approaches might produce relevant results in certain contexts. Then there might be fruitful ways to pursue interdisciplinary studies linking the social sciences and the neurosciences. It may indeed be possible to construct a neurosocial model of the self. This would entail that socialization operates on a brain-central nervous system-body (signifying an integrated entity that eliminates conventional brain/mind-body and brain-mind dichotomies) and not on a "person" *per se*. Brother's Law (after Brothers, 1991, 2002).

The Eternal Relevance Fallacy is that ancient and more recently departed philosophers should be important and even leading members of our inquiring conversations about social life. *An act of intellectual courage is needed to rid us of Plato and Hegel. Once they are eliminated, an entire pantheon of outmoded and outdated thinkers, from Aristotle to Kant, will disappear from our radar*. This move might also go a long way toward eliminating the worshipful attitude intellectuals often adopt to the more productive and visible members of their contemporary discourse communities. The caveat here is that some ancient and some modern thinkers (departed ones, as well as some who are still with us) who can be claimed for philosophy are still extremely valuable for us. Marx, Nietzsche, and Wittgenstein come immediately to mind.

The Corollary Intellectual's Fallacy is that philosophers as philosophers (and psychologists as psychologists) have anything at all to tell us anymore about the social world. In the wake of the work of sociologists from Emile Durkheim (1995/1912) to Mary Douglas (1988), all the central human problems of traditional and contemporary philosophy resolve into (not "reduce to") problems in sociology and anthropology.

The neque demonstra neque redargue Fallacy, The "Neither Provable nor Unprovable Fallacy" is that one can neither prove nor disprove some claim, proposition, or statement. In the cases where this claim is true it is because it is made in the context of the physical and/or natural sciences for a claim that falls under the jurisdiction of the social sciences. *In the context of sociology this statement is not necessarily true.* Consider: One can neither prove nor disprove the existence of God. This has not kept theologians, philosophers, and mathematicians from Anselm to Gödel from proposing proofs for the existence of God. While all proofs build conclusions into premises, God proofs are universally contaminated by this strategy. The fallacy has, on the other hand, kept social thinkers and social critics from proposing proofs for their beliefs about God as a delusion, a myth, and so on. In fact, proofs are situated, contingent, contextualized, community matters, and indeed, social constructions and social institutions. Therefore, within the world of Durkheim's *Elementary Forms* and what follows a proof that God does not exist is clearly possible.

The NOMA Fallacy is the fallacy, defended most recently by S.J. Gould, that science and religion are non-overlapping magisteria. *Once we admit social science into the science and religion dialogue this fallacy is revealed.*

The Experential Fallacy is the fallacy that experience and feeling are trustworthy modes of interrogating and knowing reality. Consider that our immediate sensation is that the earth is fixed in place; we do not experience the earth rotating, wobbling in precession, or racing through the galaxy. In order to understand and explain the earth in motion, we have to abandon our immediate experience of fixity, our feeling that the earth is stable. If we assume fixity and stability, we will arrive at absurd conclusions about the earth and ourselves. If, based on information garnered by expanding the scale, scope, and depth of our experiences, we come to admit that the earth moves, then (in Tolstoy's words) "we arrive at laws". In the case of history, society, and culture, we do not experience, we do not feel, we are not conscious of our dependence on the external world and on others. This is not straightforward. We are, in fact, more aware of our dependence on the material world than we are of our dependence on the social world. Differences in our levels of awareness across our material and social environments do not readily override our feeling that we are free-willing beings. In the prior instance, we had to discard a sense of an immobility that was not real and admit a motion we did not feel. In this instance we are required to renounce our experience of free will and admit to a dependence, and especially a dependence on social causes and forces, that we do not feel. It may be easier to admit to ourselves that we are subject to recalcitrant physical laws, that we are thermodynamic systems subject to the laws of thermodynamics than to admit that we are social systems subject to sociological laws. But we are just as subject to one set of laws as to the other set of laws. You must keep in mind the distinction between open and closed systems and the distinction between lawful and determined in order to avoid the fallacy that being subject to causes is the same as unmitigated determinism. Tolstoy's Law.

The Napoleon Fallacy is that heroic larger than life individuals make history. How we think about and experience freedom and necessity depends (here I follow Tolstoy's analysis in *War and Peace*) on three things: (1) the relationship between the person carrying out an action and the external world in which the action is carried out; (2) the relationship between the actor and time; and (3) the actor's place in the causal nexus out of which the action arises. All things being equal, there are fewer degrees of freedom for the drowning person than for the person on dry land. If we focus on the person standing apart, alone in his/her room or within the woods, his/her actions seem to us and to him/her to be free. If instead we focus on his/her relation to the things (material and symbolic) and people around him/her now and in the past we will begin to multiply the influences on who and what s/he is as a whole person. As we multiply the influences we diminish the degrees of freedom on his/her actions and thoughts and see how necessity weighs on him/her.

It is also the case that our own current actions and thoughts appear to be freer by comparison with those of someone who lived a long time ago and whose life is open to our scrutiny in a different way than is our own. That person's life appears to have fewer degrees of freedom than does our own; but from a future perspective, ours too will appear to have had fewer degrees of freedom than we can now perceive. This is the fact of the matter for untutored introspection; the trained observer can already see fewer degrees of freedom that the untutored person observing his/her own life.

The more time passes, or the more my introspections and judgments go forward, the more I will find myself doubting that I have freedom of action and thought. History makes events, actions, and thoughts seem less arbitrary and less subject to free will: as Tolstoy points out:

> The Austro-Prussian war appears to us undoubtedly the result of the crafty conduct of Bismarck, and so on. The Napoleonic wars still seem to us, though already questionably, to be the outcome of their heroes' will. But in the Crusades we already see an event occupying its definite place in history and without which we cannot imagine the modern history of Europe, though to the chroniclers of the Crusades that event appeared as merely due to the will of certain people.

Finally, attending to the unfolding of our understanding of the nexus of causal chains leads us inevitably to seeing actions and thoughts as consequences of what came before, contradicting the transparency of free will in action at the moment that a particular idea occurs to us or we perform a particular act. Understanding is the greatest enemy of the ideology of free will, ignorance its greatest nourishment. And as for "responsibility", that will appear to be greater or less depending on how much we know about the circumstances of the person under our judge's eye, how much time has passed since the judged act, and how well we understand the causes of the kind of act being judged. Tolstoy's Second Law.

Classic Fallacies from Philosophy

The *fallacy of misplaced concreteness*, described by philosopher Alfred North Whitehead, involves thinking something is a "concrete" reality when in fact it is an abstract belief, opinion or concept about the way things are.

The fallacy refers to Whitehead's thoughts on the relationship of spatial and temporal location of objects. Whitehead rejects the notion that a real, concrete object in the universe can be described simply in terms of spatial or temporal extension. Rather, the object must be described as a field that has both a location in space and a location in time. This is analogous to lessons learned from E.A. Abbott's *Flatland* (1884): just as humans cannot perceive a line that has width but no breadth, humans also cannot perceive an object that has spatial but not temporal position (or vice versa).

> ...among the primary elements of nature as apprehended in our immediate experience, there is no element whatever which possesses this character of simple location. ...[Instead,] I hold that by a process of constructive abstraction we can arrive at abstractions which are the simply located bits of material, and at other abstractions which are the minds included in the scientific scheme.

Accordingly, the real error is an example of what I have termed: The Fallacy of Misplaced Concreteness (Whitehead (1925), p. 58. also see Whitehead (1919), Part III).

A *category mistake*, or *category error*, is a semantic or ontological error by which a property is ascribed to a thing that could not possibly have that property. For example, the statement "the business of the book sleeps eternally" is syntactically correct, but it is meaningless or nonsense or, at the very most, metaphorical, because it incorrectly ascribes the property, *sleeps eternally*, to *business*, and incorrectly ascribes the property, *business*, to the token, *the book*.

The term "category mistake" was introduced by Gilbert Ryle in his book *The Concept of Mind* (1949) to remove what he argued to be a confusion over the nature of mind born from Cartesian metaphysics. It was alleged to be a mistake to treat the mind as an object made of an immaterial substance because predications of substance are not meaningful for a collection of dispositions and capacities.

Human Survival and the Big Questions

We are asking ourselves the big questions about life, the universe, and everything with more sound and fury than ever. The media are overflowing with explanations about miracles, Biblical facts, the life of Jesus, the dogma fights of the fundamentalism wars, and the creationism/intelligent design versus evolutionary theory conflict. Culture wars and science wars have darkened our intellectual horizons. Dan Brown's *The Da Vinci Code*, a work of fiction, spawned an industry of criticisms, commentaries, editions and translations, a Hollywood movie, and a lawsuit. The discourse on the *Code* continually blurred the distinctions and rules that separate fiction and non-fiction. All of this is being driven more by anger, fear, and ignorance than by sound scholarship and fearless inquiry. And even where sound scholarship gets a foothold, it does so without the fearlessness needed to get to the bottom of the issues.

> **Intervention 1:** For Germany, the criticism of religion has been essentially completed, and the criticism of religion is the prerequisite of all criticism. The profane existence of error is compromised as soon as its heavenly *oratio pro aris et focis* ["speech for the altars and hearths," i.e., for God and country] has been refuted. Man, who has found only the reflection of himself in the fantastic reality of heaven, where he sought a superman, will no longer feel disposed to find the mere appearance of himself, the non-man [Unmensch], where he seeks and must seek his true reality.
>
> The foundation of irreligious criticism is: Man makes religion, religion does not make man. Religion is, indeed, the self-consciousness and self-esteem of man who has either not yet won through to himself, or has already lost himself again. But man is no abstract being squatting outside the world. Man is the

world of man – state, society. This state and this society produce religion, which is an inverted consciousness of the world, because they are an inverted world. Religion is the general theory of this world, its encyclopaedic compendium, its logic in popular form, its spiritual *point d'honneur*, its enthusiasm, its moral sanction, its solemn complement, and its universal basis of consolation and justification. It is the fantastic realization of the human essence since the human essence has not acquired any true reality. The struggle against religion is, therefore, indirectly the struggle against that world whose spiritual aroma is religion. Religious suffering is, at one and the same time, the expression of real suffering and a protest against real suffering. Religion is the sigh of the oppressed creature, the heart of a heartless world, and the soul of soulless conditions. It is the opium of the people. (Marx, 1844).

Intervention 2: [W]hat I ask of the free thinker is that he should confront religion in the same mental state as the believer...[H]e who does not bring to the study of religion a sort of religious sentiment cannot speak about it! He is like a blind man trying to talk about color.

Now I shall address the free believer...Without going so far as to disbelieve the formula we believe in, we must forget it provisionally, reserving the right to return to it later. Having once escaped from this tyranny, we are no longer in danger of perpetrating the error and injustice into which certain believers have fallen who have called my way of interpreting religion basically irreligious. There cannot be a rational interpretation of religion which is fundamentally irreligious; an irreligious interpretation of religion would be an interpretation which denied the phenomenon it was trying to explain.
Émile Durkheim (1858-1917).

Occasionally, a self-proclaimed voice of reason emerges to bring order to the chaos of these debates and conflicts. Philosophers and journalists come to our intellectual rescue with naturalistic explanations for religion based on evolutionary theory, genetics, biology, sociobiology, and brain research. An oceanographer tells us that the Sea of Galilee may have been frozen when Jesus "walked on water". The new atheists mobilize a logic of anger against the irrationality of religion. The explanations, criticisms, theories, and ideas proliferate without end and without critical stop signs. Physical and natural scientists figure prominently in this discourse, some proving God with science, others using science to disprove God. Notably missing from this dialogue are sociologists and anthropologists.

The sociologist Rodney Stark (2008) has made it into the bookstores with his *Discovering God*, but Stark is an independent (less "evangelical" than he once was, perhaps) Christian. He begins his book with a welcome critique of the new atheists and concludes it with the claim that the universe is the ultimate revelation of God and that (following Kepler) "science is theology and thereby serves as another method for the discovery of God". And anthropologist Barbara

King (2007) has written beautifully about the social roots of the religious imagination in our evolution as a species bound by belongingness. And yet, while she believes that science has something meaningful to say about the evolution of the religious imagination, she cannot bring herself to grant that science might actually "explain" religion. So the problem persists. In spite of the overwhelming consiliency of evidences that the gods are human creations, very few people seem to have the intellectual and community contexts and resources needed to give up the belief in Godhead.

Where are the fearless social scientists in these debates, discussions, critical explorations? Why are they silent and silenced? Where are the voices of the intellectuals and scholars who see all of this transparent freedom to explain, criticize, and debate religion and God as another cover up – unintentional and intentional – of the discoveries made by sociologists, anthropologists, archaeologists, and scientific historians? One of the great consequences of the emergence of the social sciences has been the progressive rejection of the idea that there are realms of reality that transcend our everyday world, supernatural realms that escape our social, physical, and natural being.

There are two problems with the analytical and explanatory literature on religion flooding the media today. One is that even writers who are non-believers are hesitant to close off reasons to believe for their readers, even when the evidence they present fairly assessed leads to that conclusion. The second is a social blindness that keeps writers from seeing the sociology staring them in their faces as they propose one genetic or neurological explanation after the other. In his *The Faith Instinct*, Nicholas Wade (2009) demonstrates the consequences of this affliction. He reviews the contributions of the classical sociologist Émile Durkheim but doesn't actually hear Durkheim's message. On page 7 of his book he writes:

> The rules of sentence formation are so complex that babies must presumably possess an innate syntax-generating machinery, rather than having to figure out the rules for themselves. The existence of such a neural mechanism would explain why infants learn to speak so effortlessly, and at a specific age, as if some neural developmental program is being rolled out at that time.

The choice isn't between innate machinery and figuring things out for themselves. The choice is between innate, individual, and social (interactional) causes. What makes Wades's statement so curious is that on that same page he writes: "People survive as social groups, not as individuals, and little is more critical to a social species than its member's ability to communicate with one another."

The other curious thing is that Wade, like Chomsky, appears to have never been a child learning a language or observed a child learning a language. Only a severe case of social blindness could lead them to claim that infants learn to speak "so effortlessly".

The Jesus Narratives

Consider that from the perspective of a sociological materialism, Jesus was either one of the mythical solar messiahs; the solar messiah mythology was socially tattooed onto the life of an historical Jesus; or Jesus was a composite character (and therefore fictional) on whom the solar messiah myth was imposed. Outside of this perspective, one general strategy tends to be to assume the reality of Biblical stories and then set out to prove or otherwise theorize the facts of the matter. Another is to assume the good intentions of the Biblical writers as historians or journalists trying to be "objective" and then to pull apart their stories. These are empty exercises given what we know sociologically, anthropologically, archeologically, and historically about the Bible and Christianity (and all other religions and religious texts).

Contrary to what Nicholas Wade believes, religion and the social/moral order are not separate units of evolutionary natural selection, and there is no God gene. Society precedes the individual; the individual is a social unit, a social fact. It is worth repeating that humans come onto the evolutionary scene not as individuals who then at some Hobbesian point choose to come together socially by way, for example, of a social contract. Rather, humans emerge everywhere, always, and already social. And these humans emerge everywhere, always, and already religious. That is, where we have societies, we have moral orders systematized as more or less distinct religious activities and institutions. We cannot argue as Wade does that the earliest societies vary according to whether they have religion or not and that natural selection selects for religion. Natural selection does operate on the level of culture and social organization, but cannot select for religion per se because religion is one with social order.

The anthropologist Maurice Leehhardt was told by his father, a pastor and a geologist, that facts are the word of God. Durkheim taught us that God is society. We could then say that facts are the word of society. For a less mythological way of putting this, we can turn to Nietzsche (1974/1887: 35-36):

> We are not thinking frogs, nor objectifying and registering mechanisms with their innards removed: constantly, we have to give birth to our thoughts out of our pain and, like mothers, endow them with all we have of blood, heart, fire, pleasure, agony, conscience, fate, and catastrophe.

If we combine this observation with Marx's insights on the social nature of thinking and consciousness, of science and religion, and of the self itself, and with Durkheim's ideas on religion as an eminently social thing, we come up with most of the ingredients of what we can call the social constructionist paradigm for understanding religion and God.

Tolerance and open-mindedness are as much impositions as "facts of the matter". We do, however, have an obligation as scholars and intellectuals to let people know what we are up to. Education is a dangerous enterprise because it propagates new ideas that may eventually take hold in the future if they do not do so immediately. Secularization is just one sign that the old religions are dead or dying. The idea that because religions have survived secularization and even thrived in its wake and context the secularization thesis is wrong is a distraction from a powerful historical unfolding.

As I look back on what I've just written it seems to make it easy to chalk up my position as one involving individual choices about what to teach, how to teach it, and when and where to teach it. In fact, against the background of everything that has come before in this book, what I write here I write as the *we* of a thought collective, of a particular community of intellectuals. This *we* is organized and organizing in the context of this time and place, and I write at the nexus of a particular biography, and historical and cultural contexts. This book represents another iteration in the fitful movements of a secular culture and worldview trying to take root.

This moment was most recently foreshadowed by the Enlightenment, and Hobbes' defense of The Great Separation. Hobbes argued that no just and reasonable political life could be based on a Christian political theology. The modern romantics, following Rousseau rather than Hobbes, sought to implement a political theology grounded in human experience. They did not want to jettison the divine and religious sentiments but wanted instead to purify them in a rational way. In spite of their differences, Hobbes' and Rousseau's followers agreed that the Biblical God could no longer be taken seriously. Friedrich Schleiermacher tried to span this difference by claiming that we should refer to our human awareness of our dependence on "something" as God and let this replace the notion of divine revelation. It took someone with a highly developed sociological imagination and a religious sentiment, Emile Durkheim, to finally see that that "something" was in fact society, the social group.

Let us step back for a moment and recall the great controversy stirred up in ancient Greece when Protagoras (ca.490-420 BCE), a pre-Socratic sophist, proclaimed that "man is the measure of all things". This violated the prevailing idea that the universe was based on something beyond human influence. Schleiermacher takes the same Protagorean step by making man the measure of theological truth in the midst of a world ruled by a God beyond humanity and human influence, a God we could know through revelation. As Lilla (2008: 228) notes, the revolutionary idea in Schleiermacher was "the unstated assumption... that we can find God by finding ourselves". When Durkheim and the sociologists decentered the self and put society and the group at the center of the human universe, the rule became we can actually discover God by finding ourselves in society and the group. Durkheim and the sociologists benefitted from the development of modern critical Biblical studies pioneered in the German universities in the wake of the wars of liberation (War of the Sixth Coalition, 1812-1814) that sent Napoleon Bonaparte into exile. The secularization thesis and process is not dead because there are still vibrant signs of belief and faith anymore than the evolutionary thesis is dead because there is resistance from creationists and intelligent design advocates. It is the job of educators to facilitate the secular movement as part of their commitment to intellectual excellence.

Getting Things Right is Still Possible, Postmodernism Notwithstanding

It is crucial for human survival that we get certain things about how our world works right. Contrary to many of the conclusions reached by scholars and intellectuals in the postmodern world, it is still possible to tell the truth, it is still possible to distinguish what is real from what is not real, it is still possible to make a distinction between right and wrong facts of the matter. All of this has admittedly become more complicated, more subtle, more inspired sociologically. But truth telling has not become impossible. Historically, our collective capacity to solve problems of survival has depended on leaving childish things behind, on reasoning our way past the old myths and mysteries. Traditional beliefs about religion and God have survived the virtual onslaught against traditional beliefs in general by science and technology, but not without giving some ground. The nineteenth century "loss of faith" was new in scope and scale, but religious beliefs have been the object of criticism, skepticism, and theorizing from ancient times to the present. What was unusual about the nineteenth century was that assumed matters of fact started to wither in the face of new archaeological and historical evidence about and the emergence of social theories about religion and God.

What are the consequences of viewing the history of the idea of God (and of gods in general) and religion in comparative and cross-cultural perspective, and intersecting this view with advances in the social and cultural sciences over the last 200 years? More specifically, what are the consequences for the view of history as the divine unfolding of God's plan and God's voice if we adopt a view of history as a human narrative and moreover as a social and cultural narrative? What is the significance of death of God narratives in theology and philosophy for our understanding of history and time? Physical and natural scientists have had a great deal to say about such issues in dialogue with theologians and believers, both as participants in conflictful dialogues (notably though the efforts of aggressive opponents such as Dennett, Dawkins, Harris, and Hitchens using a logic of anger), and in dialogues of harmony, convergence, and détente (most notably and visibly in the works of Karen Armstrong and the Dalai Lama). The logics of anger, mystery, and uncritical skepticism have dominated debates and discussions about God, religion, and society for thousands of years. The emergence and development of the social and cultural sciences has changed the grounds and terms of heavenly discourses, but this change has not penetrated the centers of contemporary or even more broadly modern intellectual and lay circles of inquiry.

There are numerous indications that the continuing tolerance for religious ideas which even atheistic and post-atheism intellectuals and laypeople take for granted is threatening our survival. The 27 million dollar creationist museum recently opened near Cincinnati, Ohio flaunts a level of ignorance that is equivalent to putting astrology on a par with astronomy or numerology on a par with mathematics. The problems being generated in the context of contemporary global society will not yield to solutions contaminated by illusory and delusionary belief systems. The culture wars are – or should be – a battleground for survival pitting the best of educated reason against the fear of education and thinking.

Closing the Door on Pure Reason: Once More, the Manifesto of "There is no There, There": A Reiteration

I am guided here by Gertrude Stein's remark, "There is no there, there". Rebecca Goldstein's beautifully and thoughtfully fashioned study of Kurt Gödel and his famous theorems affords us yet another opportunity to wonder about the resistance of Platonic, transcendental, and supernatural thinking to the lessons of modernity and post-modernity. These lessons, admittedly, are buried beneath the rubble of the wars, holocausts, political economic failures, and ecological disasters of the twentieth and now the twenty-first century. The brilliant flare-up of the very idea of "the social" between 1840 and 1918 and the discovery sciences it gave form to has remained virtually invisible on the intellectual landscape formed over the last 150 years. Until and unless we uncover that revolution, we will continue to be haunted by the ghosts of Plato, Descartes, Kant, and God. These ghosts cannot be banished by materialism *per se*. What is required is a sociological materialism, a cultural materialism. Anarcho-sociology brings together in my worldview the lessons and perspectives of sociology, materialism, communism (Marxism), socialism, and anarchism. It is no simple ideological or political victory I champion but an adaptation, an evolutionary matter of life and death. So long as these ghosts of philosophy and theology haunt us, we will be unable as a species to take advantage of whatever small opportunities are left to us to make something worthwhile flourish on this planet for even a little while. The issues here are that big.

The more general problem we are faced with here is the problem of abstraction. How does one account for abstract ideas without falling into the traps of transcendental and supernatural realism? The solution is to stop making a distinction between concrete and abstract ideas. It is important to realize that the distinction between concrete and abstract is really a distinction between two different kinds of concreteness. A materialist sociology of abstraction reveals it to be the form of concreteness found in highly professionalized intellectual work. We must escape the idea of "abstractions", an idea that is a companion and surrogate for "purity"; for wherever we find the "abstract" and the "pure" there also we find the danger of falling into the trap of believing in supernatural and transcendental realities.

Wonder en isgheen wonder

In 1585 The Flemish proto-scientist Simon Stevin (1548/49-1620) produced a major work on mathematics and algebra. A year later he wrote The Elements of the Art of Weighing, in which he provided a good example of his desire to make things plain even to the non-mathematically inclined. He showed that if you took a necklace of metal spheres and laid it over a triangle, apex up, of which one side was longer than the other, the necklace would hang on the triangle. Then, by taking away all the spheres hanging below the triangle, you would leave only those resting on the two inclined faces. These would remain in position, even though on the short, steep side there were only two, and on the long, shallow side there were four. This was due to the relation between the downward forces on either side being in equilibrium, thanks to the differing angle of their support. This resolution of different forces is known today as the parallelogram of forces. Above the illustration of this experiment, Stevin put his scientific motto: *"Wonder en isgheen wonder"* (nothing is the miracle it appears to be). The "wreath of spheres", as it was called, gave the astronomers evidence that the forces acting on a planet could be such as to keep the planet in a stable condition as it moved.
"Infinitely Reasonable", Chapter 5, in James Burke The Day The Universe Changed. *New York: Back Bay Books, 1995; orig. publ. 1985.*

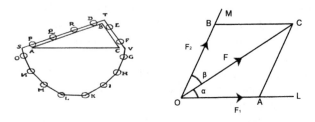

Karen Armstrong is the most intelligent and knowledgeable contemporary writer on religion. Her ecumenical strategy has much to recommend it. She wants to build a more peaceful and just world around the insight that religion is universal and its universal characteristic is compassion. She argues that since all religions are grounded in compassion it should be more or less straightforward to link up all the compassionate systems and build a world community. The problem is that compassion is a centripetal force in societies. It organizes within groups and societies and as it does so creates a more or less self-defining but variously impenetrable identifying boundary. To the extent that compassion is a centrifugal force, it is much weaker. So we need to do more than recognize the nature of compassion.

We need to recognize that compassion is not an automatic link across equally compassionate societies. Tenzin Gyatso, the 14th Dalai Lama, has also argued that compassion is the core feature uniting all religions. Interestingly, he acknowledges that a "sense of exclusivity" is part of the core identity of every religion. This is an acknowledgement of what I have called the centripetal form and force of compassion. Gyatso nonetheless believes that it is possible to preserve one's own faith tradition while simultaneously respecting, admiring, appreciating, and tolerating other traditions. My argument is that this is sociologically much more problematic than Armstrong and Gyatso suggest.

Michael Harrington noted that religiosity is surviving the decline of religion. This, in my terms, reflects the functional necessity of moral orders. There is not much difference between what Armstrong and Gyatso call compassion and what Harrington calls religiosity. But Harrington does not believe that religiosity can provide the basis for integrating a society let alone a civilization. His call for unity among believers and atheists is based on a "common transcendental" that is not supernatural but not anti-supernatural either. If religiosity and compassion are in fact synonymous, than Harrington is making the same argument that Armstrong and Gyatso make. Compassion, in other words, could be Harrington's "common transcendental". In the end, it will be our common humanity that we will have to depend on for the centrifugal force that will tie our communities of compassion together.

Conclusion

Marx said famously, "I am not a Marxist"; Thomas Kuhn might as well have said "I am not a Kuhnian"; I don't know that Descartes ever said "I am not a Cartesian", but he wasn't; and the Parmenides suggests that perhaps Plato might well have said "I am not a Platonist". (This is where *I* should proclaim "I am not an Anarchist"!).

What is the lesson of such iconoclastic negations? Perhaps it is the recognition of the complex cultural and cross-cultural interactions and interdependencies of learning networks across time, space, and society. Within such an overarching framework, it is my objective to defend a rationale for a non-essentialist but critically realistic view of mathematics (and by extension science; and by additional extension, knowledge, reasoned discourse, and education). So long, however, as we individually, collectively, locally and universally, leave room for widespread and respected beliefs about things that do not exist, things that transcend society, culture, history, and the ground we walk on and that nourishes us, we will be vulnerable to ideas about purity in our intellectual as well as our social and political pursuits.

Chapter 9
A Manifesto in Anarcho-Sociology

My manifesto takes social science seriously. In particular, I begin with the assumption or claim that sociology and anthropology are discovery sciences. The terms "discovery" and "science" have been subjected to intense critical scrutiny by sociologists of knowledge and science over the last 40 years or so. On the basis of this background research, I view discovery as a complex unfolding over time of a claim about the world, a claim that doesn't come full-blown and once-and-for-all into our consciousness and communications from an immediate and transparent experience. It comes in stages, it goes backward, it moves forward, it solidifies around a consensus, it loses solidity, and if it passes the tests of time it becomes more or less unchallengeable. Science is not a once-and-for-all phenomenon either. It is not Science *per se*, science that speaks in the grammar of the ever present tense that I defend. I defend a science that unfolds as a complex set of discourses and practices in flux; written with a small "s", "science" is "a strategy for producing defensible knowledge grounded in shared experience rather than authority – knowledge which has a strong but tentative status as the basis for action" (Loughlin and Restivo, 1997: 64).

What then is there to be said for sociology? Allow me to draw on the words of one of those sociologists you are obligated to study carefully if you are intent on convincing anyone that you know something about this field – Erving Goffman. In a detailed and one might say typically Goffmanesque lecture on the "interaction order", a lecture (his 1982 American Sociological Association presidential address) characterized by a stunning ability to bring the recurring features of everyday life into analytical focus, Goffman concluded as follows:

> For myself I believe that human social life is ours to study naturalistically, sub specie aeternitatis. From the perspective of the physical and biological sciences, human social life is only a small irregular scab on the face of nature, not particularly amenable to deep systematic analysis. And so it is. But it's ours. With a few exceptions, only students in our century have managed to hold it steadily in view this way, without piety or the necessity to treat traditional issues. Only in modern times have university students been systematically trained to examine all levels of social life meticulously. I'm not one to think that so far our claims can be based on magnificent accomplishment. Indeed I've heard it said that we should be glad to trade what we've so far produced for a few really good conceptual distinctions and a cold beer. But there's nothing in the world we should trade for what we do have: the bent to sustain in regard to all elements of social life a spirit of unfettered, unsponsored inquiry, and the

wisdom not to look elsewhere but ourselves and our discipline for this mandate. That is our inheritance and that so far is what we have to bequeath. If one must have warrant addressed to social needs, let it be for unsponsored analyses of the social arrangements enjoyed by those with institutional authority – priests, psychiatrists, school teachers, police, generals, government leaders, parents, males, whites, nationals, media operators, and all the other well-placed persons who are in a position to give official imprint to versions of reality.

Ours is an era of colliding cultures and engagements with the Other. One of the consequences of globalization has been to increase the flows of communication and information across formerly more or less impermeable barriers. In this situation, conflicts are inevitable as the forces of local and regional integrity and solidarity engage more ecumenical forces. The math wars, the science wars, and the culture wars need to be set more concretely in the sociocultural and theoretical contexts of twentieth and twenty-first century developments. Unless we have some sense of the bigger picture, these conflicts will look like small skirmishes instead of fault lines in the changing cultural geography of our world.

From Pythagoras and Mahavira to George Cantor, William Hamilton, and George Boole we find mathematics and God conflated. That this relationship has not faded away is demonstrated by the existence of God-surrogates such as "Nature", "Logic", and "Science", as well as in the works of the mystical physicists of the twentieth century. This should be viewed as part of the background against which the contemporary dialogue between science and religion has developed. Physical and natural scientists have played a major role in dialogues of harmony, convergence, and détente but they have also been aggressive opponents of religion under a banner of the logic of anger. The Anglo-American concern with science and Christianity has in recent years been linked with an emerging Christian-Islamist dialogue of ecumenism on the one hand, and warfare on the other. Nietzschean death of God narratives are in this context of conflict and cooperation between religion and science taking on a new meaning that bears on issues of education, tolerance, and international relations. What has been conspicuously missing from the study of the history of mathematics, the history of God, the science and religion dialogue, and the analysis of the death of God narratives is any significant input from the social sciences.

Science and Progressive Thought

Science is widely assumed to be a successful and valuable enterprise. But critics who recognize the need to challenge current institutions and societies should also recognize that modern science is a social problem. It is a machinelike product of industrial and technological society, and indeed the mental framework and cognitive mode of industrial capitalism (Berman, 1984: 37; Geller, 1964: 72). Its consequences have certainly not all been benign, and the negative consequences should not be brushed off as "mere side effects". Foucault's lectures and interviews provide a subtle perspective on the relations of power and truth, and point to a major source of a continuing ambivalence toward science. "What makes power hold good, what makes it acceptable, is simply the fact that it doesn't only weigh on us as a force that says no, but that it traverses and produces things, it induces pleasure, forms knowledge, produces discourse" (Foucault, 1984: 61).

Critical thinking mated with ambivalence about science is characteristic of progressive traditions. I want to draw attention to the sources of this ambivalence and to show that it reflects a fundamental bankruptcy in modern science as a social institution. I frame this inquiry in a context of structural and intellectual crises brought about by transformations in the relations of global capital, generally identified as "postmodern" (cf. Jameson, 1984). Each of the progressive traditions has complex and contradictory relations to each other and to these transformations. I want to expose the regressive tendencies of science as institutionalized inquiry and Science as an authoritarian icon.

It makes no more sense for progressives to support what is essentially state-science than it would for them to support state-church, state-justice, or any of the other core institutions of modern industrial societies. In fact, Science, Reason, Logic, Truth, and Objectivity, along with Obligation, Duty, Morality, and God are all tyrannical ideas that have been used singly and collectively to intimidate and restrict humans, and to attack the foundations for liberating human and cultural development. The use of capital letters signifies the iconic or symbolic use of science and related concepts as powerful "abstractions" that suppress dissent and constrain discourse. I recognize the complexity and multiplicity of scientific practices, but at the same time we can all, to different degrees, see and experience the hegemonic power of science as system, institution, and icon. This re-radicalizes the proposition that "Science is Culture" in social studies of science (e.g., Latour, 1988a; Haraway, 1991b: 230), but grounds it in an older tradition in radical science studies (e.g., the contributions to *Radical Science Journal* and *Science as Culture*, materializations of the slogans "science as culture" and "science is social relations"). My intention is to raise a polemic against capitalized Science (in all possible senses of the term). How do we diffuse the trap question: What are the alternatives to Science for critical thinkers?

Modern science (including the scientific role and images, symbols, and organizations of science) came into the world as a commodity, and it has developed in close association with the discipline of the machine. One of the widely ignored consequences of looking to impersonal machinelike truths and measures (relying on proof-, logic-, language-, and number-machines as validating mechanisms) to guarantee knowledge has been to transform inquirers and thinkers into machines behaving in a supposedly value-free, value-neutral wonderland. The tyranny of science means in part that while it is possible and easy to criticize and oppose "distorted" versions of science (science corrupted by capital, politics, and sexism), it is impossible and futile to criticize or oppose "true", "pure", or "unadulterated" science. Claims about "the scientific method" and "pure science" are convenient myths, ideologies, and rhetorical constructs (a tyranny of methodolatry, in Mary Daly's (1985: 11) terms) that justify objectification and alienation, and mask the constructed nature of the necessary statements scientists formulate as "laws of nature".

The tyranny of Method makes it an obstruction to inquiry. No one has made this clearer than Paul Feyerabend. His slogan, "Anything Goes" is the conclusion of a thorough search across the history of science for the scientific method, a fruitless search in the end (Feyerabend, 1975, 1978). Similarly, Foucault's (1972) search for a final cause of the emergence of "man" was thwarted by the multiplicity of medical and social practices, interests, and authorities framing discourse.

Given how science is practiced rather than how it is characterized in myth and ideology, Feyerabend argues that "reason cannot be universal and unreason cannot be excluded". This is the grounds for "Anything Goes". The idea of an unadulterated science (as institution or method) is certainly not yet dead. It has become increasingly vulnerable thanks to more than a half-century of research in the sociology of science and more than a quarter-century of research in the interdisciplinary field of social studies of science. What is not yet clearly and unequivocally resolved is: What does it mean to criticize science, and what can it possibly mean to prophesy a new science? Marx and Foucault challenged intellectuals to work toward changing rather than exclusively studying the world. And the questions plaguing progressive traditions in the era of postindustrial societies and postmodern theories are about what knowledge about the world is needed and what the bases for that knowledge must be to effect the desired changes. Today, these questions are raised in vital and volatile forms in debates and discussions about feminism and science. But they are a central feature of the history of progressive thought. Marxists, anarchists, socialists, feminists, and other progressive thinkers over the past 200 years or so have struggled with these questions in one way or another. Progressives tend to recognize that science is social relations and that it is a problematic activity in modern societies; and on the other hand they feel that they need to be "scientific" or follow scientific agendas to retain some level of legitimacy in the arenas of public (and especially intellectual) discourse, not to mention in their own eyes.

The concept of science as social relations leads to a recognition that science in modern societies is in the service of capital, patriarchy, and authority. I understand the complexity of these concepts, and of their relationship to modern science. Nonetheless, it is important that we not let this complexity veil the extent to which modern science is implicated in the social and environmental problems of our times, including alienation, dehumanization, ecological degradation, and nuclear, chemical, and biological hazards and warfare. It has played a role in increasing anomie, alienation, environmental disasters, the commodification of individuals and social relationships, and the spread of authoritarianism. In its current institutionalized form, scientific inquiry requires the control and co-optation of intellectual labor at several levels, and is inextricably linked to the agendas of the state and capital.

In recent years, scientific work has itself become the object of degradation as industrial forces have moved to complete the rationalization of the knowledge production process. This is part of the general process of reducing mental labor that is an inevitable strategy of late capitalism. The process is well underway in the university research centers I and some of my colleagues have studied. Research centers bring industrial, governmental (including military), and academic interests into direct contact, and serve as crucibles within which to begin the industrialization of universities, including laboratories, classrooms, and graduate programs, in earnest. Let us be clear that what is new about this is its intensity and breadth of application.

If, in fact, information is rapidly becoming the new "industrial base" for first world nations (Reich, 1991) we can expect to see the further degradation of science as an institution, and yet with further invocations of Science as a justification for repressive policies and authoritarian tendencies in the social relations of multinational capital and states. I don't begin by referring to some golden era of science for judging the relative degradation of scientific institutions. The question is what progressives might make of such transformations. For example, what does "Science", or technoscience, have to do with the rapid commodification of biotechnology and the erosion of peer review, public accountability, and regulation as concerns about property rights and international competitiveness in this field arise (Lewontin, 1992).

Marxism: Bourgeois versus Human Science

Karl Marx (1956: 110-111; 1973: 699ff.) introduced the potential for Marxist ambivalence about science by distinguishing between bourgeois science and human science. He did not spend much time clarifying this distinction. But a couple of points are clear. First, he recognized perhaps more clearly than any other thinker of his age that science was social relations. More importantly, he understood that scientists themselves were social relations. He thus also understood that modern science (as a social institution) was a product of and an ingredient of modern capitalist society. If there is any question about this, it is dispelled by Marx's introduction of the concept "human science". The new social order Marx blurrily envisaged would give rise to a new form of science; science-as-it-is would be negated, and a new science – dealienated, integrated (but not Unified), holistic, and global – would emerge.

Following Marx, it is relatively easy to conclude today that modern science is part of the hegemonic ideology of modern capitalism, and an integral part of the relations of production. For example, David Dickson notes that "one can detect a formal similarity between the calculus as a mathematical language, and the forms of representation required by the capitalist labour production." In the seventeenth century, algebra "provided an abstract language in which commodity transactions could be readily calculated". Later, the calculus helped to establish a quantitative relationship between process and product, exactly what is "required by capital for the full articulation of, and control over, the links between the labour process and the commodity" (Dickson, 1979: 23-24).

Science and technology in contemporary society are, for at least some Marxist scholars, systems out of democratic control, controlled by industrial and military moguls, and threatening not only to whatever shards of democracy exist but to the very existence of life on this planet (Rose and Rose, 1976; Dickson, 1988). It is also increasingly clear that it is misleading at best to continue to separate science and technology. This separation has as one of its consequences the allocation of blame for many of our social and environmental ills to technology (and engineers) while science is held aloft as an exemplar of Platonic purity. Perhaps this purity might be better understood as an indicator of alienation.

Marxist critiques of the effects of contemporary science and technology (or "technoscience") grow primarily out of studies of the workplace and the relations of production, and of the ideology of science as a justification for capitalist enterprises. Critical analyses of the historical roots of the factory, the rise of Taylorism and scientific management, the introduction of new technologies in new industries in the context of manipulations of the world labor market, unemployment, and the degradation of work all take us to the threshold of tyrannical science.

The technosciences (including the social sciences) serve capital. They have provided rhetorical ammunition for justifying social programming and policies and militarism. Technoscientific expertise has been used as "cultural capital" to justify imperialism and the patronization of weaker nations by stronger ones. And yet none of this has been able once and for all to exorcise the specter of Science the Good from Marxist scholarship.

The Marxists (here including Marx, with due respect for his objections) over and over drew attention to the facts that those who control the means of material production control the means of mental production, that new theories and technologies are grounded in social conditions, that the commodity form penetrates all areas of society, that the imperialist expansions and conquests of Capital require the development of the technosciences, and that – finally – the technosciences and capital are inextricably linked. And yet, in this same tradition, we find a tendency to exempt science and technology from the basic principles and perspectives of Marxism, to conceive of the content of technoscience discoveries as independent of social relations, and to identify bourgeois philosophies as ideological but not the empirical sciences. The bottom line seems to be, then, that the empirical sciences, based on observation and experiment, are not ideologically mediated.

The sources of these contradictory and ambivalent views should be obvious. The material successes of the natural sciences, and the recalcitrance of the material world, demand of Marxists as realistic (and perhaps in some cases, Realist) thinkers that they accept the findings of science and the methods of science that led to those findings. The dynamics of power and knowledge are simultaneous processes of coercive relations and the making of useful "goods". What many Marxists have missed is the fact that these findings and methods are inseparable from a variety of social relations. The associations of science that make it problematic for Marxists include a domineering orientation to nature and humans, and the alienation of humans from each other and from the natural world as objects of study, sexist social relations, and gendered knowledge. Within this set of problematic social relations, science is especially troublesome for feminists because it embodies the contradictory impulses of liberalism within the debates on realism, knowledge, and postmodernism.

Feminisms: Criticizing Science without Losing Your Voice

While Mary Wollstonecraft relied on evidence and the emerging discourses of rationality and science in her arguments for the equality of women, her daughter Mary Shelley created *Frankenstein*, the paradigmatic tale of male appropriation of reproduction and creativity and the terror of masculinized inquiry. The most radical feminist agendas reject science, as method and institution and as patriarchal discourse. Science requires that we objectify nature in the natural sciences and persons in the social sciences. For ecofeminists, scientific inquiry is the rape of nature and has produced not "knowledge" but rampant degradation of environments and peoples. The symbolic imagery of "penetrating arguments", "seminal theories" and "unveiling nature" is described and decried by various feminist authors. Because women and nature are associated historically, the domination of nature demanded by science mirrors, justifies, and reinforces the domination of women. For radical feminists, the scientific method is by its very nature in the service of Capital, Authority, and Patriarchy. Scientific technologies under the influence of masculinist ideologies entail the exploitation of the natural world, women, and other powerless people.

One of the problems with the radical feminist critique of science is that it leaves them without a voice, that is, without a legitimate institutional discourse. This is why in part, many feminists, like other progressives, devote considerable energy to conceiving and devising "radical sciences", in this case "feminist sciences". Sometimes the agenda is to show that what women do in the area of knowledge production is "science" that has simply not been legitimated by patriarchal institutions. Occasionally, women (or minorities) are granted (or grant themselves) a privileged epistemological status because of their experiences as objects and subjects of domination, exploitation, and oppression, a familiar perspective in Marxism. The argument then is that their increased participation in science will "fix" and "improve" science.

Science becomes a question mark for feminists because there is sexism in science as in other social worlds, and because whatever progress has fallen out from developments in technoscience has not fallen equally across the lives of men and women. The conclusion that a sexist/gendered society will produce a sexist/ gender science is not adhered to by all feminists, but it is a sensible conclusion from the sociological principles of Marxist thought. Still, the conclusion is not transparent. To make it transparent, we need to clarify some points about the phrase 'science and society'.

Society can be looked at as a set of more or less well-defined institutional sectors. The more well-defined the boundaries of a given sector, the more sense it makes to conceive of it as "autonomous". But autonomy does not entail "separation". It simply identifies the degree to which a given sector of the society is dependent on or independent of the resources of other sectors, and the extent to which it interacts with other sectors through communication, transportation, and exchange linkages. Thus, even the most autonomous of institutions is in and of the society it is part of, and conditioned by that society. Its members are initially socialized in families, schools, and religious organizations; this prepares and allows them to be socialized later in life in the technoscience professions. The social structures and value systems of those professions thus reproduce the social structure and value system dominant in the wider society. The social institution of science is thus an arena like any other institution in which power relations between social groups and conflicts in relation to value systems are reflected and acted out.

It is clear that science and the roots of liberalism were effective legitimating and liberating ideals, relative to the strictures and structures of feudal Christianity and to the confines of women's lives. Scientific knowledge has served as an ally for feminist agendas. In the writing and lives of thinkers from J.S. Mill and Harriet Martineau to Mary Wollstonecraft, and later, Charlotte Perkins Gilman, the eighteenth- and nineteenth- century roots of women's liberatory activities in the West relied on notions of rationality and the emerging rhetoric of science and proof to argue for the equality and emancipation of women.

In both the early debates of modern feminism and its current discourse, science is called into service on pro- and antifeminist agendas. Feminist scholars who have argued that science is sexist and gendered find that science is used to justify the social arrangements in contemporary society. Donna Haraway has documented the efforts of sociobiologists to argue from primatology that woman's "place" and the nuclear family are "natural" and "inevitable", and that their support and continuity are in the best interest of the human species. Norms of sexuality that justify violence, rape, and male "promiscuity", and myths of female passivity are reified in sociobiological agendas. New studies of the heritability of intelligence and personality are called on to find (and justify) novel treatments for the "ills" of drugs and poverty in modern society, and to explain away the underrepresentation of women in science, mathematics, and engineering. Much of the science of "woman" fails to adequately foster the emancipation of women, whether in the now discredited phrenological enterprises of the nineteenth century, or in present theories of sexual difference. And this is despite numerous attempts to develop feminist biologies and explicit challenges to the existing frameworks.

Recent expressions of concern about gender and science come from "liberal" traditions concerned with equity and employment. The quality and availability of work for women in the technosciences has long been questioned. Women have not had access to the professions in the same way men have; and when they have gained access, the tendency has been to marginalize them. Ethnic groups face similar problems. Many of those concerned with these issues assume that scientific practice is "objective" and that it is matters of equity and civil rights that need to be addressed. The idea is that "science" would "work" and produce objective knowledge and unambiguous progress without alienating and damaging women's lives if society were working properly. As forms of feminist empiricism, these agendas leave untouched the core ideas of science as pure and disinterested. Further, these perspectives beg questions of whether or not, and if so, why, women and feminists might be interested in or capable of doing or organizing science any differently.

The ambivalence about science is a variation on the theme (and tension) of a feminist separatist politics where we find the general problem of voice. Feminist activists have worked assiduously to give women a voice. The problem is that the language of science which is most likely to give them a voice may be inherently oppressive and exploitative, a danger to women and to democratic and socialist principles. However, few feminist critics of science support Audre Lorde's claims about the limited value of the master's tools for dismantling the master's house.

The reactions against postpositivist critiques of science are similar to other feminist reactions to postmodernist agendas. Radical critiques of knowledge leave an inquirer and activist at a loss in the face of the apparent necessity for real knowledge regarding causes, effects, and facts to be wielded in the name of emancipation. Demands for realistic assessments of science's instrumental effectiveness and for certain knowledge (and Truth) are indicative of the hegemonic power that Science as Icon has as a legitimating idea.

Postpositivist critiques of science, whether in sociology or philosophy of science and knowledge, across feminist, Marxist, and other progressive traditions, are tenuous in the face of unbridled enthusiasm for technoscience's instrumental effects. These effects are not unequivocal successes. Numerous critics echo Haraway's rejection of "epistemological anarchism". But anarchism, whether of the most limited epistemological varieties or the most radical social imaginings, does not necessarily justify anti-realism or anti-naturalism. Properly understood and applied as a sociological science anarchism can in fact contribute to building a shared politics for women.

The possibilities of partial knowledge coming from situated knowers and standpoint epistemologies illustrate an emerging sophistication about the social roots of epistemologies. The realist/relativist dilemmas are not merely intellectual conundrums, but are central to the debates about the possibility of social change and the grounds for action. They manifest the contradictory impulses of individualistic liberalism and the promises of the Enlightenment, and the problems of identity for feminists destabilized by the postmodern deconstruction of the natural category of woman. These contradictions have been reinforced by the fracture of feminist movements along racial, class, and international lines. To date, except perhaps in healing and medicine, the need for legitimate discourse has generally outweighed hesitations about the foundations of science.

The question remains about what the grounds for reliable knowledge are. Certainly, establishing such grounds requires refining the distinctions between the institutionalized inquiry we call Science, and other processes for devising reliable, sustainable knowledge about ourselves and our worlds. It is not so much a problem that the works of Foucault, Derrida, and other postmodern scholars have left those desiring social change without an "absolute" ground for action. It has, instead, become a matter of considering what grounds are available, and under what conditions. The historical contingency of our grounds can be admitted without eliminating them. The multiple visions of internationalized, progressive, feminist consciousnesses arising from the paradoxes of occupying multiple, and contradictory, social roles invites heterogeneous knowledge. These multiplicities, however, have not moved far from their roots in the social and health sciences. Such an agenda and approach toward knowledge requires a radical re-visioning and perhaps also a reengagement of the other human senses in the social relations of inquiry, knowledge, and authority. And science, sociology, and sociology of science can finally be, as the feminist sociologist Julia Loughlin has put it, "for only those groups represented in it".

Once More, Anarchism: Social Chaos or Social Theory? Review, Summary, and New Horizons

Anarchist thought emerged in a nineteenth-century milieu in which the sociological perspective was crystallizing, and was itself considered one of the sociological sciences by Peter Kropotkin. But the anarchists had trouble, along with other progressives, making and sustaining the distinctions between science as a social institution, science as a set of statements about regularities in the world, and science as a symbol for the best form(s) of inquiry. Kropotkin recognized that the state and capitalism are inseparable, and that state-justice, state-church, and state-army are inextricably linked in a network of insurance for the landlords, warriors, judges, and priests of modern society. But he was unable to see that state-science could be added to the list of capitalist institutions and that the social roles of scientists and scholars could be added to his list of exploiters and oppressors. Already in Kropotkin's time, the hegemonic ideology of pure science had contaminated anarchist thought as it had contaminated all of the emerging social sciences (including, of course, Marxism).

Kropotkin's defense of mutual aid and individual liberty was grounded in a commitment to the scientific method. By scientific method, he meant the inductive method of the natural sciences. The goal of anarchism, as a sociological science, was to use this method to reveal the future of humanity in its progress toward "liberty, fraternity, and equality". Kropotkin's ambivalence about science is reflected in the fact that while on the one hand he was a founder of scientific (and even scientistic) anarchism, he was also aware of some of the problems with using the natural scientists as role models for anarchists. Most of the scientists of his time, he argued, were either members of the possessing classes and shared their prejudices, or they were actually employed by the state. He did not, however, seem capable of imagining that science and the state were or would become so inextricably intertwined that any convergence between anarchism and "modern" science would in the end prove impossible.

The increase in scale of organizations is a consequence and cause of the organizational search for "control, discipline, and standardization". Bureaucratization rationally extends and deepens this search, and stimulates the development of conservative behavior. This prevailing logic of the organization is just another manifestation of that authority that every anarchist opposes. But what sort of opposition is this? In the face of the logic, sheer pervasiveness, and energy of state power, anarchism may seem to offer little more than the possibility of "opposing goliath" (Horowitz, 1964: 26): "Anarchism can be no more than a posture. It cannot be a viable political position".

Indeed, Horowitz (1964: 59) claims that anarchism has failed in part because it fails to address the problem of bureaucracy and in part because when it does address that problem it becomes enmeshed by it. But anarchism can be viewed more positively as the symbolic flag followed by all those on the path to liberty, as opposed to the path to authority. Tucker (1964: 173), for example, sees this in terms of the parting of the ways by Marx (state socialism) and Proudhon (anarchism).

The logic of bureaucracy is not, as might be suggested by Horowitz's argument that anarchism can only be a posture, invulnerable. Indeed, as Horowitz (1964: 58-59) is quick to point out, the inertial extension and concentration of bureaucratic logic has made it problematic as an organizational form.

Other anarchists, such as Bakunin and Proudhon, although equally enamored of science, were at the same time somewhat more sensitive to the fact that it could be a dangerous institution, one that could divide the world and tyrannize the unlearned masses in the name of Science and Truth. Many anarchists agreed with Proudhon that science was the basis of the unity of humanity, and that society should be organized on its foundations rather than on the foundation of religion or of any Authoritative institution. Science and thought, according to Bakunin, must be the "guiding stars" of any social progress. But he was skeptical of arriving at socialist or anarchist convictions only by way of science and thinking. He was critical of science because it could be divorced from life, from "the truth of life". Then, its "cold light" would produce only powerless and sterile truths. Here he is, in this moment, at one with Nietzsche.

On the whole, the anarchists were ambivalent about science because they generally recognized that science was social relations on the one hand, but that on the other it provided important anti-authoritarian ammunition in the conflict with religion and with authoritarian institutions in general. And they struggled with the fact that science seemed to be the source of truths not only about nature but about society. But it also seemed to produce a cold, harsh, violent, distant, and alien truth far removed from the human projects of love, community, and honest trusting relationships.

Nietzsche needs to be considered here because he was, in an important sense, an anarchist (in spite of his antipathy to the anarchists of his time). He was an uncompromising enemy of the State and an equally uncompromising defender of individual liberty without advocating individualism. And like many progressives, he was an advocate and an opponent of science. But even in his advocacy it is easy to detect the bases of his opposition. For example, he defends mathematics and physics – but not for the usual reasons. Mathematics is good because it helps us to determine our human relations to things, physics because it reflects the honesty that compels us to turn to physics for explanations. But he criticized modern science because even though it had helped to "kill" (anthropologize) God, it was in general rooted in the same motives underlying religion. It was not, he claimed, a way to the goodness and wisdom of God. It has not exhibited the absolute utility claimed for it by Voltaire, or any intimate association with morality and happiness. And it is not immune to evil impulses. Science is dangerous because it has the potential for divesting life of its "rich ambiguity" and turning it into an indoor mathematical diversion. He went so far as to describe science as the stupidest of all interpretations of the world because it deals with the most superficial aspects of life, the most apparent things, only those experiences that can be counted, weighed, seen, and touched. Science might yet, Nietzsche claimed, turn out to be "the great dispenser of pain", a means for making humans cold and stoic.

Unlike other students of science and society of his era, Nietzsche was able to complement his criticism with a relatively clear vision of an alternative to modern science – what he referred to as "the joyous wisdom" (or the gay science). In place of the scientist, Nietzsche put the thinker. The thinker has inclinations that are strong, evil, defiant, nasty, and malicious in relation to prevailing values. To think is to question and experiment, to try to find out something. Thus, success and failure are equally valued because they are, above all, "answers". And the thinker constantly – day by day and hour after hour – scrutinizes his/her experiences to answer the question, What did I really experience?

Love and passion, laughter, and the complementary roles of the fool and the hero rather than the detached cold light of reason are at the root of the wisdom the thinker seeks. The more emotions we bring to bear on a given problem, Nietzsche claimed, the more eyes we bring to it; and the more emotions and eyes we bring to bear the more complete our conceptions will be and thus the greater our "objectivity". Paul Feyerabend's defense of an anarchistic or dadaistic theory of science has much in common with Nietzsche's joyous wisdom, even though Feyerabend defends a limited and temporary form of anarchism: epistemological anarchism.

Toward Humane Inquiries

I myself am not immune from the ambivalence found in the progressive traditions. That ambivalence is reflected on a larger scale in the debates about the cultural meanings of science. The defenders – worshipers, advocates, apologists, and ideologues – of science have been heard; they were, and for most of us continue to be, our teachers, mentors, educators, and peers. What types of resources, then, are needed to resolve the tensions within the progressive traditions and in the networks of thinkers who create, carry, and change those traditions, caused by ambivalence about science?

The idea that there is somewhere out there a science that is autonomous and free is a pernicious myth. The more we have learned about science as a social and cultural phenomenon, and about scientific knowledge as a social construction, the better we have been able to focus our critique of science. This critique is still widely misunderstood, even within the arenas of criticism themselves. The questions that need to be answered are: What are the bases of the radical critiques of science; What if anything can we do to change scientific institutions and ideas about knowledge in line with the critiques? Does it make sense to talk about replacing science, and if so, what would a "new" or "alternative to" science look like?

The basis for radical critiques of science is the recognition that long prevailing and pervasive ideas about the nature of science are grounded in icons, myths, and ideologies. Archimedes, for example, is a leading icon of ancient science. As an icon, he is a paragon of pure science motives; as a real person, however he is a military engineer who often serves the interests of his government. Behind every icon, from Euclid to Einstein, is a more or less sinister figure or social role. It is important to understand the concept of social role because a social role can be consistent with a wide range of personal motives.

Perhaps the most pernicious myth in science is the myth of pure science. In fact, whether we are considering knowledge systems in the ancient world, cultures across time and space, or modern science, we find that in every case the most advanced forms of gathering and using knowledge in a society are closely linked with the centers of power. Just as Platonic knowledge in ancient Greece was tied into the Greek oligarchy, so modern science was institutionalized as the mode of knowing of modern capitalism and the modern nation state. The violence associated with the emergence of modern capitalism and the modern state is at the heart of the modern science generated during the ages of the commercial and industrial revolutions. Will Wright (1992) has made a contribution to expanding the criteria of legitimacy for science to include environmental and social justice in his argument for a "wild", critically reflexive knowledge. He argues that if inquiry does not improve the human socio-natural condition, it fails on epistemological and instrumental grounds; it is thus incoherent and unsustainable. Mary Daly (1978: 343-344) also insists on wild knowledge: undomesticated, asking "unfragmented" questions, ungovernable, and also extreme and prodigious. Wild knowledge entails more than linguistic revisions in codes and metaphors. It requires the liberation of human beings and a reorientation to human ecology and the social order.

Perhaps the most important aspect of the ideology of science is that it is (in its allegedly pure form) completely independent of technology; this serves among other things to deflect social criticism from science and to justify the separation of science from concerns about ethics and values. Interestingly, this idea seems to be more readily appreciated in general by third world intellectuals than by the Brahmin scholars of the West and their emulators. Careful study of the history of contemporary Western science has shown both the intimate connection between what we often distinguish as science and technology and also the intimate connection between technoscience research and development and the production, maintenance, and use of the means (and the most advanced means) of violence in society. Not only that, but what I have just written is true in general for the most advanced systems of knowledge in at least every society that has reached a level of complexity that gives rise to a system of social stratification.

Conclusion: For a Critical Inquiry

If religion is the opium of the masses, perhaps we could say that Science is the valium of the intellectual. It is the sedative, the soporific that engenders a feeble somnambulism rather than active, critical inquiry. What could it possibly mean to argue for a new science? Or to seek to destroy science-as-it-as and to replace it with a better form of science, or a new form of inquiry all together? What will we, if we are indeed become cyborgs, be capable of building and what might we indeed build? The problem is that this is the wrong way to pose this question: it is a tyrannical trap, designed to paralyze the critics who might challenge, or ignore, the hegemony of techno-scientific or -scientistic discourse.

Marx was critical of religion, but he did not see any reason or way to go out and destroy religion in particular. Create a new society with new social relationships of the kind I imagine, he claimed – a socialistic or communistic society – and religion will disappear because there will be no need for it, no function for it to fulfill, and no resources to sustain it. This is the way we should approach the critiques of any specific institution, including the institution of science. If we create a new society, we will also set the stage for a new form of knowing and new interrogative methodologies. This does not mean throwing out "science" as a symbol of our human and cultural capacity to distinguish between truth and falsity, or to learn about how our world works. Every human society generates some form of inquiry that we would recognize as including some of the basic ingredients of what we imagine "ideal", "human", or "humane" science to be; some have been demonstrably more environmentally sustainable and a smaller number supportive of more egalitarian relationships.

The best forms of human inquiry are distinguished by their capacity for criticism (including self-criticism), reflexivity, and meta-inquiry. These are basic epistemic strategies for realistic inquirers, and not for naïve realists. Truth and falsity are not determined by the so-called "purity" or alienation of the inquirer, nor by some simple symbolic or linguistic associations between things in the world and terms that refer. They grow out of social relations.

Let us admit that it is difficult to imagine exactly what a new form of inquiry would look like relative to our current understanding of so-called scientific methods. But nonetheless, just as there is something to be gained from imagining new forms of social organization and political economy, however shadowy and ethereal our imagery, so there is something to be gained by imagining what new forms of inquiry might look like.

Imagine, then, a mode of inquiry in which we grant the acceptability of necessary statements and the weight of evidence, but treat claims as nothing more than well founded; and in which we formulate necessary statements rather than laws of nature. In this way, we can begin to imagine how to erase or circumvent the tyranny and hegemony of institutions of Rationality, Logic, Proof, and Method. We can begin, then, to imagine modes of knowing that emerge out of standpoints (local experiences in everyday/everynight lives) rather than out of centers and relations of power. We need, for example, to study schools from the perspective of parents and children, rather than from the interests of existing institutional imperatives and the perceived needs of capital and social elites (Smith, 1987: 187). We need social theory grounded in the perspectives of women, the colonized, the oppressed, not the relations of ruling elites. Technological design must be carried out in terms of the perspectives and with the participation of people as users, rather than as passive consumers. Given such perspectives, we are always at the mercy of education. No progressive agenda can be realized if our populations are characterized by knowledge and epistemological deficits, as is the case in contemporary America (Barber, 2010).

The single most important thing to understand about modern science if we are going to be able to study it critically is that it is a social institution and not an abstract body of knowledge, set of Platonic-like ideas, statements, laws, or facts, or a hall of fame populated with the images of scientists with eyes – to recall Nietzsche – such as no human being has ever possessed, eyes that can see the world unmediated by society and culture. It is equally important that as we become, for a variety of reasons, more aware of the knowledge/power axis in modern science we understand that this is a feature of science and of inquiry throughout history. The charge of envisioning new sciences prior to a new society is an attempt by the hegemonizing interests of the state, military, capitalists, technoscientists, and apologists to defuse and resist potentially explosive visions of radical thinkers.

An alternative progressive science or mode of inquiry can only emerge as the mode of knowing and thinking of an alternative progressive society. Marx offered us a brief and fuzzy view of what such a science might look like when he used the term human science in conjunction with his image of a future society. Imagine, then, a social formation in which the person has primacy, in which social relationships are diversified, cooperative, egalitarian, nonauthoritarian, participatory, expressive.

The mode of knowing and thinking in such a society would be nonexploitative, nonsexist, nonauthoritarian, and nonelitist. The imperative for progressives, then, is to press forward with their social change agendas. A *nuova scienza* will follow their successes, just as it has the social changes that have gone before, only rarely as a science of the people, and then only in localized arenas.

Harding (1991: 173) challenges the science-as-a-social-problem formulation, pushing for specific proposals for the *nuova scienza* and asking what "science and epistemology are to contribute to this project" of fostering humane social forms. The recent history and current activities of progressive agents offer prototypes and examples of marginal improvements in achieving goals for a different science and society. The Boston Women's Health Collective is an example of different means and modes for achieving, legitimating, and transmitting useful knowledge. The challenges that AIDS activists posed to the National Institutes of Health and the medical community at large for evaluating protocols, and getting onto the research agenda in the first place, indicate participatory promises well beyond "the disease of the month" strategy for managing the national health research agenda. The University of Maryland's rejection of an NJH-sponsored conference on crime and genetics should be seen not as an indication that "the public" is irrational and unprepared to speak about science, but rather that the public is capable of exercising a legitimate voice in and on science. Given the poverty of education in the United States I am not especially ready to embrace the possibility of intelligent public participation in science. But this is a clarion call for better education. Outside the borders of the United States, there are experiments, however rudimentary or partial, in the participatory design of workplace technologies or public access to scientific information. And participatory discourse on science and ethics exist, however tenuously, as possible models for progressive action. I should also mention the Science for the People movement, the associated Radical Science Movement, and the Dutch Science Shops. We have many exemplars to draw on for a new science and society architecture, exemplars that do not isolate and purify science, and that ground science in new forms of life.

Epistemology, science, and the philosophy and sociology of science, as professionalized discourses separated from ethics, method, ontology, and metaphysics, and separated from community life, are likely to have little to contribute to new inquiry enterprises. Sociology, feminism, anarchism, or Marxism in bureaucratic or scientistic forms, rather than as imaginative enterprises, will likely be impediments to goals of social and environmental justice. Rather than settling on a craft model of scientific practice (as a number of feminists and progressives do) as a remedy, we need to develop organizations and other modes of supporting and legitimating inquiries.

These are difficult changes to work toward, especially in light of postmodernist theories critical of progress, and the role such theories then play in relation to the status quo (ranging from reactionary to revolutionary). The hope for a better society stumbles across problems of relativism in the service of institutional and capital inertia. Haraway (1991b) calls it a postmodern "god trick" akin to the "god trick" of the universalizing discourses of modernism. Relativism is suspicious to a number of feminist scholars, for it seems that as women, people of color, and nations emerging from colonialism begin to speak with authority and out of their experiences, they are told it's all relative and doesn't much matter anyway (Mascia-Lees et al. 1988). Further, the hopes of progressives are eroded by postmodernism's corrosive nihilism, which induces a cynical paralysis. This can be contrasted with Nietzsche's cautious and constructive use of nihilism, in a manner reminiscent of the way Feyerabend uses anarchism. If linear modes of progress and unambiguous utopias are eliminated as possible futures, we can still remain committed to struggle. We are not reduced to despair and cynicism. And indeed, we can struggle despite and in joyous defiance of our probable futility. Social progress is not a modernist, Enlightenment fantasy, despite the Enlightenment assumptions of Marx, many feminists, anarchists, and other progressives (Hekman, 1990) and despite the end of progress ideologies and utopianism rightly heralded in postmodernist critiques of culture and capital.

What are we to make of assumptions about the efficacy of the instrumental "successes" of science, in the face of widespread environmental degradation and social injustice? Let's not be awed by "great discoveries" or by the "lives of the great scientists". We need to ask the sorts of questions about science and scientists that focus, for example, on what scientists produce, who they produce it for, how they produce it, and with what social, political, economic, and environmental consequences. In the end, we will want to know not what scientists discover or invent, but what sorts of people they are and what sorts of social worlds they are associated with. These are not issues of motives and intention, but of communities and commitments, institutions and interests, and the assumptions, practices, and agendas by which we create and re-create our social worlds.

I have lived and learned across the progressive traditions in ways the blur their distinctions. Consider the distinction between Marxism and anarchism drawn by Todd May (2009: 11-12). Marxism focuses on exploitation, an inevitable consequence of the extraction of surplus value under "capitalism". The defining focus of anarchism is domination, oppressive power relations. Exploitation is by definition restricted to the economic sphere, whereas domination ramifies across all of the institutions of society. Suppose we conceive of the issue here as one that concerns class and power. If power is more elastic it is because (and Michel Foucault is probably our great teacher here) it can operate consciously, unconsciously, anonymously, and as a restrictive as well as a creative force. Whether we focus on class and power, or more broadly Max Weber's categories of class, status, and party, our objective should be to eliminate exploitation and the restrictive modes of power as well as other material and symbolic distinctions that manifest in inequalities. It is crucial that we work toward these ends not with them "in view" but with them as conditions of our immediate practices. We must be democrats, socialists, communists, anarchists, secularists, and humanists now if we are going to realize our progressive goals in the future.

Appendix 1
A Dialogue on the Syllogism With Philosopher Jean Paul Van Bendegem (JP), Free University of Brussels

In this dialogue I am SR.

JP: There are several ways to read "is" in the statement that A is B. The first one is to read "is" as an identity. If we assume identity to be symmetric – from A=B follows B=A – then, of course, the syllogism expresses the transitivity of identity: from A=B and B=C conclude that A=C. But there are logics around that do not accept transitivity, especially when dealing with vague concepts where identity becomes something like "as good as indistinguishable". In that case, it is perfectly possible that A=B and B=C, yet A is different from C. The standard example is a series of colored strips going gradually from orange to red. Take any two neighboring strips and you will accept the statement that they have the same color, but take two strips a number of steps away and they will be judged different. So, stating that from A=B and B=C, A=C must follow is not that trivial.

The second is to read "A is B" as shorthand for "All A are B", which is (I guess) probably closer to what Aristotle had in mind. Now it is the transitivity of the implication that is at stake. To conclude that "All A are C" from "All A are B" and "All B are C", presupposes that from "if A then B" and "if B then C", "if A then C" follows. Again there are logics that do not accept this rule so again it is not trivial. But what is not accepted is that from "All A are B", one can conclude that "All B are A" so that runs against the argument you presented.

All this being said, there is of course one way of reading the syllogism as a tautological statement and, if I remember right, this point has already been raised by J.S. Mill. Take the argument that from "Socrates is a man" and "All men are mortal", it must follow that "Socrates is mortal". Mill observes that in order to accept the conclusion I need to accept the premises but what reasons or arguments do I have to accept "All men are mortal" (assuming that the manhood of Socrates is not an issue)? If it is an empirical question, then I must check all available cases, but if so I will already have checked the mortality of Socrates and nothing new is gained. But, if not empirical, then how do I convince anyone (including myself) that indeed all men are mortal without having checked a number of specific cases. Seen from this perspective, the argument becomes more of an inductive argument.

The general point seems to be the following. A logic consists of a finite set of axioms and a finite set of rules, such as "From 'if A then B' and 'if B then C' conclude 'if A then C'". Then, of course, it is absolutely no surprise that when one sees two statements of the form "if A then B" and "if B then C" one thinks, aha! so "if A then C". Yes, of course, it could not be otherwise. This, I think, is what Wittgenstein meant when he wrote in the *Tractatus* that "in logic there are no surprises".

I have been thinking of whether there is another way to formulate your argument about the tautological nature of such logical arguments, but so far without success. But perhaps it is better if I wait for your comments on my thoughts.

SR: Yes, to all of this. I was thinking of Wittgenstein, and of one particular interpretation of "is", and maybe as you suggest the one Socrates had in mind. In any event, I think my case stands with my and your caveats. If you can come up with a more precise version that makes my Wittgensteinian point, I would be most grateful.

JP: Here is an attempt:
Formal deductive logic is all about necessity: if I accept this and that, what else am I obliged or "forced" to accept? But if something is necessary (in whatever sense), does that not imply that, among a variety of choices, one and only one outcome is allowed? So, if I accept "If A, then B" and I accept A, then I must accept B. So, as Wittgenstein claimed in the *Tractatus*, there can be no surprises in logic. All of this seems alright, as long as the question what guarantees this necessity is not asked. That guarantee cannot be logical for that would mean that necessity justifies itself by invoking necessity itself. That sounds all too familiar. Which leaves as the only possibility the grounding of the necessary by what is not necessary, i.e. the contingent. Which is self-refuting. Though perhaps not necessarily so.

SR: Yes. If I understand you correctly, then perhaps there is a way to resolve the self-refutation. The way this is put in sociology is in terms of the irrational foundations of rationality or rational action. See the first chapter in Randall Collins, *Sociological Insight*. Collins does not use "irrational" in the usual way. What he means here is something like this: that the roots of everyday life in ritual, solidarity, and trust give us the grounds for our logics, rationalities, and necessities. This means in part that our capacity to use language is a function of our embeddedness in these activities, which of course varies in intensity as we move along the continuum from *Gemeinschaft* to *Gesellschaft* societies and from the earliest professional associations to the most advanced professions. The line of inquiry here runs from Durkheim, Mary Douglas, and C. Wright Mills, to R. Collins; here Goffman and Garfinkel are also relevant.

Appendix 2
Bibliographic Epilogue:
Anarchism All the Way Down

As I pointed out earlier, drawing on de Acosta (2009), we can think of the very idea of society as anarchistic "all the way down"; our very humanity, "being itself", may be anarchistic. If anarchism is one of the sociological sciences, then we must engage the idea that anarchism is ontologically grounded. I have adopted a positive orientation to anarchism in this book, an orientation that must seem odd to readers who associate anarchism with chaos and bombs on the one hand and with extreme utopianism on the other. It should be clear that I do not advocate chaos and bombs. It is probably less clear that I do not view myself as an extreme utopian or a utopian of any kind. If you fear anarchism or leave it out of your social, political, and economic discourses because it doesn't look like it could ever work, perhaps you should take a wider look around (to recall a Wittgensteinian imperative). Is there any real evidence that any contemporary social system or political economy, any state or government, is in fact working and viable? How can the answer be yes when even in the best of times we have the poor always with us, gender wars, racism, sexism, conflicts and wars peppering the globe, ecological disasters on line or on the horizon, and economies of crisis the norm? Can we turn to real human societies now or in the past that offer alternatives that are at least marginally better than our own and even embody the basic principles of anarchism? In our own world, standing on the soil of the United States of America and looking abroad, we find many countries at least marginally better than we are – on matters of health care and wealth and income gaps between the rich and the poor, for example. There is hardly anywhere to stand today if one wants to continue to sing the hymn to American exceptionalism. We fare poorly in education by comparison with other countries; we lag behind in math and science scores. And even where things are apparently better, human culture seems to do more damage to people and environments as opposed to nourishing healthy human ecologies.

Perhaps, then, we would do well to learn about societies – real ones, not imagined ones – that demonstrate to one degree or another the viability of anarchism, communism, and socialism. Consider, for example, what the early American feminists were able to learn about freedom, political power, control over their own bodies and properties, and a society that knew little of rape and domestic violence. Sally Roesch Wagner documents the influence of native American women on the struggles of the early feminists, including Elizabeth Stanton, Matilda Gage, and

Lucretia Mott. See her *Sisters in Spirit: Haudenosaunee (Iriquois) Influence on Early American Feminists* (Summertown, TN: Native Voices, 2001).

The anthropologist Harold Barclay has argued that anarchism is not only common in human communities across time and space but in fact characteristic of much of our history; *People Without Government: An Anthropology of Anarchy* (London: Kahn and Averill, 1990). Barclay writes that his interest in anthropology was stimulated by Kropotkin's work on mutual aid. His book covers the social lives and cultures of hunter-gatherers, gardeners, herders, and agriculturalists. Examples of anarchist societies in the modern world often erupt in the middle of widespread conflicts that eventually chew up the experiment. This is what happened to the Makhno anarchist communities in the Ukraine in the years immediately following the 1917 revolution. We can debate the fine point about whether the collectives that sprang up in Spain during the Civil War were experiments in decentralized collectivist democracy or in anarchism *per se*, but in any event they faced the same problem the Ukrainian's faced – trying to establish an alternative social and political order in the midst of widespread conflict and open warfare. These efforts fed on the anarchism embedded in the traditional Spanish peasant collective. Anarchism has also been a part of the intentional communities movements in the U.S. from the 1800s through the 1960s.

The French anthropologist and ethnographer, Pierre Clastres, is considered by some observers as having provided a scientific grounding for the anarchist perspective. Clastres was a critic of the idea the state was society's destiny but equally critical of the Rousseauian myth of the noble savage. Among the Guayaki of Paraguay, Clastres reported, the representational role of the leader was not institutionalized. If the leader abused his authority as a spokesperson for his people, he could be violently removed from this position. Clastres is best know for his book, *Society Against the State* (Brooklyn, NY: Zone Books, 1987; orig. published in French in 1974). And on the stateless upland southeast Asians, see James C. Scott, *The Art of Not Being Governed* (New Haven, CT: Yale University Press, 2010). There are a number of online sites that provide information on the nature and history of anarchism as a positive model for social, economic and poltical discourse: see, for example,

http://dwardmac.pitzer.edu/anarchist_archives/anarchisthistory.html;
http://www.spunk.org/texts/intro/sp000282.txt;
http://flag.blackened.net/revolt/history.html;
http://www.katesharpleylibrary.net/f7m1bn.

For "conventional" anthropological studies of early human societies unburdened by ideologies of an inherently greedy human nature, see Marshall Sahlins, *Stone Age Economics,* 2nd edition (New York: Routledge, 2003); and his *The Western Illusion of Human Nature: With Reflections on the Long History of Hierarchy, Equality and the Sublimation of Anarchy in the West, and Comparative Notes on Other Conceptions of the Human Condition* (Chicago, IL: Prickly Paradigm Press,

2008). And on the possibilities for a anarchist anthropology, see David Graeber, *Fragments of an Anarchist Anthropology* (Chicago, IL: Prickly Paradigm Press, 2004).

Readers interested in this topic may also wish to consult works on the anthropology of the earliest human settlements such as Adam Kuper's critique of the idea of "the primitive" in his *The Invention of Primitive Society: Transformation of an Illusion* (New York, NY: Routledge, 1988). Kuper's sociology of science perspective leads him to conclude that in developing the idea of an original "primitive society," we constructed mirror images of ourselves. And see A.W. Johnson and T. Earle, *The Evolution of Human Societies: From Foraging Group to Agrarian State,* 2nd ed. (Stanford, CA: Stanford University Press, 2000).

Bibliography

de Acosta, A. (2009), "Two Undecidable Questions For Thinking in Which Anything Goes," pp. 26-34 in R. Amster et al. (eds), *Contemporary Anarchist Studies*. New York: Routledge.

Akrich, M. and, B. Latour (1992), "A Summary of a Convenient Vocabulary for the Semiotics of Human and Non-Human Assemblies," pp. 259-264 in W.E. Bijker and J. Law (eds), *Shaping Technology/Building Society: Studies in Sociotechnical Change*. Cambridge, MA: The MIT Press.

Amster, R., A. DeLeon, L.A. Fernandez, A. Nocella II, and D. Shannon (eds) (2009), *Contemporary Anarchist Studies*. New York: Routledge.

Amsterdamska, O. (1990), "Surely You Are Joking, Monsieur Latour!" *Science, Technology, and Human Values* 15, 4 (Autumn), pp. 495-504.

Bailey, J. (1996), *After Thoughts*. New York: Basic Books.

Bakhtin, M.M. (1981), *The Dialogic Imagination: Four Essays*. Austin, TX: University of Texas Press.

Bakhtin, M.M. (1986), *Speech Genres and Other Late Essays*. Austin, TX: University of Texas Press.

Barber, B. (2010), "America's Knowledge Deficit," *The Nation* (November 10).

Barnes, B. and D. Bloor (1982), "Relativism, Rationalism and the Sociology of Knowledge," pp. 21-47 in M. Hollis and S. Lukes (eds), *Rationality and Relativism*. Oxford: Basil Blackwell.

Bartusiak, M. (1996), "The Mechanics of the Soul," review of W.H. Calvin, *How Brains Think*, *The New York Times* (November 17), p. 12.

Bernal, J.D. (1939), *The Social Functions of Science*. New York: Macmillan.

Bernal, J.D. (1964), "After Twenty-Five Years", pp. 285-309 in M. Goldsmith and A. Mackay (eds), *The Science of Science*. Harmondsworth: Penguin.

Berreby, D. (1994), "And now, overcoming all binary oppositions, it's...That Damned Elusive Bruno Latour," *Lingua Franca* 4, 6 (October), p. 26.

Bidney, D. (1967), *Theoretical Anthropology*. New York: Schocken Books.

Bloor, D. (1976), *Knowledge and Social Imagery*. London: Routledge and Kegan Paul.

Bloor, D. (1999), "Anti-Latour," *Studies in History and Philosophy of Science* 30, 1, pp. 81-112.

Bohm, D. (1976), *Fragmentation and Wholeness*. Jerusalem: Van Lee Jerusalem Foundation.

Boulding, K. (1970), *Primer on Social Dynamics*. New York: The Free Press.

Bourguignon, E. (1973), *Religion, Altered States of Consciousness, and Social Change*. Columbus: Ohio State University Press.

Burton, L. (1996), "The Implications of a Narrative Approach to the Learning of Mathematics," paper presented at the Symposium: Learning Mathematics – From Hierarchies to Networks, conference on The Growing Mind, Geneva, Switzerland.

Calhoun, J.B. (1962), "Population Density and Social Pathology," *Scientific American* 206, 3, pp. 139-148.

Callon, M. (1986), "Some Elements of a Sociology of Translation: Domestication of the Scallops and the Fishermen of St Brieuc Bay," pp. 196-233 in J. Law (ed.), *Power, Action and Belief: A New Sociology of Knowledge*. London: Routledge & Kegan Paul.

Campbell, D.T. (1969), "A Phenomenology of the Other One: Corrigible, Hypothetical and Critical," pp. 41-69. in T. Mischel (ed.), *Human Action: Conceptual and Empirical Issues*. New York: Academic Press.

Campbell, N. (1919/1957), *Foundations of Science*. New York: Dover.

Cetina, K.K. (1979), "Tinkering Toward Success: Prelude to a Theory of Scientific Practice," *Theory and Society*, 8, pp. 347-376.

Cohen, S. (1988), *Against Criminology*, Oxford: Transaction.

Collins, H. (1979), *Changing Order*, Beverly Hills, CA: Sage.

Collins, R. (1988), *Theoretical Sociology*, New York: Harcourt Brace Jovanovich Publishers.

Collins, R. (1997), *The Social Causes of Philosophies*, Cambridge, MA: Harvard University Press.

Crawford, K. (1998), "Hierarchies, Networks and Learning," pp. 108-118 in L. Burton (ed.), *Learning Mathematics: From Hierarchies to Networks*. London: Falmer Press.

Daly, M. (1978), *Gyn/Ecology: The Metaethics of Radical Feminism*. Boston: Beacon Press.

Damasio, A. (1994), *Descartes' Error: Emotion, Reason, and the Human Brain*. New York: G.P. Putnam's Sons.

Daston, L. and P. Galison (2007), *Objectivity*, Brooklyn, NY: Zone Books.

Davidson, I. and W. Noble (1989), "The Archaeology of Perception," *Current Anthropology* 39, 2 (April), pp. 125-155.

DeGré, G. (1985), *The Social Compulsion of Ideas*, New Brunswick, NJ: Transaction Books. Edited by C.H. Levitt.

Dostoevsky, F. (1864/1972), *Notes from Underground*. London: Penguin Classics.

Douglas, M. (1966), *Purity and Danger*. London: Routledge and Kegan Paul.

Douglas, M. (1975), *Implicit Meanings*. London: Routledge and Kegan Paul.

Douglas, M. (1986), *How Institutions Think*. Syracuse, NY: Syracuse University Press.

Durkheim, É. (1961), *The Elementary Forms of the Religious Life* (trans. by Joseph Ward Swain). New York: Collier Books.

Durkheim, É. (1995), *The Elementary Forms of Religious Life*. The Free Press: New York. Trans. by Karen E. Fields; orig. published in French as *Les Formes elementaires de la vie religieuse: Le systeme totemique en Australie.* Paris: F. Alcan.

Duthel, H. (2010), *The Concise Duthel Encyclopedia of Anarchism III.* Lexington, KY: Heinz Duthel, IAC Society.

Easlea, B. (1973), *Liberation and the Aims of Science.* Brighton: Sussex University Press.

Eisenberg, L. (1995), "The Social Construction of the Human Brain," *American Journal of Psychiatry* 152, 11, pp. 1563-1575.

Ernest, P. (ed.) (1994), *Mathematics, Education, and Philosophy: An International Perspective.* London, Falmer Press.

Evans, C. (1970), *The Subject of Consciousness.* New York: Humanities Press.

Ferrell, J. (2009), "Against Method, Against Authority…for Anarchy," pp. 73-81 in Amster et al.

Feyerabend, P. (1975), *Against Method,* 3rd ed. London: Verson, orig. publ. by New Left Books.

Feyerabend, P. (1978), *Science in a Free Society.* London: Verso.

Firth, R. (1936), *We, the Tikopia.* American Book Company, New York.

Fleck, L. (1979), *Genesis and Development of a Scientific Fact.* Chicago: University of Chicago Press (orig. publ. in German, 1939).

Freire, P. (1967), *Education: The Practice of Freedom.* London: Writers and Readers Publishing Cooperative.

Freire, P. (1985), *The Politics of Education: Culture, Power, and Liberation.* South Hadley, MA: Bergin & Garvey.

Frickel, S. and K. Moore (2006), *The New Political Sociology of Science.* Madison, WI: University of Wisconsin Press.

Garfinkel, H. (1967), *Studies in Ethnomethodology.* Englewood Cliffs, NJ: Prentice-Hall.

Geertz, C. (1973), *The Interpretation of Cultures.* New York: Basic Books.

Geertz, C. (2000), *Available Light: Anthropological Reflections on Philosophical Topics.* Princeton, PA: Princeton University Press.

Godwin, W. (1977), "The Evils of National Education; & "Education Through Desire," pp. 267-273 in G. Woodcock (ed.), *The Anarchist Reader.* Glasgow: Fontana Paperbacks.

Goffman, E. (1974), *Frame Analysis.* Boston: Northeastern University Press.

Goodman, P. (1977), "Alternatives to Miseducation," pp. 274-278 in G. Woodcock (ed.), *The Anarchist Reader.* Glasgow: Fontana Paperbacks.

Greimas, A.J. (1966/1986), *Sémantique structurale.* Paris: Presse universitaires de France.

Gross, P.R. and N. Levitt (1994), *The Higher Superstition.* Baltimore: The Johns Hopkins Press.

Guérin, D. ed. (2005), *No Gods No Masters.* Oakland, CA: AK Press.

Gumplowicz, L. (1905), *Grundrisse der Soziologie,* 2nd ed. Vienna: Manz.

Gurvitch, G. (1957, 1963), *La Vocation Actuelle de la Sociologie,* 2nd eds., 2 vols. Paris: Presses Universitaires de France.

Gurvitch, G. (1962), *Dialectique et Sociologie*. Paris: Presses Universitaires de France.

Harawy, D. (1991), *Simians, Cyborgs, and Women: The Reinvention of Nature*. New York: Routledge.

Hardy, C., N. Phillips, and S. Clegg (2001). Reflexivity in Organization and Management Studies: A Study of the Production of the Research "Subject." *Human Relations* 54, 5, pp. 3-32.

Harding, S. (1991), *Whose Knowledge? Whose Science? Thinking From Women's Lives*. Ithaca: Cornell University Press.

Harding, S., ed. (2004), *The Feminist Standpoint Theory Reader*. New York: Routledge.

Harding, S. (2008), *Science From Below: Feminisms, Postcolonialities, and Modernities*. Durham, NC: Duke University Press.

Harrington, M. (1983), *The Politics at God's Funeral*. Baltimore: Penguin Books.

Hall, E.T. (1966/1990), *The Hidden Dimension*. New York: Anchor Books.

Hawkes, T. (1977), *Structuralism and Semiotics*. Berkeley, CA: University of California Press.

Heelan, P. (1983), *Space-Perception and the Philosophy of Science*. Berkeley, CA: University of California Press.

Hekman, S. (1990), *Gender and Knowledge: Elements of a Postmodern Feminism*. Boston, MA: Northeastern University Press.

Hesse, M. (1974), *The Structure of Scientific Inference*. London: Macmillan.

Holton, G. (1973), *Thematic Origins of Scientific Thought*. Cambridge, MA: Harvard University Press.

Hooker, C. (1975), "Philosophy and Meta-Philosophy of Science: Empiricism, Popperianism, and Realism," *Synthese* 32, pp. 177-231.

Hooker, C. (1987), *A Realistic Theory of Science*. Albany, NY: SUNY Press.

Hottois, G. (1984). *Le signe et la technique: La philosophie à l'épreuve de la technique*. Paris: Aubier.

James, W. (1890), *Principles of Psychology*, 2 vols. New York: Henry Holt.

Jarvie, I.C. (1975), "Cultural Relativism Again," *Philosophy of the Social Sciences* 5, pp. 343-353.

Kaalwa, J. (1999), "Culture, Environment and Mathematics Learning in Uganda", pp. 135-140 in L. Burton (ed.), *Learning Mathematics: From Hierarchies to Networks*. London: Falmer Press.

Keller, E.F. (1985), *Reflections on Gender and Science*. New Haven, CT: Yale University Press.

Kitcher, P. (1983), *The Nature of Mathematical Knowledge*. New York: Oxford University Press.

Knorr-Cetina, K. and M. Mulkay (1983), *Science Observed*. Beverly Hills, CA: Sage.

Kristeva, J. (1967), "L'Expansion de la sémiotique," *Information sur les sciences sociales* 6, 5 (October), pp. 169-181.

Kropotkin, P. (1908), *Modern Science and Anarchism*. New York: Mother Earth Publishing Association.

Kuhn, T. (1962), *The Structure of Scientific Revolutions*. Chicago, IL: University of Chicago Press.

Kuhn, T. (1972), *The Structure of Scientific Revolutions*, 2nd ed. Chicago, IL: University of Chicago Press.

Lamont, M. (1987), "How to Become a Dominant French Philosopher: The Case of Jacques Derrida." *American Journal of Sociology* 93, 3 (November), pp. 584-622.

Latour, B. and S. Woolgar (1979), *Laboratory Life: The Social Construction of Scientific Facts*. Thousand Oaks, CA: Sage Publications.

Latour, B. and S. Woolgar (1986), *Laboratory Life: The Construction of Scientific Facts: With a New Postscript By the Authors*. Princeton, NJ: Princeton University Press.

Latour, B. (1987), *Science in Action*. Cambridge, MA: Harvard University Press.

Latour, B. (1988), "A Relativist Account of Einstein's Relativity," *Social Studies of Science* 18, pp. 3-44.

Latour, B. (1988), *The Pasteurization of France*. Cambridge, MA: Harvard University Press.

Latour, B. (1993), *We Have Never Been Modern*. Cambridge, MA: Harvard University Press.

Latour, B. (1996), *Aramis, or The Love of Technology*. Cambridge, MA: Harvard University Press.

Latour, B. (1999), *Pandora's Hope*. Cambridge, MA: Harvard University Press.

Latour, B. (2002), "Gabriel Tarde and the End of the Social," pp. 117-132 in P. Joyce (ed.), *The Social in Question: New Bearings in History and the Social Sciences*. London: Routledge.

Latour, B. (2004), *Politics of Nature: How to Bring the Sciences into Democracy*. Cambridge, MA: Harvard University Press.

Latour, B. (2005), *Reassembling the Social: An Introduction to Actor-Network Theory*. Oxford: Oxford University Press.

Latour, B. (2010), "Coming Out as a Philosopher," *Social Studies of Science* 40, 4 (August), pp. 599-608.

Leggett, J. (1973), "From the Bottom: An Evolutionary View of Underclass Challenge," pp. 1-5 in J. Leggett (ed.), *Taking State Power*. New York: Harper and Row.

Lenski, G. (1970), *Human Societies*. New York: McGraw-Hill.

Lenski, G. (2005), *Ecological-evolutionary Theory: Principles and Applications*. Boulder, CO: Paradigm Publishers.

Lerman, S. (1998), "Culturally Situated Knowledge and the Problem of Transfer in the Learning of Mathematics," pp. 93-107 in L. Burton (ed.), *Learning Mathematics: From Hierarchies to Networks*. London: Falmer Press.

Lilla, M. (2008), *The Stillborn God*. New York: Vintage.

Mackenzie, D. (1981), *Statistics in Great Britain 1865-1930*. Edinburgh: Edinburgh University Press.

Mannheim, K. (1936), *Ideology and Utopia*. London: Routledge and Kegan Paul.

Marcus, S.J. (1993), "Editorial," *Technology Review*, 96, 6 (August/September), 5

Martin, B. (1977), "Ten Areas for Anarchist Initiatives," *Social Anarchism*, 24, pp. 31-33.

Marx, K. (1844/1958), *The Economic and Philosophic Manuscripts of 1844*. Moscow: Foreign Languages Publishing House.

Marx, K. (1844), "A Contribution to the Critique of Hegel's Philosophy of Right" *Deutsch-Französische Jahrbücher*, (February 7 and 10).

Marx, K., F. Engels (1975), *The Holy Family*, 2nd rev. ed. Delhi: Progress Publishers. Originally published in German in 1845.

Maslow, A. (1965), *Science and Human Values*, revised and enlarged. New York: Harper Torchbooks.

Maslow, A. (1971), *The Farther Reaches of Human Nature*. New York: The Viking Press.

May, T. (2009), "Anarchism from Foucault to Rancière," pp. 11-17 in Amster et al.

Mascia-Lees, F.E., P. Sharpe, and C. Ballerino Cohen (1989), "The Postmodernist Turn in Anthropology; Cautions From a Feminist Perspective," *Journal of Women in Culture and Society* 15, 1.

McCulloch, W.S. and W. Pitts (1943), "A Logical Calculus of Ideas Immanent in Nervous Activity," *Bulletin of Mathematical Biophysics* 5, pp. 115-143.

Mead, G.H. (1938), *The Philosophy of the Act*, edited by C.W. Morris. Chicago, IL: University of Chicago Press.

Mead, G.H. (1947), *Mind, Self and Society: From the Perspective of a Social Behaviorist*, edited by C.W. Morris. Chicago, IL: University of Chicago Press.

Melamed, D. (2009), Unpublished Manuscript, "Brain, Body and Mind: A Structural Theory of Stratification". Tucson: Department of Sociology University of Arizona.

Mendick, H. (2005), "Only Connect: Troubling Oppositions in Gender and Mathematics," *International Journal of Inclusive Education* 9, 2, pp. 161-180.

Merchant, C. (1980), *The Death of Nature*. New York: Harper/Collins.

Merton, R.K. (1963), "The Ambivalence of Scientists," *Bulletin of the Johns Hopkins Hospital*, 112, pp. 77-97.

Merton, R.K. (1973), *The Sociology of Science*, edited by N. Storer. Chicago: University of Chicago Press.

Mills, C. Wright (1961), *The Sociological Imagination*. New York: Grove Press.

Mills, C. Wright (1963), "Language, Logic, and Culture," pp. Edinburgh 423-438 in C. Wright Mills, *Power, Politics, and People*, edited by I.L. Horowitz. New York: Ballantine Books.

Mitroff, I.I. (1974), "Norms and Counter-Norms in a Select Group of the Apollo Moon Scientists: A Case Study of the Ambivalence of Scientists," *American Sociological Review*, 39: 579-595.

Nicholson, R.S. (1993), "Editorial," *Science*, 261, 5118 (July 9), p. 143.

Nietzsche, F. (1887/1974), *The Gay Science*. New York: Vintage Books.

Nietzsche, F. (1887/1956), *The Geneology of Morals* (bound with *The Birth of Tragedy*, 1872). New York: Doubleday Anchor.

Nordon, D. (1981), *Les mathematiques pure n'existent pas!* Le Paradou: Editions Actes Sud.

Noddings, N. (1993), "Politicizing the Mathematics Classroom," pp. 150-161 in S. Restivo, J.P. Van Bendegem, and R. Fischer, eds. (1993), *Math Worlds: Philosophical and Social Studies of Mathematics and Mathematics Education*. Albany, NY: SUNY Press.

Orwell, G. (1949/1983), *Nineteen Eighty-Four*. London: Penguin Books.

Polanyi, M. (1962), *The Republic of Science: Its Political and Economic Theory*. Chicago: Roosevelt University Press.

Popper, K. (1962), *The Open Society and its Enemies*. New York: Routledge.

Potter, E. (2006), *Feminism and Philosophy of Science: An Introduction*. New York: Routledge.

Read, H. (1977), "An Aesthetic Approach to Education," pp. 279-286 in G. Woodcock (ed.), *The Anarchist Reader*. Glasgow: Fontana Paperbacks.

Reich, R.B. (1991), *The Work of Nations: Preparing Ourselves for 21st Century Capitalism*. New York: Knopf.

Restivo, S. and M. Zenzen (1978), "A Humanistic Perspective on Science and Society," *Humanity and Society* 2, 4 (November), pp. 211-236.

Restivo, S. (1983), *The Social Relations of Physics, Mysticism, and Mathematics*. Dordrecht: Kluwer Academic Publishers.

Restivo, S. (1991), *The Sociological Worldview*. New York: Wiley-Blackwell.

Restivo, S. (1992), *Mathematics in Society and History*. Boston: Kluwer Academic Publishers.

Restivo, S. J.P. Van Bendegem, and R. Fischer, eds. (1993), *Math Worlds: Philosophical and Social Studies of Mathematics and Mathematics Education*. Albany, NY: SUNY Press.

Restivo, S. (1994), *Science, Society, and Values: Toward a Sociology of Objectivity*. Bethlehem, PA: Lehigh University Press.

Restivo, S. (2005), "Politics of Latour," review essay, *Organization and Environment* 8, 1 (March), pp. 111-115.

Restivo, S. and W.K. Bauchspies (2006), "The Will to Mathematics: Minds, Morals and Numbers," *Foundations of Science* 11, 1-2, pp. 197-215.

Restivo, S. and J. Croissant (2007), "Social Constructionism in Science and Technology Studies," pp. 213-229 in J. Holstein and J. Gubrium (eds), *Handbook of Constructionist Research*. New York: Guilford.

Robinson, H. (1975), *Renascent Rationalism*. Toronto: MacMillan.

Roszak, T. (1972), *Where the Wasteland Ends*. New York: Doubleday-Anchor.

Sahlins, M.D. and E.R. Service (1960), *Evolution and Culture*. Ann Arbor: University of Michigan Press.

Sanderson, S.K. (2001), *The Evolution of Human Sociality: A Darwinian Conflict Perspective.* New York: Rowman and Littlefield Publishers, Inc.

Schram, S.R. (1971), Mao Tse-tung and the Theory of the Permanent Revolution, 1958-69. *The China Quarterly* 46, pp. 221-244.

Schumacher, J. (1989), *Human Posture: The Nature of Inquiry.* Albany, NY: SUNY Press.

Schutz, A. (1967), *The Problem of Social Reality: Collected Papers,* 3 vols. The Hague: M. Nijhoff.

Smith, D.E. (1987), *The Everyday as Problematic: A Feminist Sociology.* Boston, MA: Northeastern University Press.

Smith, D.E. (1996), "Telling the Truth after Postmodernism," *Symbolic Interaction* 19, 3, pp. 171-202.

Spengler, O. (1926), *The Decline of the West,* New York: A. Knopf.

Star, S.L and Griesemer J.R. (1989), "Institutional Ecology, 'Translations' and Boundary Objects: Amateurs and Professionals in Berkeley's Museum of Vertebrate Zoology, 1907-39," *Social Studies of Science* 19, 4, pp. 387-420.

Stein, G. (1993), *Everybody's Autobiography.* Boston: Exact Change (reprint of the 1971 Cooper Square edition).

Struik, D. (1986), "The Sociology of Mathematics Revisited: a Personal Note," *Science and Society* 50, pp. 280-299.

Suissa, J. (2006), *Anarchism and Education: A Philosophical Perspective.* Oxford: Routledge.

Tarde, G. (1899/2009), *Social Laws: An Outline of Sociology.* Bibliolife, Open Source. Orig. publ. London: Macmillan.

Taussig, M.T. (1980), *The Devil and Commodity Fetishism in South America.* Chapel Hill, NC: University of North Carolina Press.

TenHouten, W. and C.D. Kaplan (1973), *Science and its Mirror Image.* New York: Harper and Row.

Tesnière, L. (1959), *Eléments de syntaxe structurale.* Paris: C. Klinksieck.

Thackray, A. (1971), "Reflections of the Decline of Science in America and on Some of its Causes," *Science* 173, 399 (July 2), pp. 27-31.

Torrance, S. (1994), "Real-World Embedding and Traditional AI," Preprint. London: Middlesex University AI Group.

Toulmin, S. (1972), *Human Understanding.* Princeton, NJ: Princeton University Press.

Trotsky, L. (2007), *The Permanent Revolution and Results and Prospects.* Limena: IMG publications. Orig. published in Russian in 1930 by the Left Opposition.

Tymoczko, T. (1991), "Mathematics, Science, and Ontology," *Synthese* 88, pp. 201-228.

Tymoczko, T. (1993), "Mathematical Skepticism: Are We Brains in a Countable Vat?", pp. 61-79 in S. Restivo, J.P. van Bedegem, and R. Fischer (eds.), *Math Worlds: Philosophical and Social Studies of Mathematics and Mathematics Education.* Albany, NY: SUNY Press.

Van Kerkhove, B. and J.P. van Bendegem (eds.) (2007), *Perspectives on Mathematical Practices*. Dordrecht: Springer.

Varela, F.J., F. Thompson, and E. Rosch (1991), *The Embodied Mind: Cognitive Science and Human Experience*. Cambridge, MA: MIT Press.

Wade, N. (2009), *The Faith Instinct*, New York, Penguin Press.

Wartofsky, M. (1974), "Is Science Rational?", pp. 202-210 in W.H. Truitt and T.W.G. Solomons (eds.), *Science, Technology, and Freedom*. Boston: Mifflin and Co.

Woolgar, S. and D. Pawluch (1985), "Ontological Gerrymandering: The Anatomy of Social Problems Explanations," *Social Problems*, 32, pp. 214-237.

Wright, W. (1992), *Wild Knowledge: Science, Language, and Social Life in a Fragile Environment*. Minneapolis: University of Minnesota Press.

Wyer, M., M. Barbercheck, D. Giesman, Hatice Örün Öztürk, and M. Wayne, eds. (2009), *Women, Science, and Technology*, 2nd ed., New York: Routledge.

Zammito, J. (2004), "Women, ANTs, and (Other) Dangerous Things," pp. 183-231 in J. Zammito, *A Nice Derangement of Epistemes: Post-Positivism in the Study of Science from Quine to Latour*. Chicago: University of Chicago Press.

Ziman, J. (1968), *Public Knowledge: The Social Dimension of Science*. Cambridge: Cambridge University Press.

Zinn, H. (1995), *A People's History of the United States 1492-Present*. New York: Harper Perennial.

Index

For Product Safety Concerns and Information please contact our
EU representative GPSR@taylorandfrancis.com Taylor & Francis
Verlag GmbH, Kaufingerstraße 24, 80331 München, Germany